Learning about School Violence

"*Learning about School Violence* provides state policymakers with the tools to define, debate and craft policies that help reduce harmful behavior in schools. This book challenges lawmakers to analyze school violence in a comprehensive way and to re-examine the problems and policies that will help combat violence. It helps move beyond the pattern of reacting to tragedy, providing legislators and others with a better understanding of the problems that lead to violence and ideas to develop comprehensive policies to address the issue."

—*Eric Hirsch, Education Policy Specialist,*
National Conference of State Legislatures, Denver, Colorado

"Greene offers one of the most thoughtful and comprehensive perspectives on the issue of school violence to date and it will further the field in important ways. I applaud his efforts to help us get beyond a quick fix, simplistic approach. By offering ways to re-define school violence and by helping us realize the importance of 'institutional learning,' Greene takes us a big step forward in finding long term, collaborative solutions to a complex problem. If we are to create safe and peaceable places for our children to learn in schools, we shall have to begin by setting goals that reflect such a positive, comprehensive approach. Practitioners and policy-makers alike will benefit from the recommendations in this book."

—*Randy Compton, Executive Director,*
Colorado School Mediation Project

"An important contribution to our understanding of school violence in the United States, Matthew W. Greene's book is a very timely and comprehensive analysis of the troubles in our society that ultimately manifest themselves as violence in our schools. Parents, teachers, and policy makers will benefit from reading this book and then acting upon its recommendations."

—*Robin J. Crews, Peace Studies Program,*
Goucher College, Baltimore, Maryland

Learning about School Violence

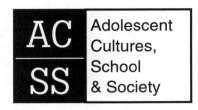

Joseph L. DeVitis & Linda Irwin-DeVitis
General Editors

Vol. 14

PETER LANG
New York • Washington, D.C./Baltimore • Bern
Frankfurt am Main • Berlin • Brussels • Vienna • Oxford

Matthew W. Greene

Learning about
School Violence

Lessons for Educators, Parents, Students, and Communities

PETER LANG
New York • Washington, D.C./Baltimore • Bern
Frankfurt am Main • Berlin • Brussels • Vienna • Oxford

Library of Congress Cataloging-in-Publication Data

Greene, Matthew W.
Learning about school violence: lessons for educators, parents,
students, and communities / Matthew W. Greene.
p. cm. — (Adolescent cultures, school, and society; vol. 14)
Includes bibliographical references.
1. School violence—United States. 2. School violence—United States—Case
studies. I. Title. II. Adolescent cultures, school & society; vol. 14.
LB3013.3 .G75   371.7'82'0973—dc21   00-030461
ISBN 0-8204-4868-0
ISSN 1091-1464

Die Deutsche Bibliothek-CIP-Einheitsaufnahme

Greene, Matthew W.:
Learning about school violence: lessons for educators, parents,
students, and communities / Matthew W. Greene.
–New York; Washington, D.C./Baltimore; Bern;
Frankfurt am Main; Berlin; Brussels; Vienna; Oxford: Lang.
(Adolescent cultures, school, and society; Vol. 14)
ISBN 0-8204-4868-0

Cover photograph: Library of Congress, Prints & Photographs Division,
FSA-OWI Collection, LC-USF33-TO1-001539-M2 DLC (B&W film dup. neg.)

Cover design by Lisa Dillon

The paper in this book meets the guidelines for permanence and durability
of the Committee on Production Guidelines for Book Longevity
of the Council of Library Resources.

Printed in the United States of America

To my wife and partner in life, Margret, and to my family, whose love and support have sustained me; and to making peace and nonviolence the reality.

Contents

Tables

Foreword

I began my journey into learning about school violence seven years ago. As a graduate student with long-standing interests in conflict resolution and policy-making, I began gradually to link my study of theories of nonviolence, such as those of Ghandi, King, and Sharp, with my fascination for politics, policy-making, and education. I became convinced that education was the primary way that we as a society, and government, representing American families and communities, could foster positive changes in values among our children. I joined the spheres of education policy and conflict resolution by researching peer mediation and school conflict resolution programs.

What I learned very quickly was that teaching students nonviolent methods for solving their problems was just the tip of the school violence iceberg. The problem, as such, was much more complicated and intricate than was suggested by the media, educators, and many academic scholars. Where I had begun my inquiry with an earnest goal of supporting the development of positive, practical means of problem-solving for youth, I opened a Pandora's box of value disagreements, education policy dilemmas, and fear and concern on the part of educators, parents, and students.

Learning about School Violence traces my personal path toward grasping the many intricacies of this complex issue as much as it provides a road map for concerned parents, policy makers, students, communities, and educators, a map that guides them toward a fuller understanding of this important social policy problem. The book orients the reader with a discussion of the process of policy learning and problem definition, supporting the development of a comprehensive definition of school violence, and a process of learning more effectively about what works in preventing school and community youth violence over time. It uses examples from the national stage and more detailed discussions of the school violence policy processes in the state of Colorado and the Denver and Colorado Springs school districts, to illustrate lessons for addressing school violence in a more productive manner. Learning about School Violence is based on my many discussions with educators, students, teachers, legislators, juvenile justice workers, and others, and my integration of the policy sciences literature with school violence data and debates.

This study began at a point in time that we would now identify as "pre-Columbine." That horrific incident marks a profound change in our nation's thinking about and attention to the school violence problem. I have not seen anywhere near this level and extent of focus and concern about school violence, even as we move beyond Columbine to other tragedies and other worries. And Columbine itself represents in some awful way the culmination of a spate of dramatic school shootings linked with names like Springfield, Pearl, West Paducah, and Jonesboro. What I find striking in reviewing the story I trace through 1997 here in detail are the ways in which much of the current public shock and outrage are foreshadowed by earlier events, earlier reactions, and earlier outrage, particularly in Colorado itself.

This book does not have all the answers. There are partial answers available, but communities, educators, and policy makers must commit themselves not only to taking advantage of the existing research on violence prevention, but also to gathering new and accurate information on effective solutions and to sharing in the learning process on this issue in the future. My hope is that this book will offer individuals and communities guidelines toward changing the definition of the violence in their midst and thus solving their problem more effectively over time.

Why Write (and Read) about the School Violence Problem?

In American communities across the country, the problem seems to be growing. Schools and school districts are confronting kids with guns, kids without compassion, kids with serious substance abuse and criminal issues. Why do children as young as eleven years old kill their classmates and teachers, and what can schools do to prevent such tragedies in the future? Schools and districts are adopting policies and approaches that are increasingly complicated and complex to deal with an ill-defined and poorly understood problem. One administrator for special education in an urban school district recently described the situation:

> Our alternative programs have really grown lately. You know, we even opened a collaborative school this year with Denver Juvenile Court. All sixty kids have to be on probation. They have a full-time probation officer. We have a task worker who is a drug and alcohol person there from juvenile court, that's full-time. We have a mental health person. [The district] provides the building and the teachers and the paraprofessionals, and these are kids that the [probation officers] were saying to us, you know, they go

into school and they just don't make it. They aren't welcomed, they don't feel welcomed, they don't want to be there. *It's obvious the school doesn't want them there. They've got ankle bracelets on.*

What should we do about school violence? Should we throw those dangerous kids out of school to keep the rest of the "good" kids safe? When we expel a student, where does he or she end up? How much and what kind of violence is occurring? How can we prevent that violence from happening in the first place? What is the nature of the school violence problem?

Crime, violence, and education consistently top polls as chief concerns among Americans. High-profile acts of violence in the schools have led to much soul-searching, tough reactions on the part of schools, communities, and the justice system, and intense media scrutiny of troubled youth and their schools. With much blame being placed on the various systems associated with violence prevention and punishment, teachers, parents, students, policy makers, and other stakeholders interested in and confronted by this complex problem need help in understanding, defining, and learning how to learn about school violence.

Of a more academic nature, policy scholars have long attempted to understand how individuals and institutions learn about policy problems over time. Many theoretical perspectives have been put forth, and often the work has not been done to join these perspectives and examine them in actual contexts. There, the issues are real and complicated. In one city school district central office, a district administrator described the changes that were being implemented in the various district and school departments since the arrival of new district leadership:

> Well, I know there's a lot more communication and collaboration. A lot more. And the education folks would probably say there's a lot more sharing. I just call it flat out communication and coordination. Yeah, there's a lot more, and there's a lot more trust, the trust level has gone up . . . Based on what I've heard, you know, *there was a lot of parochialism, even departmental parochialism*, and [the superintendent] said we're not islands. We don't do island management here. We're all on the Titanic, and we're not going to hit an iceberg. He's at the helm, and we're steering clear of those suckers, and this thing's moving.

What we see here is the tension between specialization and integration of an institution's departments and responsibilities. Yet there are many questions as to how the definition of a policy problem can be connected to learning about how to manage that problem over time. How can the definition of the school violence problem become more comprehensive, integrated, and accurate, and why is that necessary?

Purpose of the Book

This book sets out to answer these questions and others for those involved in or impacted by the school violence problem. It will help schools, school districts, and communities better understand, define, and approach this complex policy issue as they work to prevent and reduce the violence and harmful behaviors occurring in their midst. This is both a general audience and a practitioner-oriented book, emphasizing lessons learned for school administrators, teachers, parents, and policy makers. It highlights the narrative detail from my over fifty interviews with those in the midst of dealing with the school violence problem in two urban school districts and the state of Colorado. I discuss policy and program stories, and how institutional learning takes place in various school systems. The focus is on school violence as a practical policy concern, helping stakeholders to redefine and approach this policy problem. At the same time, readers will gain a sense of the importance of taking a "problem definition" perspective in critically approaching such educational issues as school choice, special education, equitable funding, and college preparation.

As an issue of serious and continuing concern, the school violence focus of this book will attract readers who are interested in gaining a handle on this problem. They will learn alternative ways of thinking about and approaching this issue. They will see what other states and school districts are doing in this area and will be able to bring key lessons and experiences back to their own schools, communities, districts, and states. The book presents a national overview of the school violence problem, an overview that is accessible and relevant for communities across America.

As an approach to policy problems, this book gives readers the conceptual tools to rethink not only education issues, but also such complex social policy problems as welfare, substance abuse, and teen pregnancy. Thus, this book is not only about the school violence issue, it is also a model for how to redefine and thus learn about complex issues.

Clarifying the School Violence Debate

To the overall debate on school violence in America today, this book adds depth, breadth, and a more well-reasoned and comprehensive perspective on and definition of the problem. It offers both a summary of existing perceptions and research on school violence and a detailed exploration of this problem in actual school contexts. This book provides a much-needed consensus-oriented perspective on how to approach school violence. It combines practical research and suggestions with a sensible conceptual framework.

This book offers researchers, teachers, students, and decision makers case studies through which to see how problem definition and policy learning can be examined in real contexts. Political decision makers might also see this book as an indication that learning about complex policy problems needs to involve an intentional redefinition of those problems, rather than just the typical legislative tinkering approach. Decentralization, for example, needs to be reconsidered in light of the evidence brought forward here. The argument for policy scholars and decision makers would be that if you really want to learn about policy problems, you have to engage in a comprehensive and dynamic definition and redefinition of that problem over time. Thus, the book offers hope and lessons for more productively and positively approaching complex policy problems such as school violence.

I expect that the main audience for Learning about School Violence will be teachers, community members, school administrators, students, educators, policy makers, and parents. The middle school teacher, the volunteer board member who runs a local business, the high school student, the parent of three children entering the public schools, the state legislator, the principal, and the director of the youth services agency, for example, will all find this book useful in helping them to grasp and redefine the school violence problem so that they can better manage it. All across this country, communities are struggling to understand violence and to think about it in a more rational and comprehensive manner. They want to move beyond the simple prevention-punishment debate in order to more effectively communicate with each other and multiple public agencies across different policy issues. This book helps them move in that direction.

Another audience for this book will be policy scholars and other academics interested in the nature of organizational learning and problem definition. This will likely include those concentrating in public policy and administration, political scientists, sociologists, those with a focus in the politics of education and education policy, and business and management experts and students. This book contributes to the debate on learning across state and institutional boundaries, drawing lessons from successful or unsuccessful programs and policies and defining policy problems. This book is appropriate for classroom use as case study and theoretical material in undergraduate or graduate public policy classes, undergraduate classes in organizational management, classes in conflict resolution theory, education policy seminars, and so forth.

A tertiary audience for this book will be journalists and other media members interested in examining a real-world study of this important issue and reporting on various viewpoints on school violence.

This book, then, has both practical and academic uses. For example, for the education practitioners, it offers guidance in how to foster a learning organization, not only in the area of school violence, but also in such complex arenas as bilingual education, special education, decentralization, and school choice; for academics, this book offers a useful framework for considering the policy learning and problem definition literature together, reconceptualizing policy learning as a process of problem redefinition. Such a theoretical shift presents a logical and practical means through which to study the evolution and construction of complex policy problems over time.

Outline of Contents and Chapters

Learning about School Violence is organized to provide a foundation for how to think conceptually about defining school violence and other complex problems; an overview of the school violence problem nationally; a focus on stories about individuals, school districts, and states; and overall lessons for the reader about how to improve learning about school violence through redefining this policy problem.

Chapter 1 introduces the reader to the problem of school violence through compelling stories and a national portrait of the issue. Here, I set out an overview of the school violence problem in terms of goals associated with school violence policies, trends in school violence over time, causes of school violence, predictions for levels of future violence, and current and proposed solutions to the problem. I argue that the debate over school violence is inconclusive and vague, tied up with cultural and political assumptions and values, and in need of further elaboration and focused study.

In chapter 2, I set out the dilemma of learning about complex policy problems like school violence and how we might better think about more effective learning as a process of constructing a more accurate, well-integrated, and comprehensive problem definition. I define essential concepts, such as problem definition and policy learning. I then set out school violence as an example of a complex policy problem. I argue that the public and policy debate over school violence will benefit from a focus on policy learning and problem definition.

Chapter 3 focuses on a particular state, Colorado, its debates over school violence and its attempts to manage the problem, as an example of what is happening in states across the country. I use narrative interviews and research to tell this story as an example of the challenges that states are facing in dealing with this issue. The chapter shows how fragmentation of state institutions and political groups prevents more complex learning overall about school violence at the state level.

Continuing the work of the previous chapter, chapter 4 focuses on the school district level and individual schools in Denver to assess school violence and the definition of this problem on a closer community basis. Chapter 5 continues that work in Colorado Springs. Again, we see through analysis of rules, policies, and history, and discussions with school district and community stakeholders, that a focus on and record of learning about this policy problem are generally lacking in the area of school violence.

In chapter 6, I summarize lessons from the previous chapters. I then present an overall assessment of the school violence problem and how we can learn about and redefine it. Lessons are outlined for policy makers, practitioners, and concerned community members on how to best engage such complex policy problems as school violence within and outside of public and private institutions. Finally, I include an afterword on the shootings at Columbine High School in Littleton, Colorado, an incident that so dramatically brought the issue of school violence to the forefront of the public's attention.

Acknowledgments

I would like to acknowledge the guidance and perceptive comments of my graduate advisor, Professor J. Samuel Fitch, and the wisdom and support of Professors Susan Clarke, Dennis Eckart, and Rodney Hero. I would also like to thank the educators, policy makers, and members of the community who agreed to share with me their views on school violence. Without their concern and hard work, the children would be lost.

Chapter 1
The School Violence Problem

Introduction: School Violence and Education Policy

Crime and education top today's list of national concerns. Violence in the schools is one of the hot issues in education policy today. How much violence is there? How does it affect learning? How can it be curtailed? As educators, legislators, and community members strive to assess the damage and limit future harm, they look for some indication of what works and what does not. In a situation of social complexity and limited knowledge, the extent of the problem and the efficacy of different solutions are trees hidden in a forest of uncertain information.[1]

School violence is a *complex social policy problem*, as defined in chapter 2. It is a complicated and poorly defined policy issue. The school violence problem is characterized by limited, competing, and intensely held problem definitions. Further study and clarification of this issue is required, and this book makes a contribution in that direction by examining and comparing the school violence problem in one state, two school districts, and six local schools. It connects the problem definition and policy learning processes in this area and shows how learning can be conceived and measured as problem redefinition.

This chapter assesses the general state of understanding surrounding the school violence issue. It emphasizes such elements as incomplete and conflicting information about the extent and causes of the school violence problem to reveal the nature of this issue as a complex social policy problem. The effects of violence on learning, the causes of violence, and projections for future levels of violence are discussed. The problem of insufficient or incomplete data is portrayed as the context for any school violence dialogue. A general assessment of some policy alternatives is presented, as is a sampling of state and school district action across the nation. Finally, the need for further study and clarification of the school violence debate is emphasized.

The Social Context and the Goals of School Violence Policies

School violence is not unrelated to youth violence or societal violence in general. The causes of school violence include many factors that are not amenable to school-based intervention. On the other hand, the education system can play a prominent role in producing nonviolent youths. A recent survey of the literature identifies myriad societal conditions and strategies that families, communities, and governments can address regarding violence reduction.[2] Schools are only one link in a chain of family, community, and governmental actions in areas from domestic violence prevention to the media and from poverty alleviation to criminal justice reform. However, schools can be an important link. They can play a role in many of the violence reduction strategies that this chapter identifies.

This book recognizes the societal context for the school violence problem, the need for collaboration and cooperation between schools and other agencies and the community, and the basic parental and social genesis for much violence. However, it focuses on the schools and the education policy arena in order to address the question, What can schools and education policy makers do to contribute to the reduction of violence in schools, as well as in society as a whole?

Goals of School Violence Policies

The goals associated with the school violence problem are wide ranging and complex. Most ultimately focus on fostering the well-being of children and school staff. They often connect this basic premise to improving education. Well-being is measured in terms of violent incidents that occur in the schools and harm teachers, staff, and students. The reduction of gun incidents and reports of guns in schools, and the suspension and expulsion of disruptive students, are examples of focusing on dangers in the school environment. To improve students' well-being, secondary goals involving learning to handle conflict without violence are suggested. The creation of a culture of peace in schools and society as a whole is promoted.

The National Education Goals were established in 1989 at a national education summit. A bipartisan coalition then listed six goals that would be set for the year 2000. Originally, goal six, the school violence goal, read: "Every school in America will be free of drugs and violence and will offer a disciplined environment conducive to learning."[3] As the Clinton administration took over the goals program, two more goals were added, and goal six became goal seven: "Every school in the United States will be free of drugs, violence, and the unauthorized presence of firearms and alcohol and will offer a disciplined environment conducive to learning." Goal seven is also known as "Safe, Disciplined, and Alcohol- and Drug-Free Schools."[4] The language is generally consistent, but we see the prevention of gun incidents and alcohol abuse as two additional policy priorities of the Clinton administration.

These goals should be examined critically in order to understand and balance the values that are involved in a discussion of school violence. Nationally, the key goals are safety, discipline (defined as order and security) and the avoidance of harmful behaviors. Such goals as building "peaceful communities" and changing the American culture of violence, elements of alternative problem definitions that are held by peace educators, are not part of the dominant American problem definition.[5] Additionally, as part of the national education goal, learning takes a prominent position in this assessment of school violence. In addition to physical safety and personal well-being, concern about the effects of violence on education represents a major element of the school violence problem.

Negative Effects on Education

Violence negatively affects the learning environment. Both actual violence and the fear of future violence can be detrimental. A recent national poll of teachers, students, and law enforcement officers found that one-third of teachers felt that because of violence or the threat of violence, teachers and students were less eager to go to school. One-third of teachers felt that their colleagues were less likely to discipline students because of violence. Half of all teachers felt that students paid less attention to learning in the classroom. From the student point of view, 22 percent admitted that violence and the threat of violence made them less eager to go school. Twelve percent said it made them stay home or cut class. Sixteen percent said they were less eager to talk in class. Twenty-five percent said it lessened the quality of education at their school. Forty-two percent of students said violence made them feel angry.[6]

A report by the National Governors' Association, commenting on the seriousness of the youth violence problem in America, states:

Children who are exposed to violence often have difficulty focusing on school work or engaging in other activities that are the treasured experiences of childhood . . . These findings pose serious impediments to the nation's ability to reach the National Education Goals . . . Children must be safe at school in order to learn successfully.[7]

And, more dramatically, Ronald Stephens of the National School Safety Center has argued that: "Twenty-nine percent of our nation's teachers have stated they have considered leaving the teaching profession because of violence. School crime negatively impacts students, teachers, the school and community, our economic viability and national defense, not to mention quality of life."[8] It is argued that violence in the schools can hamper learning, and physically and psychologically harm students. Violence can impair students' social and intellectual development and cause further violence to erupt.[9]

Dangers to Students and Staff and the Fear That Results
Violence in the schools involves more than just a discussion of hampered learning potential and educational distractions. School violence results in tangible physical and psychological harm to students, teachers, administrators, and staff. The U.S. secretary of education has said that about three million thefts and violent crimes occur on or near school grounds each year. This translates into about sixteen thousand incidents per school day.[10] It seems that such violence occurs in rural and suburban school districts, though with slightly less frequency than in urban districts. One study, for example, found that differences between these areas in reported school crime victimization over a sixth-month period in 1989 were minimal. The rate was 10 percent for youth in central cities, 9 percent for those in suburbs, and 8 percent for those in rural areas.[11] School board reports of the types of violence that their district has experienced show similar patterns, with violence occurring in all areas, but the most violence occurring in urban areas and the least in rural areas. Student versus teacher violence, gang violence, and weapons offenses showed the greatest differences in reported occurrences between areas.[12] While the victims of violence suffer physical loss and mental trauma, the multiple witnesses to violent acts are also subject to the negative effects of violent scenes and the psychological harm they produce.

Those attending schools where violence is a potential risk face the daily question of whether they will be confronted by a violent act. They may react to this situation in different ways. Some teachers may ignore the risk, while others may leave the school permanently.[13] This fear of violence, reluctance to maintain discipline, hesitation to go to school, and desire to leave school cannot but impede a teacher's performance in the classroom.

Students are the most immediate victims of school violence, violence that is most often perpetrated by youth against youth of similar ethnic and socioeconomic backgrounds.[14] One reaction among student victims is to stay away from school. But some research suggests that those youth who are afraid in school may be more likely to become future aggressors.[15] While only 7 percent of all students in the Harris poll and 17 percent of those with poor grades reported feeling unsafe at school, 13 percent of all students reported that they had carried a weapon to school at one time.[16] Thus, possible student reactions to violence include, but are not limited to, future violent aggression, carrying a weapon, and avoiding school work and participation.

The Data Problem: An Uncertain Context for the Violence Debate

The school violence debate suffers from a great deal of uncertainty and confusion due to the lack of clear data as to the nature and extent of the problem. Projections for future levels of violence, normally a difficult and faulty process, are even more complicated due to the disagreement over the present character and past trends in the levels of violence in our schools and communities. Has violence gotten worse? If so, in what ways? Where is violence concentrated? Among whom? I have already discussed some of the self-reported survey data showing the perception that violence in schools is a problem. What about "hard evidence"? I begin with a narrative account of a year's worth of violence and education in one American city.

A Snapshot of America

It is a typical year. In January, the police avert a gang war in one of the larger city boroughs. The police commissioner outlines an anti-crime program to his department officers. Police statistics show that felonies and misdemeanors are up 5 percent from two years earlier. High school officials are worried about the resurgence of "secret student clubs" that have been banned for over thirty years.

Nationally, corporal punishment is debated and becomes the subject of several court cases.

In February, in another city borough, the police avert another teenage gang fight, and the present and former police commissioners are praised for "restoring honest reporting of offenses." School officials expound the value of parental visits to school after their child's poor behavior or work. Truancy officers now can take graduate classes at the local education school to help them deal with offenders. Causes of school absences are discussed. A committee of school principals reports on the problems associated with delinquency and makes some suggestions. The Teachers and High School Principals Association then asks the mayor to appoint a study committee to look into the problem further. School officials deny that teachers are warned not to report "incidents" to "outside agencies."

A report from Columbia University finds that 10 percent of students are "emotionally disturbed and in need of guidance." Most schools are found to lack the personnel or facilities to deal with these students. The report calls for "mental hygiene" to become part of the academic program of the schools.

In March, forty-six boys gathering for a teenage gang war are arrested. High school principals confer with law enforcement officials on how to protect students from loiterers. Smaller classrooms are suggested for the schools. A local assemblyman requests segregated classes for "delinquents." The education board and local school officials deal with the problems of recent immigrants who have limited education and limited proficiency in English language skills. Two youths, who are former junior high school students, are held and later sentenced for assaulting a teacher. Continuing an ongoing debate over the role and mission of schools in the area of moral and religious values in education, two authors argue that the demands placed on schools to "solve diverse social problems" distort the main mission of the schools. They argue that this mission is "to help develop skills for living."

In April, it is argued that the delinquency problem, while serious, is not the "sole responsibility" of the schools. Educators and local civic leaders suggest more "all-day neighborhood schools" as a way to reduce delinquency. Some claim the "delinquency problem" is exaggerated. Nevertheless, the city is asked to provide increased social and psychiatric services to help fight it.

In May, a school academic argues that keeping the age that youth can leave school at sixteen aggravates the delinquency problem. After April's Federal Bureau of Investigation *Uniform Crime Report* put the previous year's city crime total up 4.5 percent over the year before, the police foil more gang wars in May. In July, the quality of education in predominantly minority schools is debated. Segregation, integration, and improving educational quality in the schools will be a topic for discussion through the year, due to recent court decisions.

In August, the police commissioner cites "an alarming rise in youth offenses," and pledges to meet the problem without violating civil rights. The state controller argues that the police are trying to mislead the public through their claims that the crime "crisis" stems from a lack of funds for police. A city judge argues that the federal government's failure to enforce narcotics legislation is a major factor in the city's "crime wave" and urges that enforcement be shifted from the Treasury Department to the FBI.

A city councilman now urges the mayor to appoint an emergency anti-crime commission that would coordinate the city's law enforcement program. The city council president warns against referring to the city as a "community of violence and crime" and urges prevention, not arrests, as the solution. He calls for new recreation and social organizations and urges other city departments to assist the police in their efforts against "undesirables." The courts stiffen penalties. The deputy administrator, while acknowledging that the crime rate is on the rise, holds that it is still below that of other major U.S. cities. A citizens commission is planned, as is a conference of officials and criminologists. A letter to the editor questions whether police action alone can solve the problem.

On August 20, the newspaper reports that a seventeen-year-old was shot when his identity was mistaken by a teenage gang that was fighting a rival group. Police act to avert an escalation of the war after a member of one of the gangs involved is arrested for arms possession. This boy argues that he withdrew from the gang after the shooting. A letter to the paper urges stronger punishment as a deterrent to crime. A state assemblyman argues that the rising teen crime rate shows the need for stricter prohibitions on the sales of publications that showcase violence.

A county grand jury, after studying the issue for two years, reports that the adolescent court is too lenient with repeat offenders. It urges that the court be limited to "wayward minor cases," and urges the higher courts to be responsible for misdemeanors and indictable offenses. A letter urges more play schools as a preventive measure. In a television interview, the education board president calls for boys clubs to curb youth crime. A local private organization pledges to donate half a million dollars for a prevention program. Letters to the paper argue that amusements "glorify crime." The chief justice of the U.S. Supreme Court recommends crime prevention as a strategy.

In September, a permanent planning agency is suggested in the mayor's office as a means to curb crime. A study is planned focusing on high incidence areas and causes of crime. A letter to the paper argues for improving social and economic conditions as a crime prevention measure. A city mental health association urges support and assistance for mental health associations that are trying to develop "broad programs to curb offenses." The Housing Authority and education board announce plans to increase recreational facilities in twenty-five public housing developments to help decrease youth crime. Four girls are seized after a fight involving one hundred students. A borough district attorney announces the formation of a special youth squad, consisting of two assistant district attorneys, to hold open forums in all the high schools in order to discuss students' problems.

The state education commissioner defends the state Education Department from superintendents' charges that it is trying to dictate local education policies. School buses are used as classrooms in one high school due to overcrowding. In a nearby state, one education board bans "informal garb" in high schools, letting parents decide on the dress of elementary students. In another neighboring state, a high school lets parents decide on whether students can smoke during lunch periods.

The media debate over the youth violence problems suggests that improving family life and family relationships with the help of community agencies is a key factor in lowering juvenile offenses. A doctor denies that "faulty parental discipline" is a major cause of youth crime. He suggests that society puts pressures on kids over which the family has "little control." A minister links youth crime to gambling.

By October, pledges are made to seek state aid for local organizations fighting youth crime. The chairman of a commission on youth offenses is named. A doctor and a judge suggest that high school students learn "duties as future parents" as a way to decrease youth crime. A rabbi urges "greater parental effort to secure more schools and playgrounds." The Women's City Club, after visiting correctional facilities, calls for the establishment of a "youth center" to rehabilitate young offenders who are awaiting trial, to separate them from sentenced prisoners. The bar association begins a study of youth offenses. A doctor blames narrowly focused political interest groups for the rise in youth crime, arguing that they failed to make improved housing, education, and other institutions into political issues. A judge calls for more trained social workers and psychiatrists to help the courts aid youthful offenders.

Recent films about "bad" policemen are blamed for negatively impacting the fight against juvenile crime. The plan for recreation centers is opposed by a number of groups who favor "staffed facilities at new schools and housing projects." A state Parents and Teachers Congress calls for "better care, protection, and detention and rehabilitation facilities for young offenders."

Meanwhile, a prominent sociologist urges a "more careful search of basic causes of youth offenses." He argues against putting too much blame on the media. A doctor discusses the potentially harmful effects of teasing. Other doctors present research that links "brain impairments" to youth crime, citing the abnormality of youth offenders' brain waves in electroencephalograph tests. The public is warned that 20 percent of males of military age will have a juvenile court record if current youth crime trends continue.

In November, the president of the community councils calls for opening schools five nights a week. "Operation 25," a several-month-long crime reduction experiment in one of the city's boroughs, is praised as costworthy and effective. Replicating the experiment calls for more money and police personnel, but the increase is defended. The governor-elect assigns the lieutenant governor-elect to develop an "anti-delinquency program," arguing that youth offenses are a major problem in the state. The National Probation and Parole Association begins a five-year, six hundred thousand dollar program to "curb delinquency" with a Ford Foundation grant. The state Teachers Association issues a guide for teachers on punishing pupils. One nearby town offers "joint courses for parents and children." And the state Education Department plans to modernize its elementary school program by stressing "informal teacher-pupil ties, more student-initiated activities, and flexible standards in teaching basic skills."

In December, a youth forum is sponsored by the paper; at the forum youths provide recommendations for decreasing juvenile crime. In one town, a high school football coach is charged with third-degree assault for hitting a student. The superintendent argues that the pupil broke an agreement to let school officials handle the case when the pupil went to the courts. The coach pleads innocent. The charge is later dismissed. A state Temporary Commission on the Courts subcommittee supports a plan for "rehabilitation" over a "punitive approach to youth offenses." The state is found to be slow to adopt "positive methods," with inadequate probation and detention practices and a lack of diverse institutional care. A plan for treatment and youth courts is proposed. It proves immediately controversial. In a neighboring state, it is argued that a number of youth crimes are caused by laws that prevent those under eighteen from working.

1954 . . . 1999

The year ends. Its stories are sad, convoluted, and familiar. What is surprising is the year during which these actual events took place: 1954.[17]

The main city was New York. And, although some of the language and the specifics have changed, it is remarkable how many issues that were faced there and then continue to be discussed today around the country. It helps one to keep in mind that the youth violence "problem" in this country is not a new phenomenon. Looking at the number of articles indexed by the *New York Times* under the heading "Violence–Education and Schools" between 1968 and 1996, for example, illustrates periods of attention in a major paper to the school violence issue. Such an examination shows a peak in school violence-related articles in the late 1970s, in the mid-1980s, in 1990, and, most strongly, in 1992 and 1993.[18] While crime in the city has decreased dramatically in recent years, the New York school system today is a place where some students fear to go outside because of the threat of attack from students at another school. Many students there are not meeting standards, and the state has ordered the city's schools chancellor "to take direct control of New York's 42 worst schools."[19] But the city has been to at least some of these places before.

Violence Trends

I turn now to more systematic measures of school violence across the country. What is the relationship between the perception of risk and actual violence rates?[20] One newspaper cites the "Crime Puzzle: Lower statistics belie rising fear."[21] The perception of risk is up in this country, perhaps due to massive media focus on crime and the general assumption that the exceptional crime is the norm. One author claims that the media have constructed, at least in New York City, the perception among the public of a massive threat to white, middle-class citizens. This resulted in a shift to the right toward the "law and order" approach.[22] Others argue, "Haphazard and sensationalistic portrayals of violence in schools contribute to a distorted perception of the reality of school violence."[23]

Overall Crime and Violence

It is clear that overall violent crime is up significantly since the 1960s and that the level of the problem is psychologically and physically troublesome for many Americans. Crime now rates at the top of concerns in polls.[24] As a country, the United States is generally, in terms of homicide rates and prevalence rates for physical assaults, much more violent than other industrialized countries. With 25,500 homicides in the United States in an average year, the U.S. homicide rate is seventeen times that of Japan or Ireland, ten times that of Germany, France, or Greece, and five times that of Canada. The homicide rate for teenage males is at a historically high level.[25]

Yet crime and violence reporting overall is problematic, due to such issues as a lack of comparability of data, victim self-reporting hesitancy or uncertainty, agency interests in crime reporting, and a lack of funding for data collection.[26] The school violence problem is a specific case of the youth violence problem, which itself is a specific manifestation of our national violence problem, which is only one aspect of the overall crime problem. And while measurements of youth violence are bad, those of school violence appear even worse.

Almost one-third of the nineteen million crime victimizations that persons aged twelve and over reported in the 1990 National Crime Victimization Survey (NCVS) involved violence. The majority of these violent crimes were aggravated and simple assaults. While actual numbers of violent crimes and homicides are higher than ever, homicide rates have peaked and declined twice in this century; they peaked in the 1930s and between 1979 and 1981. The homicide rate rose again after the mid-1980s and reached its 1980 level. Nonfatal violent crime rates also rose during the late 1980s, but only the aggravated assault rate in 1990 exceeded the 1980 rates in cities of all sizes. Minorities are at much greater risk of violent victimization and death in this country, with young black males recently some twenty times more likely to be victimized than older white females. Violent offenders tend to share similar characteristics with their victims, and although a few individuals do commit violent crimes frequently, these persons account for only a small portion of the overall violence committed in the country.[27]

More recently, overall crime in the United States has dropped, by almost 2 percent in 1995 according to the FBI. Longer-term trends in the violent crime rate (which includes offenses of murder, forcible rape, robbery, and aggravated assault), the murder and nonnegligent manslaughter rate, and the aggravated assault rate are mixed. The murder rate was lower in 1995 than the historically high 1980 rate. However, the violent crime rate was higher in 1995 than in 1980, and the aggravated assault rate was much higher in 1994 than in 1980. The more recent trends seem to represent some consistent declines over the past few years but may in part be due to a smaller proportion of youth in peak offending years in the overall population during this time period.[28]

Table 1 shows percentage changes in selected crime rates over different periods of time, illustrating the declines in the murder and violent crime rates through the first half of the 1990s in particular.

Overall Youth Violence

In terms of overall youth violence, Elliott summarizes the recent trends as follows:

> The evidence suggests the following conclusions about trends in youth violence over the past decade: 1) There is a substantial increase in the violence victimization rates for adolescents, particularly for 12–15 year olds; 2) There has been a relatively small increase (8–10 percent) in the proportion of adolescents involved in some type of serious violent offending; and 3) There has been a dramatic increase in adolescent homicide rates, beginning in 1988.[29]

Elliott points out that the lethality of youth violence is what has

Table 1

Change in Selected Crime Rates over Time

	Violent Crime (%)	Murder (%)	Aggravated Assault (%)
1994–1995	- 3	- 7	- 1
1991–1995	- 6	- 13	n/a
1986–1995	+ 21	n/a	n/a

Note: Violent crime includes murder, forcible rape, robbery, and aggravated assault. Murder includes nonnegligent manslaughter.
Source: Federal Bureau of Investigation, *Uniform Crime Report* (Washington, DC: Department of Justice, 1995).

significantly increased. The national rate of juvenile violent crimes, while persistently high, dropped slightly in 1995 for the first time in almost a decade, while the juvenile homicide rate dropped for the second year running, by over 15 percent, according to the FBI. The arrest rate for homicides for youths ten to seventeen years old fell almost 23 percent between 1993, an all-time peak, and 1995.[30]

School Violence

What are the trends in terms of school violence specifically? Again, the data are scattered, piecemeal, and unclear. Different types of data collection techniques abound. They include surveys of school officials on rates of offenses, school and student victimization surveys, and general opinion surveys. These differences combine with variations in question wording, length of time covered by the survey question, and higher levels of perceived violence compared to victim self-reports. This all leads to multiple uncertainties about the levels of violence in the schools now and in the past. They lead one set of researchers to caution: *"Thus, we strongly urge healthy skepticism when reviewing any set of statistics about school violence."*[31] The paucity of solid numerical data, combined with the plenitude of narrative and anecdotal reports from the schools, has led to a level of public concern about this problem that, while consistent over time, may or may not be justified. Americans ranked discipline as the number one problem facing schools for sixteen of the first twenty years of the Gallup education poll, which was first taken in 1969. Recently, drug abuse has taken first place.[32]

School violence is not a new problem. In 1995 Reese stated, "Discipline . . . has been a perennial educational concern, often unrelated to drugs."[33] Reese traces the school violence, discipline, safety, and drug abuse problem over time. He finds evidence of these concerns even in the nineteenth century. School discipline and fighting were issues through the 1940s, which witnessed corporal punishment, ethnic gangs, and legal expulsion. Schools increasingly took on societal troubles as school attendance became mandatory in the 1950s and 1960s, and Americans feared increasing juvenile crime and delinquency. Such movies as *Blackboard Jungle* (1955) highlighted popular fears about violent youth. There were some weapons in the schools. Ethnic and racial tensions were prevalent. Discipline was discussed in academic journals, but little research was conducted in this area. School and youth violence increased through the 1960s, but it was in the mid-1970s that school violence and vandalism appeared to reach an apogee.[34] Thus, while concern about school violence, safety, and discipline is certainly high, this concern is not a recent phenomenon.

A sampling and synthesis of some of the available data and actual numbers does provide a general picture of the extent of violence, victimization, and some trends over time in the schools. The results of a survey of school boards taken by the National School Boards Association in the 1992–1993 school year showed that a large majority, 82 percent, thought that student violence had increased in the last five years, while only 4 percent thought that it had decreased. This broad national sample found similarities across urban, suburban, and rural school districts. However, fewer types of violence and lesser increases in violence were reported in suburban and rural districts. The types of violence experienced by districts overall included student versus student (78 percent); weapons in school (61 percent); student versus teacher (28 percent); racial/ethnic (28 percent); gang (24 percent); shooting/knifing (13 percent); drive-by shooting (9 percent); rape (7 percent); other (6 percent); and violence against gays/lesbians (3 percent).[35]

The responses of students, parents, teachers, and law enforcement officers to a question in two successive Harris polls about changes in levels of violence at school, although students were the only group polled in both years, lean toward perceived increases in violence levels. In both 1993 and 1994, large proportions of each group felt that violence levels had remained constant. Significant proportions of all groups reported increases in violence, with law enforcement officers most likely to report increases. Smaller proportions of all groups reported decreases in violence. Many students in both years were unsure about changes in violence levels at school.

Table 2 shows student reports of the types of violent acts that they had ever committed at school. Verbal insults and pushing and shoving behavior were the most common. Few students reported having threatened a teacher or having threatened someone with or used a knife or gun. More students had threatened other students, however. Males and those with poor grades were more likely to have reported engaging in all types of violent behavior.

Violence in schools is reported to occur across all school levels. For example, the National School Boards Association reported that one-fourth of all suspensions from school across the country were for violence committed by elementary school children. Children are reported to be at risk of robbery at school on a regular basis: "Evidence on school crime and other studies suggest that attempted as well as actual robberies of children under age 12 and of schoolchildren at all ages are quite common."[36]

Gun incidents on school property involved high school students 63 percent of the time, junior high school students 24 percent of the time, elementary students 12 percent of the time, and preschoolers 1 percent of the time.[37] The Center to Prevent Handgun Violence examined media reports from 1986 to 1990 and found that 65 students and 6 school staff members were killed by guns on school campuses during that period. Another 201 were severely wounded by gunfire, and 242 hostage situations involving guns were reported.[38] While these figures sound terrible, however, they are dwarfed by over sixteen thousand homicides, eighteen thousand suicides, and about fifteen hundred accidental deaths involving firearms in the United States in 1990. In 1990, firearms contributed to more teenage deaths than all natural diseases combined.[39] Thus, most gun-related deaths occur outside of schools.

Another baseline comparison is estimates of the effects of domestic violence, including four thousand women and fourteen hundred men killed annually and a minimum of thirteen children, most under the age of one, killed daily.[40] Recent trends examined in a

Table 2

Types of Violent Acts That Students Have Committed

Violent Acts	Total Students (%)	Those with Good/ Fair Grades (%)	Those with Poor Grades (%)	Male (%)	Female (%)
Verbally insulted someone	50	51	69	60	40
Threatened another student	23	22	50	34	12
Pushed, shoved, grabbed, slapped someone else	42	42	63	54	30
Kicked, bitten, or hit someone with a fist	26	25	48	37	15
Threatened a teacher	5	4	21	8	3
Threatened someone with a knife or gun	3	3	10	6	1
Used a knife or fired a gun	1	1	4	2	1
Stolen something from someone	14	13	23	18	9
Base number of students	1151	1021	42	534	610

Note: Students may have reported having participated in more than one type of violence. Students responded to the question, "Have you ever done any of the following things, in or around school or not . . . ?"
Source: L. Harris, *Metropolitan Life Survey of the American Teacher, 1993: Violence in America's Public Schools* (New York: Louis Harris and Associates, 1993), 72.

study published by the *Journal of the American Medical Association* show that while the total incidence of accidental youth deaths has declined, by 39 percent from 1992 to 1994, that of non-accidental deaths has increased, by 47 percent during the same period: 4,805 youths died from homicides and suicides combined, a 67 percent increase in the former and a 17 percent increase in the latter. Deaths from gunshots accounted for almost all the increase. One hundred five children died violently in or near secondary schools during this time period, the majority as a result of homicides involving guns.[41] Again, the number of youths actually killed by violence in the schools represents a small proportion of the total number of childhood violent deaths in the country.

In measuring the trends in school violence based on National Education Goal Seven, the National Education Goals Panel (NEGP) found that disruptions in class by students remained constant between 1992 and 1995, with 17 percent of tenth graders reporting that during an average week, misbehavior by other students interfered with their own learning six times or more. In 1991, 37 percent of all secondary school teachers reported that student misbehavior interfered with their teaching. That number had increased to 46 percent in 1994. In 1991, 10 percent of public school teachers reported that they were threatened with physical injury or were physically attacked by a student from their own school during the preceding twelve months. In 1994, that number had increased to 15 percent. The NEGP also found that tenth graders increasingly reported illicit drug use during the previous year, 36 percent in 1995, up from 24 percent in 1991. They reported consistent alcohol use during the previous year, at 64 percent, and increasing sales of drugs at school, up from 18 percent in 1992 to 28 percent in 1995.[42] According to this data, one must conclude that progress on goal seven has been poor or mixed. The only measure that shows improvement is student victimizations.

A collection of data tracked on a variety of student school violence victimizations includes the following:

- Students victimized by violence, in or around school, ever
- Students in any physical fight, past year, any setting
- Tenth-grade boys attacked while at school or on a bus
- Eighth-grade boys attacked while at school or on a bus
- Students attacked while at school or on a bus
- Students victimized by violence, 6-month period, ages 12 to 19, "in or around" school, mostly simple assaults without weapon
- Students victimized by crime, 6-month period, ages 12 to 19, "in or around" school
- Students injured by weapon at school
- Students threatened by weapon at school
- Students victimized, tenth graders reported being threatened or injured, with or without a weapon, at school during previous year[43]

The NEGP figures show a decrease in tenth-grade students who reported being threatened or injured from 1991 to 1995. The Harris poll shows a decrease in lifetime victimizations by students between 1993 and 1994. Other figures are generally single-point-in-time statistics that need to be carefully compared, as they all measure school violence in different ways over different periods of time. While not equivalent, these figures provide a sampling of the kind of statistics that are available on school violence trends. They also indicate the aforementioned difficulties in tracking and comparing information on the extent of the school violence problem.

Problems and Issues Associated with Assessing School Violence Trends

This discussion of trends and perceptions surrounding violence highlights the inadequacies of the current information regarding levels of violence in our schools. The information currently used is not fully dependable, nor does there seem to be an adequate understanding among policy makers of the uncertainty surrounding violence statistics. The assessment of violence involves the use of conflicting analyses to support competing positions.[44]

In the broader context of measuring levels of societal and youth crime and violence, levels of school violence are perhaps even less clear. What is school violence? Does it include violence that begins in school and is settled later in the day behind the local supermarket? Does it include gang violence that is carried into the school from the surrounding community? What is violence itself? Does it include fistfights? Verbal abuse? Racial slurs? Intimidation? Weapons possession? What about class disruptions? These are questions that legislators and school administrators decide differently in conjunction with their communities in order to set the basis for measuring what type of violence, and how much of it, is occurring in their midst. Only with this information, preferably in a nationally comparable form, can a full assessment of the levels and nature of the school violence problems be conducted and delineated over time.

One summary of surveys on school violence has shown a general trend of increasing violence as reported by schools across the country. It is clear that levels of violence and victimization have at least remained high, even if they have not increased.[45] Perceptually, the problem seems to have gotten worse. Anecdotal evidence refers to increases in the intensity, if not the level, of violence among youth in school. Weapons have contributed to this trend and perception, but other forms of fighting seem to have taken on a new, more visceral quality. Beyond these perceptions, which vary across communities, it is difficult to find broad statistics that are reliable on school violence. Fewer non-accidental deaths, at least, occur in schools than in homes and the community as a whole.

School districts must monitor their own levels of violence if they are to understand the nature of the problem, or nonproblem, that exists in their schools. States can help by providing funds for these information initiatives, by providing for some standardization in the information-gathering process, and perhaps by mandating that all districts track certain data in their schools and report it to the state. Until a more comprehensive information-gathering process is fully implemented, starting at the school level, it will continue to be difficult to assess the comparative levels of violence over time and between schools, districts, and states. Even then, comparability of measures and varying interpretations of definitions will likely cause problems in analysis.

Possible Causes of School Violence

Violence in the schools is primarily perpetrated by youth. Thus, the causes of school violence must be considered in terms of the broader complex of youth violence and, ultimately, societal violence. There are specific conditions which may inhibit or promote a more or less violent atmosphere in schools. Additionally, schools may take actions that may prevent violence from occurring or lessen its effects. It is important to note that, in the problem definition perspective that this book takes, the causes that one identifies as underlying the violence phenomenon will tend to lead to conclusions about the policies one should adopt to confront the problem.[46] Whether one defines the issue as one of a dangerous physical environment and a lack of personal awareness of safety, for example, or one of psychosocial development and a lack of behavioral conflict resolution skills in individual students will influence one's final selection of policy alternatives. This section first outlines the prevailing "liberal" and "conservative" understandings about the causes of school violence. It then focuses on more comprehensive, research-based knowledge about the causes of violence and the role of the school as a risk factor in a child's life.

The Liberal Approach

Liberal assumptions and arguments about the causes of school violence focus on social conditions and strategies to prevent violence. In this view, students have learned violence, but not other ways of solving problems. They have been abused and neglected by their parents and their communities. They psychologically react to that treatment. They enter school unprepared to learn. Once there, they find themselves disconnected from school and their classes for various reasons, including cultural and racial bias. This alienation leads them to act out to get attention. The prevalence of guns makes violence easier and more deadly. This is combined with the availability of drugs that students have little knowledge or incentive to resist. Teachers and schools do not have the skills or resources to properly handle potentially disruptive students. They are not providing the means through which individual violent students and the schools as a whole can become more peaceful. The more liberal problem definitions concentrate on the needs of students, the lack of caring for students with problems, and the poor response of the school system to behavioral issues.

The Conservative Approach

The conservative approach concentrates on the lack of order and discipline in the schools and the loss of authority of teachers and principals. Poor parenting, a lack of traditional values, and compulsory education have led to too many kids in school who do not want to be there. The basic school role has shifted away from teaching core subjects. Students have been corrupted by violent and immoral media influences. At school, there is not enough focus on security needs to protect schools and their inhabitants from violence and vandalism.

The conservative approach to school violence involves deterrence and control by school authorities. The causes of violence in the school in this regard include a lack of an anti-crime policy, a personal lack of awareness about safety, and a physical environment that allows crime to flourish. Compulsory attendance laws are blamed for keeping too many uninterested students in schools. Lax punishment has resulted from too much concern for due process. Combined with a weakening of authority and a hesitancy to assert control and discipline, this focus on keeping all children in school has led to increasing disorder and subsequent violence in the schools. It is argued that the abandonment of teacher responsibility for disciplining students has contributed to the erosion of authority in the schools; this has led to an increase in disorder and violence.[47]

While liberals stress poverty and racism, conservatives emphasize the decline of moral values and the breakdown of the traditional family structure as causes of violence. The rise of single-parent families or families that, due to economic circumstances, require both parents to work outside of the home, is blamed for inadequate supervision of children.[48] The loss of working-class jobs and the movement toward universalization of education are blamed for introducing students and families into schools where learning may not always occur. Desegregation is blamed for bringing racial and ethnic groups together and fueling animosities through court-ordered busing.

Thus, both liberal and conservative commentators and researchers connect school violence to broad societal trends in America. Both sides have indicted violent media and television access and the presence of weapons. Teachers, students, and law officers claim that students carry weapons for four reasons: for protection to and from school, to impress friends, for self-esteem, and for protection in school.[49] These general societal trends include fiscal constraints, integration, and suburbanization. Combined with the "loosening" of authority during the sixties, the rise in drug availability, and the rise in single-parent families and illegitimate births, these trends form the environmental context in which school violence is situated.[50]

Four Major Academic Perspectives on Violence

Beyond the simplified and overlapping liberal and conservative causal understandings and arguments about school violence, one can identify at least four major perspectives on violence in the literature on violence and several other perspectives within these broader categories. These perspectives not only situate school violence conditions in the larger context of violence, but also provide a more structured framework for understanding the causes of violence in the schools.

The Comprehensive Approach

The National Research Council (NRC) issued a recent report that summarized and synthesized the existing research on violence. This inclusive volume is itself an example of what I will call the "comprehensive" perspective on violence. The NRC identifies three basic perspectives on violence: psychosocial-developmental, biological-genetic, and social-environmental. The NRC argues that most studies of violence focus on only one element of the problem. In other words, they approach the issue from only one perspective. Few studies, it claims, study the important interactions among the elements prioritized by each perspective.[51]

The NRC exemplifies a comprehensive approach, arguing that all three perspectives, or "levels of explanation," should be examined together. The interactions between factors are keys to understanding and preventing violence. Yet these interactions are understudied. Programs that simultaneously operate on the three levels are too rare.[52] The comprehensive approach is a multidisciplinary, inclusive perspective on violence. It moves beyond particular categorical attempts to explain and reduce violence. It integrates elements from various types of research to argue for a broad examination of the causes of and solutions to the violence problem.

A focus on risk and protective factors is the theoretical perspective that underpins the NRC's approach. The risk and protective factor approach is a widely shared understanding of the development of the potential for violence. In modern society, there are myriad conditions that emerge as risk factors that tend to produce violent youth.[53] Many of these conditions converge on the family and the child's place therein. However, the comprehensive perspective holds that families are but one of the so-called "risk factors" that contribute to delinquency and substance abuse.[54] These behaviors are strongly correlated with violence. Risk factors in the area of violence indicate the possibility of harmful behavior. And while no one can yet construct a perfect causal model for violence, one can recognize that individual skills and characteristics are joined by social contexts in contributing to behavioral outcomes. Thus, Hawkins et al. identify as risk factors "community factors such as poverty and neighborhood disorganization; family factors including poor family management and negative parental modeling; school factors like lack of student involvement and low expectations for success; peer influence; and individual factors such as early antisocial behavior and alienation."[55] Of much interest to schools, then, is the fact that they themselves can be risk factors. They can also play a role in confronting some of the other risk factors once these are identified.

Psychosocial-Developmental Perspective

The comprehensive perspective encompasses several constituent perspectives. The psychosocial-developmental perspective that the NRC identifies incorporates elements of social learning theory. It focuses on the early developmental experiences of the child as the key factors in explaining later violent behavior. This approach sees such factors as family modeling of behavior, television viewing, and perinatal and early school experiences, such as failure or rejection, as later predictors of aggression and violence. In other words, modeling of violent behavior occurs early in the child's life. If you notice certain attributes of violence early on, then you tend to see them again later in adolescence or adulthood. The psychosocial-developmental perspective, then, can be more or less global in its frame of reference, but it tends to focus on early childhood experiences as influencing later integration of behavioral skills.[56]

Biological-Genetic Perspective

The biological perspective that the NRC identifies focuses on both permanent and temporary neurological, hormonal, genetic, or other biological influences on predispositions toward violence. Examples of permanent factors include genetic predisposition, fetal or prenatal development, accidents, and brain trauma. Temporary factors include stimuli, alcohol and drugs, hormones, genes, effects on neurotransmitters, and diet. The NRC points to unclear findings in this area, and acknowledges that biological factors may be causing, and may be caused by, violence.[57]

Karr-Morse and Wiley's recent book, *Ghosts from the Nursery*, exemplifies a combination of the biological and early psychosocial-developmental perspectives on violence and aggression. Synthesizing current research on brain development, they argue that the prenatal period and first two years of a child's life are crucial in the development of empathy, emotional well-being, and cognitive growth.

She traces the roots of child, adolescent, and adult impulsive violence to the earliest months of life.[58]

Social-Environmental Perspective

The social perspective is perhaps the broadest category that the NRC identifies. It includes at least several identifiable views on causes of violence. The general approach examines the environment beyond personal and family factors. From this perspective, such elements as gang influences, schools, and cultural values influence the amount of violence perpetrated by individuals. The NRC argues that socioeconomic status accounts for ethnic and racial differences in violence, for example. Poverty, mobility of the population, and change in the community combine to produce violence. The prevalence of guns, drug networks, overall weak social organization and cohesion, high population density, and family disruption lead to violence. In other words, community influences combine with poverty to produce violence; ethnic and racial factors "disappear" when controlling for these broader variables. The social perspective identifies many interactions, such as those between family, community, individuals, culture, and social institutions.[59] The most relevant point for an examination of school violence is that violence in the schools reflects violence in the larger community. It interacts with it, causes and is caused by it, contributes to it and can decrease it, but generally cannot escape it.

The work of William Julius Wilson (1987) is representative of the social perspective. Wilson takes a broad, environmental approach to urban violence. He focuses on the "concentration effects of ghetto poverty." Such factors as social isolation, economic polarization, alienation from the mainstream, and the development of a different set of cultural norms provide the broad context for inner-city violence. A prevalence of drugs, the lack of jobs, and a weak value system interact with individual and other social factors to produce violence.[60]

The Physical Perspective. One clear perspective within the social approach is what I will call the "physical" perspective. The NRC describes one version of this as a concentration on the physical environment in which violence takes place. For example, areas such as public housing complexes and the schools near to them and spatial characteristics such as openness to intruders and drug trading present more favorable places in which violence can occur. Therefore, there is a prevalence of violence in locations such as these.[61] Physical aspects of a school, such as poor lighting, secluded and unpatrolled hallways, and unlocked doors and windows, can contribute to violence.

The NRC suggests that the following four spatial characteristics of schools can affect levels of violence: (a) a relatively high number of individuals occupy a limited space; (b) the capacity to avoid confrontations is reduced; (c) the imposition of behavioral routines and conformity may produce feelings of anger, resentment, and rejection; and (d) poor design features in the school may facilitate violent behavior.[62]

The Order-Expulsion Perspective. The National Institute of Education's (NIE) 1978 report to Congress was one of the first and most comprehensive surveys and studies of violence in America's schools. One of its conclusions was that rates of student violence were higher in schools in which students had low attachments to values and where they perceived that school authorities were ineffective in imposing social controls. Signs of such weak control included a lack of discipline in classrooms, lax or arbitrary enforcement of school rules, and a weak principal.[63] Out of this initial conclusion about the need for a reassertion of authority emerges what I will call the "order-expulsion" perspective.

Toby, for example, explains the variance in violence across schools by focusing on disorder as a predictor of violence. He makes a slippery-slope argument that an environment characterized by disorder eventually leads to violence. He cites Wilson analogously on communities and presents an authority construct of violence in the schools. He identifies two trends that contribute to disorder: the increasing numbers of students in school who lack behavioral conformity to school rules and the weakening of authority of teachers and adults over kids at school.[64] These two trends causally interact to produce disorder. The main variables on which Toby focuses are the larger size of schools and their subsequent disconnection from community values; he argues that schools are disconnecting from their surrounding communities and that students in these schools are disconnected from each other. He emphasizes the lack of "defensible space," police, or security guards in the schools. He argues that compulsory attendance laws have unintentionally made education a right, thus increasing the focus on due process for disruptive students. This has ultimately weakened disciplinary action on the part of teachers and administrators. Teachers themselves have relinquished much of their responsibility for authority.

Devine notes that in addition to other elements of the school environment, apart from the community in which the school exists, an atrophy in the role of the teacher contributes to school violence. Responding to recent surges in violence, "teachers have relinquished their traditional obligation of caring but firm moral tutelage, of challenging inappropriate adolescent behavior, from rude and offensive language to serious violence."[65] What now occurs is a deportation of students out of the school building by security personnel.

Other research on causes of violence has identified disorganization, a lack of attachment or commitment to the school, and the age of the principal. Apparently, the older the principal is, the more vandalism there is in the school, although the causality here is unclear. Research has pointed to teacher apathy, poor physical condition of the school itself, and the style of leadership or governance of the school as causes of violence. A firm, fair, and consistent style seems to be more closely related to lower levels of violence than arbitrary and severe leadership.[66] One problem with these conditions is the possible circularity of their reasoning. While seeing cause and effect as interdependent and interdetermining is important in understanding violence and its complexity, finding solutions to violence may require some determining of the primary direction of causality as well as a broader focus on the problem. "It is not clear whether the ineffective control [of school authorities] gives a kind of permission that encourages violent behavior, or whether high violence levels create fear among authorities that undermines their will to impose discipline."[67] It may be a downward spiral.

The Comprehensive Approach as More Inclusive

Overall, the NRC's recommended comprehensive approach toward understanding and preventing violence is the most inclusive and structured means of understanding the causes of violence. It recognizes the complexity of the violence problem. It places school as a social-environmental factor affecting violent tendencies in children. Schools can, however, play a role in improving the psychosocial and even the biological-neurological development of children. They can also restructure themselves physically and environmentally and change patterns of authority in order to affect the conditions that underlie violence.[68]

Another good example of the comprehensive approach to school violence comes from Elliott, Hamburg, and Williams, who present an overview of the public health approach to school violence, synthesizing a variety of approaches to school violence from different academic disciplines, and looking for consensus among them on what violence is and what works in preventing it.[69]

Projections for Future School Violence

Projections for the future extent of the school violence problem have little to rely on in the way of specifics. Thus, they focus on broad societal trends. Fears of future increases in violence among youth and at school are strong. Demographically, the proportion of youth in the overall population is expected to grow, due to the baby "boomlet" or "echo." Many observers expect overall rates of violence and crime to increase since violence initiation rates are highest among those aged fifteen to sixteen and violence participation rates are highest for those aged sixteen to seventeen.[70]

One indicator of the increasing number of youths in the overall school population is the number of students expected to graduate from high school. According to the U.S. Department of Education, the total number of high school graduates is predicted to rise steadily from 2,564,000 in 1997 to 3,015,000 in 2007. According to the Western Interstate Commission on Higher Education, this represents an increase of over 50 percent in states like California and Florida, consistently strong increases in New England and Northwestern states, and decreases in some Midwestern and Appalachian states.[71] According to the U.S. Census Bureau, the number of youths aged fourteen to seventeen will increase from an estimated 13,311,000 in 1990 to a projected 16,986,000 in 2005. This represents an increase in this group's proportion of the total U.S. population from 5.3 percent in 1990 to 5.9 percent in 2005.[72]

Observers also track the rise of a new generation of violent youth and criminals, so-called "monsters" and "super-predators." These offenders are said to have no remorse, guilt, empathy, or attachment to other human beings. They are thus more dangerous, deadly, and fearsome. Predictions are that these monsters or "super-predators" will grow in number and in societal impact.[73] Expectations for future school and youth violence can seem grim indeed if one considers some of the challenges facing us today. We see the prevalence of firearms as an enabling factor for violence in American society. We consider the arguments that infants exposed to violence, substance abuse, and lack of education and emotional support will be prone to impulsive violence during later years. We note that violent media assault children and adolescents with images and models of violence every day. And we watch as schools and classrooms grow in size to accommodate all those new students, thus becoming more impersonal and offering less support.

Policy Alternatives

Administrators, school boards, legislators, and superintendents hold perhaps the ultimate responsibility for the safety of those in their schools. They face pressure to select among alternative policies to confront school violence. Such a choice is complicated by a number of issues. However, variation in responses is evident. In the 1940s and earlier, schools enacted policies on dress codes, uniforms, obedience, and moral education. Schools then began to add security guards, surveillance systems, and "target hardening" instruction to prevent victimization. They enacted bans on gang paraphernalia, bought metal detectors, and established curricular approaches to violence prevention. A National School Safety Center was even created in 1983 by the Reagan administration in order to disseminate information about school safety approaches and research.[74]

Identification of Policies and Programs

Following the expanded NRC framework outlined above, policy solutions can be organized according to the comprehensive, psychosocial-developmental, biological, social, physical, and order-expulsion perspectives. The types of policy interventions, for example, that arise from the psychosocial-developmental perspective focus on counteracting negative developmental experiences or substituting more positive training for them. The violence prevention curriculum developed by Prothrow-Stith, for example, is an example of a public health perspective that is comprehensive but operates largely from a psychosocial-developmental standpoint.[75] This program intervenes at the community, school, and family levels to emphasize the undesirability of aggression. It teaches, for example, new problem-solving methods, different television-viewing practices, and social skills. This is an example of a more global approach in this area.

The NRC identifies some more singularly focused alternatives in the psychosocial approach, such as attempts to prevent early-grade failure, intensive early childhood education for disadvantaged students, and early identification of learning or behavioral disorders. Other psychosocial approaches include training parents in consistent discipline and family practices, Head Start–type programs, and anti-bullying campaigns. Biological interventions include the psychosocial alternatives mentioned above as well as the prevention of brain injuries through the promotion of bicycle helmets, for example. Researchers focus on reducing of substance abuse by pregnant women, providing adequate nutrition programs, and removing dangerous chemical substances from the school environment. They argue for implementing drug education and substance-abuse prevention programs and other practices to reduce the effects and presence of potentially violence-inducing chemical substances on the body.[76]

Some school districts have adopted alternative education programs for habitually disruptive students or students who have problems functioning in the regular school environment. These programs can vary from focusing on psychosocial-developmental and social-environmental issues to representing a more order-expulsion response, as described below. The Tupelo Public School District in Mississippi, for example, has established two alternative schools to reduce violence, crime, disruption, and expulsion. Continually disruptive students are sent to the Bissell Center, where they receive behavioral counseling in addition to the regular academic program. At the Youth Discipline Center, more violent or criminally prone students receive behavioral counseling, guidance, and an emphasis on personal responsibility from a school district program that works with law enforcement and the court system.[77]

The policy conclusions of the "physical" approach involve architectural innovations, defensible space, target hardening, and environmental management.[78] School administrators, for example, can light hallways, install video surveillance, make entry into the school difficult, and design schools without hidden areas for mischief. Schools can teach faculty and students to avoid certain areas, report violence, and defend themselves. Schools can attempt to remove guns through the use of metal detectors, locker searches, and security guards, thus removing an enabler of serious violence. Recent innovations in this area include the banning of backpacks, buying a second set of textbooks so that students do not have to carry books from home to school, mandating only see-through backpacks and bags, and returning to the use of school uniforms and dress codes.

The public health perspective discussed above includes physical factors. It focuses on primary, secondary, and tertiary interventions. Primary interventions are designed to prevent violence from occurring. Secondary interventions reduce the harm caused by violence. And tertiary interventions repair the harm. Staggering school hours to keep older kids in class while younger kids walk home is a primary intervention. Keeping guns out of school is a secondary physical intervention. Rehabilitating victims and training crisis or trauma teams is a tertiary physical intervention.[79] Thus, the physical perspective can be somewhat global when constructed on the three-stage model. However, the physical perspective can take on a more limited form when it focuses only on weapons reduction, expulsion for offenses to remove violent kids from school, or locking doors and windows to keep intruders out of the building. Another limited form of the physical perspective is a focus on authority and disciplinary control as a solution to violence.

This order-expulsion perspective is exemplified by Toby's argument. His perspective is not unique. It leads to physical and cultural policy actions that are designed to change the climate and the inhabitants of the school building.[80] He argues for voluntary attendance policies that will lead to higher academic and behavioral standards, a greater willingness and ability to remove disruptive students from the classroom, and a student population that is limited to those who want to be in school. Culturally, he argues for a reassertion of order and authority on the part of adults in the school, the presence of adult learners in school to act as monitors and role models, and an assertion of disciplinary responsibility by school officials.[81]

The goals of school violence policies are numerous and diverse. The language that individuals use to describe policies in this area often hints at the underlying perspectives of these individuals and policies. School safety policies, for example, highlight the need to keep all students and staff in and around schools safe from harm, a mostly physical, social approach. School security policies focus on preventing and deterring crime; protecting school campuses from vandalism, outside intrusions, and deviant student behavior; and fostering both daily administrative authority and crisis management skills. These are social and physical approaches emphasizing environmental management.

School discipline policies concentrate on promoting an orderly school environment, ensuring proper student behavior, identifying proscribed behaviors and consequent punishments, and thus furthering a good context for learning in the school. School expulsion and suspension policies aim to protect the majority of well-behaved students by removing dangerous and disruptive students from classrooms and schools. These policies often attempt to change the future behavior of individual students by punishing them for their actions and have been refered to as *peacekeeping* approaches.

Additional policies include peace education, violence prevention, and conflict resolution. Programs have been created in the areas of peer mediation, parent involvement, and gang awareness and substance abuse education. These policies fit into the social, psychosocial-developmental, comprehensive, biological, and public health perspectives. Peace education attempts to teach students about alternatives to violence and to build within students the desire to act nonviolently. It fosters a comprehensive worldview about peace and violence, a view that at its most complete level, a *peacebuilding* approach, instills in children the desire to act nonviolently. Violence prevention curricula try to teach students about the risks and dangers of violence so that they will avoid violent behavior. Conflict resolution programs promote alternative methods of nonviolent conflict resolution so that students have choices other than "fight or flight." Peer mediation programs try to give students the skills they need to solve their own problems successfully and positively, through structured mediation sessions. Again, these programs seek to promote alternatives to violence. They can be referred to as *peacemaking* approaches.

Parental involvement programs try to engage parents in the education and discipline of their children, teaching them new methods of discipline, making them take responsibility for their children's actions, and helping them work with the schools to effectively educate their children. Gang awareness programs seek to educate students and staff about the signs and dangers of gang life in order to prevent future gang involvement. Similarly, substance-abuse education programs aim to build resistance in children to the allures of alcohol and other drugs.[82]

School districts around the country have responded in widely varying ways to school violence. Table 3 illustrates the choices these districts have made. The National School Boards Association's 1993 survey, on which it is based, shows that suspension of disruptive students was the most common overall response to violence in schools nationwide. Expulsion followed closely behind. Interagency collaboration, such as that between schools and social service, mental health, and criminal justice agencies, was also common. Many districts reported conflict resolution, mediation training, and peer mediation as a policy response. School security personnel were utilized in fewer school districts, as were metal detectors. These policy responses are not mutually exclusive, but they serve to show the variety of actions that administrators have undertaken to confront school violence. Notably, these responses occurred across urban, rural, and suburban lines nationwide. However, urban districts were more likely to report using almost every policy response. The proportionate commonality and rankings of responses remained fairly constant across all three groups.

Evaluation of Alternatives

In evaluating the numerous policy alternatives that have been proposed to deal with school violence, discipline, and safety, one must first consider that measuring which policy alternatives work is probably more difficult than measuring levels of violence. In part, this is because evaluating the policy alternatives relies at the most basic level on finding out whether the intervention decreases levels of violence in the school and community over time. Isolating cause and effect in such a complex social situation is nearly impossible. Measuring something that one has prevented is especially complicated. How much violence would there have been without the intervention? Has the program affected aggregate levels of violence, as well as individual attitudes and propensities toward violent behavior?

One of the major fault lines in the violence debate is between "prevention" and "punishment." This mirrors the national debate over crime and imprisonment.[83] The perspectives on violence outlined above are broader than the dichotomous debate between prevention and punishment. However, they can still influence the evaluation of programs that do or do not fit within a particular viewpoint. It is essential that all policy alternatives be evaluated to understand whether and how they accomplish their various goals. The NRC argues that evaluation of violence prevention programs is segmented and fragmented, inconsistent, underfunded, and too short in time span. It argues that preventative strategies are just as important as punitive measures and that more research needs to be devoted to understanding individual and social influences on violence.[84] Elliott argues that prevention programs take longer and are harder to implement but that the violence reduction effects of prevention programs are substantially greater and probably cost no more.[85]

Some Evidence on School Violence Policies and Programs

Tolan and Guerra argue that evaluation of programs aimed at adolescent and school violence reduction is incomplete, flawed, and politically and institutionally biased.[86] They offer a comprehensive review of the effectiveness of various prevention alternatives, ranging from individually based social skills training to efforts to address media violence. They discuss specifics of various programs. They identify a number of programs that have accumulated what they see as solid evidence of long-term effectiveness. It is worth noting that some of the programs not identified may work, but there is not sufficient evaluation evidence on which to base a sound judgment of worth. The programs identified as having demonstrated long-term desired effects include interventions to train children to think differently to promote problem-solving skills; family relations and family problem-solving interventions; work in schools to increase students' motivation; and diversion programs in residential institutions. Reorganization programs that involve families and students in the schools and set up programs to deal with individual student needs demonstrate some success, as do structured interaction programs among peers. Changes in teacher practices, such as classroom management training and environmental security programs, are in need of more studies or are untested.[87]

What is interesting in the Tolan and Guerra report is the diversity of intervention programs available and the extensive need for more study of the various programs. While programs that focus on changing youth roles in the community and giving youth social skills training seem successful, intensive social casework programs involving close supervision and counseling and programs involving guided

Table 3

School District Policy Responses to School Violence

Policy	Overall (%)	Urban (%)	Suburban (%)	Rural (%)
Suspension	78	85	78	75
Student conduct-discipline code	76	87	79	70
Collaboration with other agencies	73	93	73	62
Expulsion	72	85	68	70
School board policy	71	76	69	71
Alternative programs or schools	66	85	66	57
Staff development	62	74	66	52
Conflict resolution, mediation, peer mediation	61	82	63	49
Locker searches	50	64	43	49
Closed campus for lunch	44	46	48	37
Mentoring programs	43	65	44	31
Home-school linkages	42	55	45	32
Dress code	41	52	42	33
Law-related education programs	39	57	36	33
Multicultural sensitivity training	39	62	49	18
Parent skill training	38	51	39	28
Search and seizure	36	51	35	28
Security personnel in schools	36	65	40	18
Support groups	36	47	37	28
Student photo ID system	32	41	39	20
Gun-free school zones	31	46	26	26
Specialized curriculum	27	48	25	18
Drug-detecting dogs	24	27	18	27
Work opportunities	23	34	21	19
Phones in classrooms	22	31	21	16
Metal detectors	15	39	10	6
Volunteer parent patrols	13	17	14	8
Other	13	16	15	11
Closed-circuit TV	11	19	8	8
Establishing safe havens	10	16	9	6

Note: School districts reported more than one policy response.
Source: National School Boards Association, *Violence in the Schools: How America's School Boards Are Safeguarding Our Children* (Alexandria, VA: National School Boards Association, 1993), 7.

group interaction among peers do not seem to work.[88] But there are many programs available that are untested, have conflictual or unclear results, or which may have only short-term effects.

In general, the NRC argues that such psychosocial interventions as Head Start, parental discipline training, and attempts to prevent early grade failure are more likely to work if they are comprehensive, culturally relevant, and developmentally appropriate. Early implementation and community involvement are also more successful strategies.[89] The usefulness of focusing only on the physical inhibitors or facilitators of violence, on the other hand, is limited. These physical approaches to violence prevention and reduction, including architectural innovations, target hardening, and environmental management, are insufficient in the long term. While in the short term they may deter some aspects of violence, they have not been found to be effective in themselves. "The reason for the inconsistent and temporary effects appears to be that crime and violence arise from interactions between the social environment and the physical environment, which cannot be controlled entirely through manipulations of the physical environment."[90]

Thus, the order-expulsion perspective is limited in that it focuses only on social aspects of violence and ignores what happens to expelled children in the community. It does not foresee the possibilities of integrating elements of this order-expulsion approach with biological and psychosocial-developmental alternatives, working with families and the community, and attempting to solve the individual problems of disruptive students.[91] Perhaps most importantly, from the comprehensive, risk-factor perspective, the order-expulsion perspective does not adequately address the evidence that dropouts are more prone to violence, and it does not see that school failure is a risk factor in itself.

In contrast, with a goal of returning students back to the regular classroom when they are ready, the Tupelo alternative education programs for habitually disruptive students have apparently been successful. They have reduced expulsion and trained students in life skills and discipline, which may prevent later problems. They have lessened disruption in the regular classrooms, increased school disciplinary enforcement by offering the alternative school as an option, and increased community safety by keeping kids in a structured program rather than on the streets.[92]

Elliot, Hamburg, and Williams emphasize five themes in their discussion of an "integrated approach to violence prevention." These themes lead to some conclusions about specific programs and strategies that work and clearly illustrate a comprehensive approach:

1. The family, peer group, school, and neighborhood are closely interconnected: "A comprehensive strategy that attends to the multiple social contexts in which youth live and function, including schools, has much greater promise for successfully stopping or reducing youth violence."

2. There is dynamic interaction between individuals and these social contexts: "social contexts can shape the process of human development," and "violence may express frustration or hopelessness for some youths striving but failing to master the tasks relevant to their developmental stage."

3. Collaboration is the key to effective violence prevention: "the prevention of violence involves building relationships among representatives of all public and private sectors that touch on the lives of youth."

4. The public health approach works best: "The public health strategy should be used to assess the nature and extent of the youth violence problem and to plan and carry out violence prevention programming."

5. Promising intervention strategies are organized around "systemic changes for schools, programs for individual youths, and public policy positions." Some of the school change strategies that recommended include schools serving as multiservice centers in communities; schools promoting the norms of nonviolence; schools developing clear, safe school plans; schools staying open after hours to be safe havens and to offer educational and other programs. Programs for individuals include developing the social resources of students; targeting interventions around gun-related events, in addition to interpersonal disputes; targeting early childhood education and family support.[93]

Difficulties in Evaluating Programs: Mediation and Conflict Resolution

The evaluation of peer mediation and conflict resolution programs further illustrates the difficulties and inadequacies of current evaluation efforts. Major issues that arise are difficulty in finding staff time and money to conduct and process evaluations and troubles with obtaining accurate quantitative data. The near impossibility of maintaining distinct experimental and control groups and difficulties in trying to clearly associate results directly with a program further complicate these evaluations. Reports indicate that students have generally responded well to peer mediation programs, have kept to the terms of mediation agreements, and have not violated stipulations of confidentiality that are part of mediated agreements. Faculty and staff, as well as students, have reported feeling safer in their school environment, having a more positive school experience, and seeing less violence in the schools. Students felt empowered, as have local schools and communities.

Mediation, conflict resolution, and peace education programs ideally want the use of program techniques to spread throughout every classroom, but it also seems important to have a comprehensive class that is required and reaches all students. The idea is to create a different culture throughout the school and even the community. These programs appear to be more effective in schools that foster a general "climate of peace" overall than when implemented as an isolated lesson in school.[94]

However, as one researcher writes,

> School mediation program administrators and participants have made fantastic claims for the success of their programs, asserting that students' lives have been changed dramatically, as have school climates. However, as in the early stages of most innovative programs, little attention has been paid to systematic research and evaluation. Anecdotal evidence of program successes are overwhelmingly positive.[95]

Lam confirms the fact that using a control group within the same school in order to determine the effects of a mediation program on an experimental group is nearly impossible, due to the fact that training influences nonexperimental group students. Since one of the implied goals of these programs is to empower and educate all the students in a school, however, it may seem counterproductive to try to measure isolated effects of a program. Paradoxically, if the program is affecting students positively across the board, then this result is desired and positive. Lam reports that findings from the studies suggest a 75 to 90 percent success rate for mediation programs, as measured by the number of mediated conflicts that resulted in an agreement that was still being upheld at the time of the follow-up.[96]

"In general, the research has paid little attention to the effectiveness of the actual mediation programs, tending to focus instead on the impact of mediation training on student trainees."[97] Lam reports mixed evidence of positive effects on school climate, fighting, attitudes toward conflict, and other goal areas of these programs. She calls for better designed, executed, and reported research, suggesting the following six improvements: (1) random assignment to experimental and control groups; (2) the use of two comparable schools as comparison groups to avoid intra-school contamination; (3) the use of interviews with mediators, students in the control group, student disputants, teachers and administrators; (4) more systematic gathering of qualitative data; (5) field observations of mediation sessions and training; and (6) studies of school records on such factors as discipline and attendance:

> An evaluative research effort which makes use of four forms of data— surveys, interviews, school records, and observations—is more valid and reliable than one or two sources of data. When all four sources are used, researchers can make a more persuasive argument about the impact of school mediation programs, and the changes that such programs bring to the school community as well as to individuals within that community.[98]

This argument applies equally well to any program designed to reduce violence, prevent violence, build within students a desire to act nonviolently, make schools safer places, punish students for disruptive or dangerous behavior, and so forth. Not only should programs be evaluated carefully according to their stated and implied goals, but these goals should be examined critically in light of a community's values and the effectiveness of adopted interventions.

It seems essential for individual communities, districts, and states to assess their needs, to examine the research related to specific programs, and to find the program that best fits their own context and violence problem. It is also essential for them to evaluate and assess these programs from the beginning in order to determine their efficacy. Whether the program involves peer mediation, boot camps, family counseling, metal detection, or mandatory expulsion, administrators and policy makers should build in an evaluation component in order to determine whether the program works. This information should be utilized in making decisions about program effectiveness and worth and in future funding decisions. What information is gathered and how that information is used are essential components of the policy learning process.[99]

A Sampling of State Policy Actions

Across the country, states are also formulating and implementing a variety of policies and programs designed to react to and to prevent school violence. This section presents an overall picture of legislation at the state level and then highlights a few examples of programs that have received some general publicity and praise in various states.

Legislation Tracking Chart. Table 4 illustrates specific state legislative actions taken in the areas of alternative schools for disruptive students, school uniforms and dress codes, transfer of student discipline records, banning pagers and cellular phones, and weapons and gun control. As one can see, numerous states have undertaken a broad array of policies to handle school and youth violence. Many of the laws were passed in recent years, indicating some of the "tough" legislative responses to the heightened attention given to the school violence problem in the early 1990s. Fewer examples and evidence of legislative actions are available in the "prevention" area, although Iowa, Minnesota, and Washington had passed laws fostering conflict resolution, mediation, and violence education programs by 1994. A number of states, including Hawaii, Kentucky, Nevada, and Tennessee, have taken such nonlegislative actions as university-school partnerships in mediation, task forces, gang awareness efforts by police, and professional development programs focusing on the school climate and dispute resolution.[100]

Specific Examples of State Actions. On the state level, Illinois has taken action to amend its school code to require that districts provide conflict resolution or violence prevention education for grades four through twelve. The Illinois Council for the Prevention of Violence formed a curriculum task force that includes representatives from many state and local groups. "The task force is creating a framework for reviewing violence prevention curricula, identifying gaps, and making recommendations for the use of such curricula in Illinois schools. It will also pilot violence prevention programs in five districts to determine what kinds of technical assistance and other resources are most helpful."[101] The Illinois model is inclusive of many participants in the state and local community. It is compulsory, by requiring participation of all school districts, but seemingly flexible, allowing for variation across districts within a state framework. It positions the

Table 4

State School Violence and Discipline Legislative Actions

School Violence Policy	States with Related Laws	States with Related Law or Laws (Year or Years Enacted)	Laws up to
Alternative schools for disruptive students	35	AZ(82), AR(93 95), CA(95), CO(96), DE(94), FL(93 95), GA(94 95), HI(95), IL(95), IN(96), KS(74), LA(94), MD(95 96), MN, MS(95), MO(95), NE(95), NH(95), NJ(95), NC, ND, OH(96), OK(92), OR(95), PA(95), SC(95), SD(95), TN(94 96), TX(95), UT(95), VA(95), WA(94), WV(96), WI(93), WY	Sept. 1996
School uniforms and dress codes	12	CA(94), IA(95), IN(95), LA(92), MA(96), MN(95), NJ(96), TN(95), TX, UT(94), VA(95), WA(94)	Oct. 1996
Ban pagers/cell phones	16	AL, CT, GA, IL, IN, MD, MI, NV, NJ, OK, PA, RI, SC, TN, TX, VA	Aug. 1996
Transfer of student discipline records	30	AL(82 94), AR(95), CO(96), CT(94 95), DE(95 96), FL(95), GA(95), HI(85), ID(95), IL(95 96), IN(95), IA(95), KS(94), KY(94 96), MD(95 96), MS(95), MO(96), NV(94), NM(94), NY(95), OH(95), OK(95), OR(96), PA(95), SC(94), TN(96), VA(96), WV(96), WI(94 95 96), WY(94 95)	Aug. 1996
Zero tolerance/ gun control	51	AL(95), AK(95), AZ(95), AR(95), CA(95), CO(93), CT(95), DC(96), DE(95), FL(95), GA(95), HI(95), ID(95), IL(95), IN(95), IA(95), KA(95), KY(96), LA(95), ME(93), MD(96), MA(93), MI(95), MN(95), MS(95), MO(95), MT(95), NE(95), NV(95), NH(95), NJ(95), NM(95), NY(95), NC(95), ND(95), OH(95), OK(95), OR(95), PA(95), RI(95), SC(95), SD(96), TN(95), TX(95), UT(95), VT(95), VA(95), WA(95), WV(95), WI(95), WY(95)	Dec. 1996
Discipline of special ed students	10	CO(93), CT(95), FL(96), ID(95), IL(95), KY(96), MD(96), NJ(95), NM(81), WV(96)	Aug. 1996
Teacher protection/ limits on liability	16	AL(94 95), AR(95), FL(96), GA(95), IA(94), IN(95 96), MD(96), MI(94), NC(95), NH(96), NV(94 95), NY(96), OR(95), TX(94 96), UT(94), VA(95 96)	Aug. 1996

Note: Some states passed multiple laws in the same year.

Source: Education Commission of the States, Clearinghouse Notes: Violence (Denver, CO: Education Commission of the States, 1994, 1996).

state as a resource provider, forum constructor, and information warehouse. It will evaluate pilot programs in order to discover what is needed by districts and how the state can best facilitate violence prevention programs at the district level. The Illinois program begins early, at the fourth grade, and generally represents a psychosocial-developmental approach.

Some thirty states are providing more comprehensive services for children and their families as part of an attempt to focus on prevention. These programs include early intervention programs, family support and preservation programs, and the expansion of public preschools.[102] Again showing a psychosocial-developmental approach, these types of programs make a connection between family structure, support, and positive child development. They then invest at the front end rather than the back end of violence prevention or intervention. States are also reforming their justice systems to deal with violence as it is already occurring. Colorado and Florida, for example, have continued to emphasize that juvenile offenders are different than adults and thus need to be treated differently. Florida created a special Juvenile Justice System with the input of diverse agencies, including the Department of Education, the Florida Network of Youth and Family Services, and the Office of the Attorney General. This interdisciplinary, interagency initiative represented both a psychosocial-developmental and a social-environmental view of the violence problem in Florida.[103]

South Carolina passed a Safe Schools Act in 1990 that increased penalties for carrying weapons at school or distributing drugs near schools. Minors fifteen years of age or older who violated sections of the act were subject to trial in general sessions court instead of family court. The Safe Schools Act also required school districts to report incidences of school crimes and to follow a checklist to monitor safety strengths and weaknesses. In 1992, Act 506 made it possible for schools to keep out students who were convicted of possession of a weapon, drug trafficking, or crimes defined as violent. In 1993, Act 117 added "assault and battery of a high and aggravated nature" to this list of crimes that could keep students out of school. This was an order-expulsion approach focusing on social and physical punishments and interventions. More recently, however, in 1996 the Schoolhouse Safety Alliance Act moved South Carolina toward a more comprehensive approach to violence prevention. It emphasized interagency collaboration, parental involvement, and judicial responsiveness. Finally, the sharing of information about offenders was facilitated between schools and law enforcement.[104]

In 1990, Ohio's governor, Richard Celeste, spent $1 million on a "peace commission" that included the study and implementation of mediation programs. This was apparently the first instance of a governor spending tax money on a peace project.[105] And in New Mexico, the state has financed a conflict resolution program for thirty thousand students in over one hundred elementary and secondary schools.[106]

The variety of responses to school violence is as varied as the communities in America. From peace education in Milwaukee to mandatory weapons expulsion in Colorado, states and school districts are implementing many different programs to deal with school violence. One way to look at these various programs is to see them as tools in a toolbox, each designed for different purposes and each serving different needs. Just as every problem is not a nail requiring a hammer, school violence is not the same in every community, requiring neither the same punitive nor educational solution. Often, punitive, rehabilitative, preventative, and security interventions need to be implemented together as part of a broad strategy to deal with violence. School violence is never in every case a gang issue, a weapons issue, a values issue, or a poverty issue. Violence tends to cut across these lines and to manifest itself differently in many communities. Nonetheless, some broad strategies that tend to work better have been identified, the primary one being overall comprehensiveness in perspective and collaboration between agencies.

Conclusion: The Need for Further Study and Clarification

School violence represents a complex education policy problem that involves strong value disagreements and emotions. Competing problem definitions and policy prescriptions are deeply held and are not always explicit. Problem definitions in this arena are influenced by core values and beliefs involving personal responsibility, justice, punishment, learning, care, community, and safety, among others.[107] Looking at school violence in local contexts, I have found that a limited definition of the problem leads to a limited consideration of alternatives. Much of the public debate on school violence defines the problem as one of guns and disruptions in schools; this leads to a debate over expulsion or non-expulsion. In contrast, many individual stakeholders have a much more comprehensive definition of the problem, one which includes such issues as a lack of family support, a lack of education in alternatives to violence, and a failure of the juvenile justice system to hold children accountable for their actions. A broader definition of this problem leads to a broader debate on options and a consideration of alternatives including conflict resolution training, stiffer probation sentences, and so forth.[108]

Rose suggests that value disagreements create a climate that is subject to change over time, but a climate that nevertheless mitigates against the successful transfer of a program that represents a set of values from one location but that cannot find the support of a majority in another place.[109] School violence represents such an area of value disagreements. Thus a policy program that aims to "solve" the school violence "problem" is subject to competing assessments of its underlying values and goals. Within the school violence arena, competing problem definitions, both intentional and subconscious, provide the screens through which actors filter assessments of potential "lessons" from other jurisdictions. Lesson-drawing, the conclusion that a program or policy is or may be successful sometime or somewhere else and thus may work in another time or location, is a component of policy learning. Strong value disagreements may have a significantly negative impact on lesson-drawing through their influence on program assessment and definition.

In general, it is difficult to reach clear conclusions about what works and what does not in addressing the school violence problem. One must be willing to examine qualitative as well as quantitative data, all of which can be inconclusive or sketchy. The multiple perspectives or approaches to violence constitute different goals, causal understandings, and policy preferences. Communities and states must assess their own specific needs when contemplating violence prevention initiatives, but can learn from available research if they are willing and able. There is obvious political benefit to taking some sort of action, but taking appropriate and meaningful action is important for long-term success, cost-effectiveness, and future community support. Short-term solutions may only serve to push the problem into the future while symbolically appearing to take a stand on violence today.

As a complex social policy problem, school violence is a problem where the problem definition process is vitally connected to policy outcomes. In this situation of uncertain trends and future projections, multiple causes, multiple and variable policy alternatives, and conflicting goals and values, problem definition powerfully structures approaches to and learning about school violence. The initial question posed in this chapter was, What can schools and education policy makers do to contribute to the reduction of violence in schools as well as in society as a whole? We can now clarify this question further: How is the education policy decision process to be improved in order to contribute to the reduction of violence in schools and in society as a whole, considering the connections between definitions of school violence and learning over time within this issue area?

In the next chapter, I focus more extensively on the problem definition and policy learning processes. For the reader interested in improving local, state, and national policy and programmatic approaches to school violence and other complex problems, this will provide helpful background understanding on how to rethink and reform the policy-making process. Those primarily interested in the school violence problem and lessons from the local and state levels may wish to jump directly to chapter 3.

Chapter 2
Problem Definition and Policy Learning
Why the Definition of the School Violence Problem Matters and How We Can Conceive of Learning about School Violence over Time

A Conceptual Approach to School Violence

This book focuses on educational policies designed to impact school violence by setting out the school violence debate in a national context and then telling the stories of legislative, policy, and program developments in Colorado and two of its largest school districts during the 1990s. In doing so, it examines the relationships between the policy problem definition and policy learning processes. These interrelated processes impact individual and institutional policy decisions. The book suggests that the values and experiences of individuals, and the broader institutional and cultural context in which they operate, shape the definitions of such complex policy problems as school violence. These definitions affect the ways in which decision makers draw lessons from their own and others' experiences for policy improvements.

I have focused on the institutional learning processes associated with both complex and simple change. *Policy learning* is defined as a process whereby a policy system adapts and improves its policy decisions over time according to information, evaluation, and lesson-drawing across time and space. *Problem definition* is the process and result of framing, labeling, and constructing a particular policy issue. I view policy learning as a process of problem redefinition. I have found that in the school systems I examined, pockets of complex learning exist, but a systemic, comprehensive redefinition of the school violence problem does not.

The essential question at the heart of this approach involves institutional learning. This book attempts to offer insight into the ways in which institutions, and the individuals within them, define policy problems and learn or do not learn over time how to more effectively handle these problems as defined. What factors help or hinder the learning ability of an institution, such as a school district, and the individuals who comprise it? What are the institutional barriers to complex learning? Through a comparative case study involving elite interviews and archival research, I will discuss the relationship between problem definition and policy learning. We will examine institutional structures that may be more or less conducive to comprehensive problem redefinition and complex learning. Complex learning is viewed as a multidimensional process whereby problem definitions become *more comprehensive, accurate, and integrative.*

What emerges from this in-depth discussion of school violence, nationally, in Colorado, and in several school districts and schools, are key recommendations for educators, parents, community members, policy makers, and others who seek to better understand and address the problem of school violence. The lessons drawn here transcend this particular policy issue. One can apply them not only to the broader issues of youth violence and corrections, but also to other such complex problems as poverty, homelessness, drug abuse, and environmental degradation, for example.

This chapter discusses briefly the theoretical literature on which the book's approach is based. It then presents a set of propositions that guide the study of problem definition and policy learning through the case of school violence policy-making in Denver, Colorado Springs, and the state of Colorado.

Public Policy Theoretical Background

This study draws on public policy theory in the areas of *problem definition* and *policy learning.* It links explicitly these two bodies of theory. This work takes the conceptual view that complex learning is a process of comprehensive problem redefinition. The linkages between problem definitions, policy learning within institutional systems—such as school districts—and policy outcomes inform and are clarified by the study of school violence policy-making in Colorado.

Problem Definition

One can talk about problem definition as a process as well as a specific conceptualization of a policy issue. Defining problems involves identifying, framing, structuring, categorizing, labeling, capturing, and describing policy issues. The process of problem definition involves language, symbols, political action, and power struggles.[1] The resultant problem definitions are dynamic conceptualizations of a policy issue and impact the policy actions that decision makers choose in that policy area. The main point of the problem definition approach is that problem *definition* is essential in the problem-*solving* process. The selection or acceptance of a particular definition leads logically to certain policy actions. Thus, most scholars recommend the adoption of a critical posture toward both the problem definition process and resulting problem definitions.

The Problem Definition Process in the Policy Sciences: Building a Contextual Map

Problem definition is often seen as both a process and an empirical phenomenon to be examined. Policy problems such as school violence are subjectively determined and goal oriented:

> Problems vary enormously in value scope and range. By definition a problem is a perceived discrepancy between goals and an actual or anticipated state of affairs. The first awareness of a problem may originate with a policy scientist who is exploring connections between proclaimed aims and factual circumstances. More commonly, however, direct participants discover a problem and begin to think or do something about it.[2]

In the policy sciences perspective, problem definition is an evolving process of examining goals and how these goals relate to actual states of affairs. One examines the state of a problem in terms of its development over time (trends), the possible causes of changes in the problem outcomes (conditions), forecasts of future changes as the result of some policy action or a continuation of the status quo (projections), and potential policy solutions (alternatives). The policy analyst, who can be an academic, a consultant, or a concerned stakeholder, for example, encounters "problems" as initially defined by participants, who may already be acting to "solve" the problems they have perceived. Analysts can play a role in specifying, evaluating, and clarifying these definitions that may relate to the same or different problems.[3]

Problem definition, then, involves building the contextual map, the understanding of an actual problem in a real place, in a comprehensive manner and clarifying problems for decision makers. "To some extent we are all blind and no doubt will remain so. But there are degrees of impairment, and so far as decision outcomes are concerned, it is the responsibility of the policy scientist to assist in the reduction of impairment."[4] The goal of this process is to avoid being overly reductionist in analysis, so as not to miss important elements of a problem.[5]

Problem Definitions as Framing Reality and the Policy Debate

"[P]roblems are not objective entities in their own right, 'out there,' to be detected as such, but are rather the product of imposing certain frames of reference on reality."[6] Problem definitions, as the results of analysis or perspective, thus capture a subjective perception of reality, a perception influenced by one's values and not just established facts or data. The problem definer is like a legislator, who looks to the future, setting out rules by which actors orient themselves, and unlike a judge, who looks to these past rules for guidance. In terms of this problem definition perspective, we look forward to set the stage for solutions through new problem definitions.[7]

The other point to make clear is that our values, the "oughts" in this world, are not fixed. Our goals and values, as well as our understanding of particular facts, can change.[8] "Problem definition, in other words, is a medium through which we discover what we realistically want and how we may go about obtaining it, and not merely an indication that certain means are inadequate to serve a given goal."[9]

Problem definition plays a powerful role in the policy process by determining the nature of the debate, influencing how the debate is framed, how empirical data are interpreted,[10] how causes and effects are identified, how alternative solutions and interests are perceived, and how the political game is structured. Researchers have offered a number of fairly equivalent concepts that describe problem definitions and the problem definition process.[11] Problem definitions simplify complex problems so as to make them easier to analyze, but this simplification process can result in errors and bias. Thus, a critical focus on problem definition and redefinition becomes essential as a means of better understanding policy issues and producing new policy alternatives that can be more effective.[12]

The Role of Institutions and Advocates in Shaping Problem Definitions

Important elements in the problem definition process are the role of institutions, such as school districts and state legislatures, in problem definition and the ways in which problem definitions, once institutionalized through policies, laws, and established procedures, provide governing norms and rules for individuals. Institutional interests and norms may impact the behavior of individuals or groups in the problem definition process by predisposing them to accept a given institutional problem definition or by leading them to define a problem in a way that serves the perceived interests of the institution, for example.[13] Even labeling a problem as a problem, and as a particular type of problem, is an important process in terms of solving a problem. "[P]roblems have their own life through a complicated labeling process. . . . A problem definition is used continuously as a ball by different players playing different games."[14] Players use personal strategies that reflect interests that they perceive to be at stake.

Advocates often explicitly or implicitly use problem definition narratives in an attempt to establish the universe of discourse around a particular issue. In effect they limit the logical or acceptable policy solutions that will be considered. "As advocates seek to attract attention to new policy proposals, they may do so by proposing substitutes for the definitions guiding existing policies."[15] Definitions compete over time. Policy-making may become preoccupied with which definition will win. Becoming the surviving definition is important. "At whatever stage a new problem definition gains significant support, it shapes the ensuing action."[16] If a particular problem definition is accepted, certain solutions will logically flow, according to the advocate's position, from that specification of the issue. The advocate thus carries out the problem definition process for the public, the decision makers, and himself or herself in order to present a framing of the issue for popular and elite consumption.[17]

The Institutionalization of Problem Definitions

A problem definition itself may become "institutionalized," guiding future policy action and becoming resistant to change.[18] Thus, "these [policy narratives] . . . often resist change or modification even in the presence of contradicting empirical data, because they continue to underwrite and stabilize the assumptions for decision making in the face of high uncertainty, complexity, and polarization."[19]

It is argued that problem definition plays a central role in any policy process. Problem definitions can limit and dictate which alternative courses of action will be considered. Symbols,

categorization, and metaphors simplify thinking and mobilize the
public and professionals alike, but can also lead to inadequate analysis
and understanding of problems and manipulation of the public by
elites. The framing role of problem definition, a process that is
essentially political, is one of its more important qualities.[20] Facts and
causal claims may be used politically in an advocacy fashion to define
a problem according to individual or institutional interests. Problem
definition as an output of the policy process represents a more stable
equilibrium in the policy process, much as the political myth becomes
"frozen meaning."[21] And issue definitions, when connected to
particular institutional structures that uphold them, play a role both in
maintaining stability over time and, through redefinition, in
generating rapid change in particular problem areas.[22]

Policy Learning

Learning has been examined in terms of processes of political
learning on the part of elites, institutional and organizational
adaptation and evolution, and policy evaluation and revision. Overall,
one can define the policy learning process as one through which
institutions and the individuals within them gather information about
policies and their implementation and then change those policies on
the basis of that information as well as their own and others'
experiences.[23] Learning may impact the ways in which both
institutional systems and individual values change.

Perspectives on Learning
    This book focuses on the substantive policy aspects of learning
and their relationship to institutional structures and the individuals
within institutions.[24] Studies of learning generally seek improved
decision-making, deeper understanding of the consequences of past
behavior, more effective and efficient use of public and private
resources, and so forth. However, learning is almost never assumed to
occur automatically, nor is the outcome of learning a certainty.
Learning can be "good," in terms of a better or more realistic
comprehension of a problem, "bad," in terms of a lack of
improvement in understanding, or "incomplete."[25]

Individual and Institutional Learning

Common among studies of learning are an emphasis on the search for solutions to problems by actors and institutions and a regard for the institutional bias toward the status quo.[26] In examining learning, researchers generally focus on either the individual and his or her cognitive change or an organization and its institutional progress.[27] The relationship between individual and collective learning is a key concern. This book looks at both the individual and institutional levels, while focusing primarily on the latter. It attempts to clarify the relationship between the two through the problem definition concept. "Individual learning is usually considered a necessary, but not sufficient condition of collective learning."[28]

Types of Learning

Three major dimensions of learning have been identified: the type of learning, the source of learning, and the outcome of learning. The first dimension involves the *type* of learning that takes place. This can range from incremental, normal, procedurallybased operation to crisis-driven, extraordinary change.[29] Crisis takes the form of failure so absolute that it cannot be ignored or denied, such as the loss of a war or a radical change in the external environment, either sudden or built up over time. The crisis forces an organization and the actors within it to confront the massive discrepancy between their beliefs about what was the right course of action and the evident outcome of those beliefs. At the "procedural" end of the scale, learning takes place in the course of regular operation according to established rules and procedures.[30]

Sources of Learning

The second major dimension involves the *source* of learning and includes success and/or failure experience; group power conflict; personnel change; lesson-drawing/contagion; uncertainty/complexity; and direct and/or indirect experience. These can be discussed as sources of learning, since they are often portrayed as the foundations upon which both individual and institutional learning occurs. For example, "experiential" learning is "trial and error learning," where actors and institutions keep the rules that work, and abandon those that do not.[31]

"Conflict" learning results from "confrontation, bargaining, and coalition." It is a "bargaining and negotiation model" based on preferences, power, and resource and mobilization changes among groups or individuals.[32] Conflict in its many forms can expose competing groups and individuals to alternative viewpoints, interests, and policy solutions. Coming into contact with these alternatives, and being forced to compromise, can lead to greater understanding about a policy problem.

"Lesson-drawing" is essentially an element of "contagion" learning in a policy system, where policy makers look for parallel programs across time and space in order to solve what is perceived to be a common problem, or to satisfy what is seen as a common need. "Lesson-drawing is about the diffusion of what was once an innovation elsewhere."[33]

Two other important sources of learning involve the *uncertainty* or *complexity* of a policy issue or political situation and the impact of *direct* versus *indirect* experience on learning. Situations of uncertainty occur when complex issues offer no immediately recognizable solution, or when past or present attempts to manage a problem have failed. In these circumstances, actors might look to the experts, if they can be found, for solutions.[34] On the other hand, uncertainty, polarization, and complexity may hinder the policy learning process. "*[C]omplexity* is the issue's internal intricacy and/or its interdependence with other policy issues, while *polarization* crystallizes as the concentration of groups around extremes in the issue . . . . All too frequently . . . complexity and polarization cause uncertainty, and efforts to reduce uncertainty or polarization end up increasing the issue's complexity."[35]

The division between direct and indirect experience as types and sources of learning is less stark but is similar. While it may appear logical that learning would be produced most substantially by direct experience with failure or success, for example, indirect experience in the form of information about policies can have a strong impact on attitudes toward policy solutions. Evaluatory information, produced through what Lasswell referred to as the "intelligence" and "appraisal" functions, may lead to learning within an organization about what policies are working and which are not.[36]

Outcomes of Learning

The third major dimension of learning involves the *extent* of change that occurs as a result of learning. One generally can differentiate between changes in more surface-level attitudes and policy solutions and deeper values, norms, beliefs, and goals. Measures of learning are often vague, ad hoc, or ill-defined.

For example, Hall delineates the policy process into three parts: guiding goals, means used to attain those goals, and precise levels of action attributed to those means or instruments.[37] Essentially, researchers are trying to understand how to identify and measure when, why, and how simple learning versus complex learning occurs.

The differentiation between simple and complex learning hinges on values, belief systems, and the overall understanding of a policy problem. At the heart of the study of policy learning is a need to understand values and beliefs and their relationship with policy problems. Learning is posited to be a conscious, intentional, deliberative, and thus a somewhat rational process associated with examining causal relationships based on new information and experience. However, it is acknowledged that values, beliefs, and prior experiences may influence the learning process, the types of lessons learned by different individuals and institutions confronted with the same facts or experiences, and the ability to learn overall.[38] This conceptualization of values and beliefs as intimately connected to learning about policy problems is the nexus that links policy learning and problem definition.

Linkages between Problem Definition and Policy Learning

Problem definition and policy learning are often analyzed separately from one another, but it is apparent that many linkages between the two concepts and bodies of knowledge can be drawn. These linkages can assist in compensating for some of the weaknesses or holes in the two sets of theories. First, a discussion of these gaps is necessary. Then some of the potential connections between these ideas will be presented, along with a set of general propositions.

Problems with Problem Definition

The problem definition literature suffers from a lack of practical specificity. It hinges on an assumption that the way problems are set or framed influences their latter resolution or attempted resolution. This assumption has become conventional wisdom, if not a cliché. What is less common is empirical verification and examination of the processes by which problem definitions are formed, compete, succeed or fail, and directly or indirectly impact policy alternative formulation and selection. Often, the problem definition process is truncated to involve only the expression of vague values, cause-and-effect assumptions, or alternative solution positions. The problem definition process as a whole, including goals, trend information, cause-and-effect arguments, predictions of future outcomes, and promotion of various alternatives, for example, is often not examined.

Researchers have studied examples of symbolic politics, advocacy problem definitions based on distinct assumptions, and static problem definition. They have focused less frequently on the dynamic processes of problem definition evolution, connections between problem definitions and continuing emphasis on particular problem solutions, and aspects that may affect the final selection of a dominant problem definition in a particular issue area and arena. The effects of strong value disagreements on competing problem definitions and problem resolution, the effects of mistaken problem definitions perpetuating themselves, and the sources of various problem definitions are issues that are insufficiently addressed.

Learning about Policy Learning

Similarly, the literature on policy learning shows a lack of specificity and attention to empirical study of actual learning processes. While the literature emphasizes the need to examine the role of cognitive beliefs, ideas, and changes in perceptions among decision makers, often the mechanisms by which changes take place are vague and unknown. Researchers have not fully answered the questions of how certain ideas and experiences promote learning and why some actors learn some lessons and others learn different lessons or do not learn at all. Learning is an evolutionary process, but few longitudinal analyses have shown the changes in policy action in an issue area due to learning. Additionally, the concept of learning itself is often vague. The connections between individual learning and group or organizational learning need to be further elaborated. The impact of ideas and values of both individuals and institutions on the learning process needs to be explored.

Furthermore, the literature does not make clear what learning is as a process, particularly in the area of public policy. What does policy learning look like? How do we know when it has occurred? Rose, for example, presents us with a number of hypotheses regarding the drawing of lessons across time and space, but he does not clearly show the processes by which such learning takes place. In other words, while the literature provides us with some ideas as to what kinds of *programs* are more or less easily transferred from one context to another, we are unsure what learning involves when it does take place. We are unsure how to define and measure the extent of learning, beyond the distinction between simple (changes in means) and complex (changes in goals and priorities) learning. We are left wondering about the *institutional* characteristics that make learning as a whole more or less difficult.

Policy Learning as Problem Redefinition

With these issues in mind, it is possible to link the two concepts under discussion in order to compensate for both of their weaknesses. Perhaps then we can arrive at a better understanding of both the problem definition and policy learning processes.[39] The important link between policy learning and problem definition here is the notion of value systems. I would argue that values are manifested in different locations in different problem definitions.[40]

A comprehensive problem redefinition involves a more radical change in the goals and instruments of policy. This magnitude of change occurs when a crisis or an accumulation of events or failures that cannot be explained coherently by the current paradigm build up to the point where the old paradigm is discredited and actors search for alternative ways of ordering the policy world.[41] Interest groups and political actors share the stage with policy entrepreneurs and institutional bureaucrats, joined and divided by definitions and redefinitions, of policy problems.

In general, individuals and organizations may be biased toward the status quo, what McCoy calls "the *entrenched belief systems* of individuals and the *collective myths* of organizations that are both expected to be very resistant to change."[42] However, problem definitions may provide the means through which actors and institutions learn over time. *This study presents the view that policy learning can be conceived of as an evolution in the conception of a problem and, fundamentally, involves problem redefinition, or the acceptance of a new policy paradigm, over time.*[43]

Learning is a process of problem redefinition. Learning causes actors, as individuals and then as components of institutions, to redefine problems. Institutional elites, on the other hand, could also adopt a new problem definition and then disseminate that definition throughout the institution. The processes and extent of learning become more visible and comprehensible when one conceives of learning as a change in the way actors, and institutions in which they serve, perceive and define problems. I define *complex learning* as comprehensive redefinition of a problem involving changes in five categories: goals, trends, conditions, projections, and alternatives.[44] *Simple learning* involves changes in only one of these categories.

In reality, learning is assumed to take place somewhere along a continuum from simple to complex. This conceptual perspective allows us to consider complex policy learning as a goal that institutions and individuals should strive to attain. Complex learning is a multidimensional and inclusive process involving a redefinition of a policy problem that is *comprehensive, accurate, and integrative.* Such a problem definition is superior to that produced through simple learning. It ensures that all of the five categories are considered. It avoids such mistakes as relying on outdated information to support understandings about multiple and confusing causes of policy change or adhering to policy solutions that do not match current organizational goals. *A problem definition produced through complex learning comprehensively addresses a complex social policy issue, simplifies it adequately and accurately for analysis, and integrates institutional structures and large amounts of information into a coherent form.*

The key here is the reduction of a problem to the extent necessary for the individual or institution to comprehend and assess it. However, oversimplification that leaves out key parts of the problem must be avoided. The use of the five categories helps in the conceptualization and organization of a complex policy problem. The final step in assessing complex learning as defined here is examining the extent to which actors and institutions have integrated the many elements of a comprehensive problem definition into a coherent whole. Have they made explicit connections between seemingly disparate parts of a policy problem? Have they made attempts to join potentially complementary perspectives on a problem to create a more complete understanding of the issue at hand? Have they connected the multiple "bricks" that are involved in any complex policy problem to build a solid foundation for a comprehensive problem definition?

Individuals and institutions cannot see or know everything. They are not presumed to live in a world of perfect information that they can understand completely.[45] Yet they are capable of more than just incremental "muddling through" until a least bad solution is reached.[46] We understand that we cannot know everything about a problem, so we simplify it. Problem definitions are these simplifications. Problem definitions vary in terms of the aspects of a policy issue that they include or exclude. A more comprehensive problem definition, and thus more complex learning, takes into account more than just the solutions to a policy problem.[47]

Incrementalism and piecemeal behavior is seen here as insufficient if it continues to attempt to solve the same problem. This problem definition perspective is about expanding the ability of individuals and institutions to more comprehensively assess a problem over time within the constraints of limited time and information. Furthermore, the problem definition perspective focuses on the need for institutions to integrate elements of a problem definition that they have segmented for analysis or action. Institutions that are more complex learners join disparate aspects of the problem they are confronting into a more complete problem definition. This problem definition simplifies a problem without adopting too simplistic an approach. It is complex without being hopelessly complicated. Public and private institutions should be capable of this kind of learning, using problem definitions both to simplify complex social problems and to integrate the various pieces of the problem they have identified.

How information is structured and presented to individuals and institutions can strongly affect its eventual impact. Problem definition simplifies a complex policy problem so that it is manageable. Complex learning is about defining a problem in a way that is comprehensive, accurate, and integrative. That is, complex learning is a multidimensional concept. Learning can be more or less comprehensive in terms of its addressing all five categories (goals, trends, conditions, projections, and alternatives). A problem definition, and thus the learning process, can be accurate, or it can be inaccurate and based on outmoded data or assumptions. Finally, a problem definition can be integrative, in terms of its connecting various partial problem definitions, or fragmented, in terms of its continued segmentation of a complex problem into oversimplified pieces. A comprehensive, accurate, and integrative problem definition of a complex social policy problem, or complex learning, is possible.[48]

Complex social policy problems include poverty, violence, and drug abuse. These problems involve multiple, often conflicting values based in varying contexts, with no clear agreement on the meaning or priority attached to policy goals. Complex social policy problems are associated with uncertain, incomplete, and conflicting information about past trends and future predictions and have outcomes that are difficult to quantify. The causes of these problems are multidimensional and interdependent, with a lack of agreement and empirical evidence on which causes are most important. Multifaceted alternatives to these problems abound, with little knowledge about costs and efficacy of these policy prescriptions and a lack of understanding about how the application of these alternatives will vary in different policy contexts. There exist no "silver bullet" solutions. These are the kinds of problems that policy makers are confronting. The debates over welfare reform, notification about sexual offenders in the community, medical usage of marijuana, and, importantly, school violence, illustrate this. These are the kinds of problems that are amenable to complex institutional learning through the simplification of a problem into its component parts across multiple dimensions and the integration of those parts into a comprehensible, coherent whole.

The Appraisal of Complex Learning as Problem Redefinition within Institutions

It is now possible to organize our conceptual understanding of learning more clearly, and to organize our empirical study of learning and problem definition more systematically. Are actors and institutions only discussing one aspect of a problem, such as the search for various alternatives to serve a given goal or the search for a goal to justify a given program with assumed causes of assumed outcomes? Or are actors linking the various components of the problem definition together and examining their priorities, understandings of cause and effect, future projections, and consideration of alternatives in light of new information or experiences regarding a particular problem?

Something I have focused on in examining school violence is the institutional characteristics that facilitate, hinder, or block the learning process. While individual learning may be a necessary condition for collective learning, it is not a sufficient one. I have not been primarily concerned with the individual cognitive processes that are involved in individual learning. Rather, I have been more concerned with the institutions in which actors operate, in order to understand the environmental constraints and incentives that influence individual learning, as well as collective change. I take a policy perspective that will allow for practical insights into ways to promote the learning process within governmental and nongovernmental organizations. For the purposes of this book, *institutions* are defined as public and private agencies and organizations that are engaged in the formulation, administration, and/or implementation of rules and laws.[49] These include state legislatures, school districts, schools, and state departments of education, for example.

Guiding Hypotheses of the Study

It is important to organize a contextually based study of problem definition and policy learning in the area of school violence, itself a complex social policy problem, with sufficient conceptual clarity to allow for reflection on both practical and theoretical implications. To that end, I offer five propositions that allow for an examination of policy learning as a process of problem redefinition in an institutional context. I use these study hypotheses to guide our inquiry.

> 1a. An institutional focus that emphasizes problem solving rather than problem setting leads to a lack of innovation and learning, and produces or continues an insufficient or limited definition of the problem.
> 1b. A critical awareness and discussion of problem definitions within an institution will lead to more complex learning.

The first proposition is derived from the notion that policy makers within institutions should be "problem setters." That is, they should be aware of problem definition as a process in order to critically assess goals, values, causal understandings, solutions, and so forth. It is argued that such an emphasis on problem setting, rather than on solving problems as given, will lead to less irrational acceptance of problem solutions and a better overall definition of a policy problem. This is derived from the notion that problems are not somewhere out there, waiting to be discovered, but rather need to be defined as such by policy makers. Here, this argument is joined with an institutional setting in order to assess problem redefinition as learning within institutions.

An institutional focus emphasizing either problem setting or problem solving can be identified through both the expressed mission of the organization and the formal and informal procedures through which individuals in the institution approach policy problems. The key here is determining whether an institution orients itself primarily toward solving problems as given, as opposed to identifying and defining new and old problems through meetings, discussions, planning sessions, and information gathering, for example. It is argued that a focus on problem solving could lead to not solving the problem, or solving the wrong problem, while problem-setting behavior will produce a more accurate and comprehensive definition of a policy problem.

Joined to this, a critical awareness of problem definitions in an institution would be evidenced by explicit discussion of the policy problem definition process in particular issue areas. The language of differing viewpoints, paradigms, approaches, or constructs, for example, would indicate that an individual or an institution is aware of problem definition as a process and that the definition of a policy problem is not a moot point. Sponsorship of a conference or retreat focused on discussion and integration of various perspectives on a policy problem would indicate an institution's attempt to actively learn about a problem through redefining it.

> 2a. Institutions that promote processes of reflection, diagnosis, and analysis based on evaluation of information and experiences will be more likely to experience complex learning.
> 2b. Program evaluation alone may lead to solving or not solving the same problem, or the wrong problem, rather than a redefinition of the problem as a whole.

The second proposition focuses on the "normal" type of institutional learning and what processes of evaluation are in place in an organization. Promoting processes of reflection, diagnosis, and analysis could take place in a department of planning, evaluation, and research. These processes could be evidenced by high-level emphasis on and involvement in the direction, use, and dissemination of research-based information, say at the superintendent and board or legislative and state department of education levels. This proposition emphasizes the need for conscious digestion of experience and research-based information. Program evaluation, when used in a manner that does not allow for broader interpretation and redefinition of the problem at hand, may not lead to learning. It may only confirm suspected, predicted, or desired results.

> 3. Institutional interests and norms of behavior will constrain and bias the learning process.

The third proposition examines an argument that is based in both the problem definition and policy-learning approaches.[50] In this case, it is hypothesized that the problem definition process, as carried out in an institution by individuals, will be affected by the perceived interests and formal and informal rules of that institution.

It may be in the interest of a school, for example, to keep reports of violence among students at a low level. The school could be concerned about scaring away parents. Principals could be concerned about losing their job. A school's customary norm of keeping incidents and issues quiet and within the institution could prevent open and productive discussion of a problem such as that of violence. Thus, the learning process in a particular school, and then across many schools to encompass the district, could be stifled by hesitancy to promote an open process of problem redefinition and policy learning. The learning process could be biased toward the school's interests in removing "dangerous" students from school and showing evidence of academic achievement within the school. Evaluations and data reports would then track expulsions and suspensions over time. Schools would be rewarded for improving test scores.

> 4a. A decentralized institution that allows its component parts to experiment with new policies, evaluates those policies, uses that assessment information to inform its policy decisions, and disseminates that information throughout the organization is more likely to experience complex learning.
> 4b. Institutions that promote only the gradual accumulation of knowledge through trial-and-error study will produce simple learning.
> 4c. Incremental change will be less likely to produce complex learning (overall problem redefinition).

The fourth proposition is based on arguments that decentralization will produce better policies through allowing smaller units of government to experiment with strategies that work best. Theoretically, it is argued that a decentralized institution, such as a school district that allows its individual schools significant powers in the areas of budgeting, personnel decisions, and curricular planning, is more likely to change in positive and rapid ways over time according to information fed back to the parts of the institution closest to the institution's constituents. That is, local schools will respond better to individual families than will the central school district. Here, however, intentional processes of utilization of and reflection on information that is gathered centrally are argued to be essential components of more complex learning.

Hypotheses 4b and 4c point out that processes of incremental learning and muddling through are insufficient in and of themselves. Theories of incremental learning are examined within institutions by arguing that basic trial-and-error study will not in itself produce problem redefinition without the more extensive processes outlined. The fourth proposition suggests that incremental change and decentralization, divorced from more intentional processes of information usage and problem setting, will continue to lead to attachment to the status quo and the established problem definition. Such incremental change and decentralization will produce learning only in one or two areas of the problem orientation, such as policy alternatives or trends information.

> 5. Complex learning may require changing the structure, direction, and mission of an institution itself to make it more open to a problem-setting approach.

Finally, the fifth proposition examines problem definition within institutions, assessing whether there are certain elements of institutions themselves which might facilitate or hinder the learning process. The ways in which some institutions are designed or structured could predispose them toward an approach that emphasizes solutions rather than more accurate and comprehensive definitions of the problems at hand.

For example, institutions may be segmented into specialized departments, each trying to solve a particular problem in its own way within its own designated area of expertise, or turf. More or less complex learning may occur within these segments, or pockets. But to establish complex learning throughout an institution such as a school district, these segmented structures may need to be opened up. Lines of communication, both formal and informal, may need to be established between them. Organizational leadership may be required to clearly define the institution's mission in terms that emphasize cooperation, coordination, and communication between disparate departments. In other words, the segmented structure of the institution would need to be reintegrated, at least in the realm of policy problem definition, on a regular basis.

The Approach of the Book

A Comparative Case Study of Two School Districts and a State

This book employs the comparative case study method in order to examine variations in problem definition and policy learning. Such a study is an effective means of contrasting causes and outcomes in densely illustrated cases.[51] Such a contextual, in-depth study of two cases allows for detailed examination of the complex linkages among problem definitions, policy learning, and policy outcomes. Examining two cases, the Denver Public School District 1 and the Colorado Springs School District 11, with many state-level factors held constant but specific outcomes that vary, allows for more valid conjecture as to the processes associated with producing that variation. In this case, actual school violence policies, problem definitions, and learning histories may vary, while many state policy mandates are similar.

Thus, the book's propositions can be examined through two cases in order to illustrate their accuracy in context. Potential conclusions can be drawn as to the linkages between problem definition and policy learning. Such a comparative case study does not attempt to "prove" these hypotheses in a manner that is valid across all cases. It also acknowledges the interpretive role of the researcher in drawing conclusions about the cases under study.[52] It does, however, allow for a better and deeper understanding of the processes and dynamics under evaluation, such that similar processes in other contexts might be more amenable to comprehension and perhaps change and improvement.

The School District Level and Linkages to the State and Schools

This study focuses on the school district level as the most relevant for understanding direct education policy action and the learning process, utilizing the comparative approach to highlight the institutional and definitional factors that are involved in school violence policy-making. The city school district is small enough to allow for detailed observation and confident conclusions. Yet the focus is large enough to make a meaningful contribution to understanding the processes under examination in other decision arenas. The decision level is authoritative enough so as to have a real impact on the school violence issue, and independent enough to make many of its own policy decisions. It has been a primary decision location in this policy area. The district is not so removed from the "policy action" as to make it too irrelevant to specific policy proposals. Districts are also the subject of much of the literature on school restructuring and systemic reform.[53]

These school districts exist in the larger context of both state and national policies, yet they have substantial independence in making curricular and disciplinary decisions. However, there are important interrelationships between the state and the district and between the district and its schools. This study utilizes a vertical comparative approach as well as the cross-district horizontal comparison. It examines learning at the state level and at the local school level in Denver, contrasting the institutional forces at each level and exploring the linkages between the three levels.

The specific research focus is on decision makers within the education system, and on other relevant actors who impact school violence and policies. These individuals include school board members; upper level school district administrators, such as the superintendents and assistant superintendents; prominent principals and teachers; community activists; state legislators; and representatives of state educational organizations. These individuals are identified as controlling primary decision-making within the state, the school district, and the schools.

The Denver Public Schools

The two districts under study are major urban centers in the state of Colorado. Denver, the central focus of the book, has a diverse urban population, a history of court-ordered desegregation, and an independent school board.[54] A contiguous city-county entity, Denver is experiencing rapid population growth and associated demographic changes. It is a city that is exploring issues of violence and education, site-based management of schools, the end of its desegregation order, and the growth of state education initiatives. It thus provides an interesting case through which to explore education policies designed to impact violence and discipline.

Denver, driven in part by changes in Colorado state laws, has been in the process of changing its school discipline policies. Additionally, there are prevention efforts underway driven in part by federal Safe and Drug-Free Schools and Communities money. This process of change, in addition to other recent, highly publicized events, offers a good basis from which to analyze policy learning. Additionally, the state has played a strong central role in compelling district policy changes in this policy area. It is important to examine the relationship between the district and the state and the forces driving legislative changes at the state level.

As a district with site-based management, Denver has given a great deal of leeway to its individual schools in making violence and discipline policies. There is an interesting dynamic, between state mandates and decentralized local authority, that has left the district somewhat in the middle of two counterbalancing forces. It is at the school level that some experimentation, diversity of approach, and learning is taking place. There is an interesting tension and contrast between a district preference for a broad policy that complies with state requirements but that allows maximum flexibility for the schools, the desire of some in the schools for more district guidance in this area, and the complaints of some in the district about the lack of consistency in the ways in which schools implement discipline policies overall.

Colorado Springs Public School District 11

Additionally, I examine Colorado Springs School District 11 as an example of a similarly sized urban district within the same state as Denver, in order to study varying responses between districts to the same state mandates. Colorado Springs is not quite as large as Denver and does not play the same central role in the state. While not as diverse as Denver, Colorado Springs has a significant minority population. However, Colorado Springs is also experiencing rapid growth. It has been forced to respond to similar social and demographic issues and state laws. Colorado Springs, as a diverse urban center in the same state, provides an interesting counterpart and test case through which to contrast and compare Denver.

The State of Colorado

In terms of the state context, Colorado represents a western Sunbelt state. It is ethnically diverse with a relatively large Hispanic population.[55] Even though Colorado has a strongly growing economy, the state's government is under significant resource constraints due to factors such as Colorado's 1992 Amendment 1, which limits the ability of state and local government to tax and spend. Colorado may provide a good comparative model for other states that are experiencing growth, population change, and fiscal constraints in the West and the South.

School Violence Policy

School violence represents both an interesting and appropriate complex social policy issue through which to examine policy learning and problem definition. An emerging policy problem that has captured the public's attention, the issue of school violence returns us to studies of discipline and classroom management, security, and behavior modification. It leads us to explore "newer" approaches to conflict resolution, violence prevention, mediation, parental and community involvement, and interagency coordination. School violence is a complex social policy problem that involves strong value disagreements and competing problem definitions.[56] It is primarily an education policy issue. As such, it involves numerous elements of institutional change and reorganization.[57] The state and the two districts chosen present informative cases through which to study variations in problem definition and policy-learning processes, as well as school violence policy outcomes.

Overall, this project compares across policy-making levels in the state system and across the district level within the same state system. I focus on the state of Colorado, the Denver school district, and particular Denver schools, fully assessing this particular case at three decision-making levels that impact school violence policy-making in the Denver schools. I study six Denver schools, including three pairs of middle and high schools, in more detail in order to examine how and whether learning is occurring at the individual school level.

To provide for comparison, the discussion of state, district, and school violence policies nationally sets the substantive context for my discussion of Denver and Colorado Springs. It shows the complex nature of the school violence policy problem, indicating the particular importance of problem definitions and a problem definition policy perspective in this area. In Colorado, I look at two districts in order to examine variation among districts within the same state context. This provides a check on the extent to which it could be argued that Denver is a unique, or anomalous, case. I focus on how actors at the state, district, and school levels have defined this policy problem and how that has impacted their decisions to pursue particular policy actions. I examine the personal and institutional factors that affect learning at the state, district, and school levels. This study reveals differences in how learning and problem definition take place in these subsystems. Additionally, it produces a better understanding of how learning may be improved in the system as a whole.

Research Methodology

Given the hypotheses presented, this study assessed (1) the extent and type of program evaluation and experiential reflection in the school violence issue area; (2) the extent and character of learning within the state, the school districts, and the schools surrounding school violence policy; (3) the school, district, and state school violence problem definitions and the extent of problem redefinition over time; (4) the level of decentralization of decision-making power and authority in the state and school districts; (5) the use and dissemination of assessment information in decision-making by state and school district components; (6) the use of pilot programs and intelligence gathering; (7) the extent of incremental and extraordinary change; (8) the relative emphasis of decision makers and institutions on problem setting and problem solving; (9) the level of explicit recognition and analysis of problem definitions; (10) changes in institutional structure, direction, or mission, and; (11) institutional interests and norms of behavior and potential relationships to policy-learning.

This book used three primary sources of information to examine these processes: open-ended and structured interviews with state, school district, and school-level decision makers and stakeholders, and a brief postinterview questionnaire; archival evidence from the school district, individual schools, and other state and local agencies, including memos, published and unpublished reports, and program evaluations; and media reports, including commentary and analysis, data gathered, and school violence problem characterizations.[58] This information was used to reconstruct the history of the school violence policy process in the two cases at each of the three decision-making levels, providing the background for the actions and viewpoints of the institutions and the individuals within them. Cross-checking among such information sources as interview comments and policy documents in an inclusive, interpretive manner allowed me to draw conclusions about the study propositions and the learning process in these contexts.

Program Evaluation and Reflection

All three information sources were used to assess the level and nature of program evaluation and reflection on experiences. School district records and media reports provided summary evidence of program evaluations. Follow-up interview questions with decision makers filled in gaps as to the use of these evaluations, the extent of reflection on personal and institutional experiences with school violence, and consequences of new information and experiences for decision-making.

Extent and Character of Learning, or Problem Redefinition

Learning, as problem redefinition, was measured by assessing changes in problem definition from simple to complex. Interviews with participants took the form of structured, open-ended questions, to reveal how decision makers defined the school violence problem, engaged in learning activities, and took policy actions over time. In order to reveal participants' values, problem definitions, and areas of consensus and conflict between participants, a set of questions was developed and structured around Lasswell's problem orientation categories. Thus, in addition to such general questions as "How do you see the school violence problem?" and "Has the district changed its policies toward school violence?" there were questions that focused on goals, trends, conditions, projections, and alternatives.[59]

For example, participants were asked, "What do you think are the causes of school violence?" "Has violence gotten worse in the past decade?" "How do you think the nature of the school violence problem will change in the future?" "What do you think should be done about school violence?" Follow-up questions asked participants to list the most important policy solutions, causes of changes over time in policies, and influences on learning. These questions allowed me to conduct several analyses.

First, responses were examined along the dimensions of the problem orientation. This revealed the extent of change in each problem orientation category. A problem redefinition that involved significant change in all categories was identified as complex learning. A problem redefinition that was limited to one or two categories was categorized as simple learning.

Second, this allowed for the identification of areas of conflict and consensus between problem definitions. This revealed institutional and individual patterns of problem definition, whether an institution such as a school district maintained a monolithic problem definition among its decision makers, and the potential flux in problem definition in the group as a whole.

Third, direct responses on the most important factors of change and the problem orientation statements were used to associate types of problem definition changes with institutional and individual characteristics, such as levels of decentralization or position in the school district. This data was also used to track learning over time and to consider, for example, the numbers of individuals and the institutional components representing accurate, integrative problem redefinition in at least three categories (relatively complex learning).

Fourth, text analysis of the interview transcripts, using the NUD*IST program and general text searches, revealed key language and symbols underlying the problem definitions, as well as prominent elements that individuals associated with the learning process.[60] This analysis showed linkages that the stakeholders themselves made between learning, problem definition, and the processes and factors associated with them. In other words, when an individual discussed learning, what kinds of components did he or she associate with learning? Did other individuals mention similar factors when discussing learning? Did the participants themselves associate learning with problem definition issues?

The literature on policy rhetoric discusses the ways in which assumptions underlying policy issues influence the definition of those issues, the presentation of those issues to the public and to decision makers, and the nature of the issues themselves. Decision makers, advocates, and analysts use rhetoric, as persuasive language, consciously and unconsciously to describe policy issues. This language not only describes an issue, but, in many respects, constructs the problem. The language represents underlying assumptions about human behavior, governmental authority, and social goods and values. Symbols and narratives are some of the types of language that actors use to influence the perception, and thus the definition, of policy problems. Thus, an analysis of the narratives and symbols utilized by stakeholders in a policy issue provided a window through which to view actors' and institutions' problem definitions.

Fifth, questions on learning and the history of the issue allowed for interpretation as to the connections between problem definitions, changes among those definitions, and policy-learning. While the study examined one data point in each case, a longitudinal component was added through the archival trends analysis and through questions pertaining to changes in policy actions, causes of those changes, and changes in personal definition of the problem over time.

The recollections of relevant participants, gathered through interview questions, were utilized to elaborate on the policy record. Their memories of actions taken to confront school violence indicated the character and development of the learning process. The human interactions in policy-making are important and vary with the context of the decision process. Discussions with relevant stakeholders illuminated the decision process and provided insight about the motivations of participants as well as individual and institutional barriers to learning. Relevant stakeholders were identified through an analysis of the decision-making process, district information, and reputational recommendation as the study progressed. Participant recollection was used to further illuminate the history of the school violence policy area in order to examine learning over time.

Decentralization, Use of Information, and Pilot Programs

The level of decentralization in each school district was assessed according to the following criteria: the presence and level of voluntary intra-district public school choice programs for students, charter schools in the district, and deregulation through waivers from district rules and localization of education codes; and the presence and extent of school-based management, localized budgeting responsibility, and shared decision-making among local administrators, teachers, and parents.[61] An ordinal ranking level using these factors was developed to rate the overall and comparative levels of decentralization in these two districts. All three information sources mentioned above were used to assess decentralization.

Additionally, these three information sources were used to interpret the extent to which assessment information was being disseminated among and utilized by the state, the school district, and its component parts, the schools. The number, type, and impact of pilot programs offered insight into the processes of experimentation and evaluation in the district. Were pilot programs in use? If so, were they evaluated? What happened to the evaluation information? Did respondents indicate any influence of pilot study results on decision-making and problem definition? Did the district gather information from other school districts through, for example, "restructuring networks" that shared information about large-scale school reforms?[62] Did the district use that information to draw lessons about policy changes and problem redefinition?

The level of complex and simple change in school violence policy-making in the school district over time was assessed by examining the policy record as represented by archival evidence, media reports, and participant recollection.

Emphasis on Problem Definition

Interviews and school district records were utilized to interpret the relative emphasis on the problem definition process itself, as opposed to a narrow focus on solving an established or given problem. An awareness of problem definition processes, critical assessments of current or competing issue definitions, attempts to redefine problems comprehensively through open and informed dialogue, and other attempts to challenge the "established wisdom" were looked for in examining the interview results. Awareness of and critical attention to problem definition was indicated by statements and actions in most of the problem orientation categories.

Institutional Structure, Direction, and Mission

Institutional structure, direction, and mission, and changes in them over time, were assessed through looking at school district policy and procedure manuals and through participant responses. Connections that individuals and the district record made between specific information or experiences and changes in institutions were sought out. The impact of learning on the overall nature of the institutions themselves was similarly assessed.

Institutional interests and norms, both in terms of "turf battles," budget priorities, political competition with other agencies, public image, and the established procedures described above, were interpreted as they might influence institutional and individual problem definitions. The three sources of information were integrated in order to determine whether the learning that had occurred was

congruent with or opposed to general expectations about the interests
of these school districts.

Telling the Story

The first chapter of the book presented an overall discussion of
the complex social policy problem of school violence from a national
perspective. The general outlines of the school violence debate were
constructed, including the goals and values represented by proposed
policies and participants. Trends in school violence over time were
discussed, as were some of the causes identified as underlying those
trends, and predictions as to the future extent of the problem. Some of
the proposed and implemented policy prescriptions for the problem
were then detailed. The chapter ended with an argument that the
school violence debate requires further clarification through
empirical, contextual study and the evaluation of policy alternatives.
This book itself has been oriented toward clarifying the school
violence policy problem.

Moving on from the more theoretical approach discussed in
chapter 2, in chapter 3, the overall context of the state of Colorado is
discussed. Trends in crime and violence are presented in order to
ground the overall discussion of school violence problem definitions
as accurately as possible. This provides a backdrop against which
individual and institutional problem definitions and particular policy
choices can be compared. The state institutional structures relevant to
school violence policy-making are described, as are recent changes in
state laws affecting district and local school violence policies. This
chapter then begins the process of integrating the results of interviews
with a discussion of institutional design, state policy history, and the
propositions presented in this study.

Chapter 4 moves to the district level and a detailed analysis of the
Denver Public School District (DPS). First, trends in crime and
violence are detailed. Then the structure and institutions of the district
are discussed. The history of school violence policy-making in the
district is tracked, including a summary of recent changes in district
policy. The integration of the interview results continues, with
reflection on the study propositions for DPS. The chapter then
integrates an examination of school violence policy at the local school
level in Denver. Interview results from these six schools provide

material for further reflection on the problem definition and policy-learning hypotheses.

The fifth chapter introduces the cross-district comparison within Colorado by discussing the Colorado Springs School District 11. Again, trends in crime and violence, the institutional structures of the district, its history of school violence policy-making, and interviews in the district are described and analyzed according to the framework so far established.

The sixth, concluding chapter of the book brings together the comparative analysis of problem definition and policy-learning at the state, district, and local school levels. An overall discussion of and reflection on the major themes of the study is presented and the implications of the research findings for the analysis of the problem definition and policy-learning processes are detailed.

Chapter 3
The State of Colorado
How One State Confronted School Violence in the '90s

This chapter presents a discussion of the Colorado state institutions involved in school violence policy-making, setting the context for district policy-making in this area.[1] Trends in violence and policy reactions are outlined, as are changes in state laws impacting district school violence policies. Policy and legislative changes are critically evaluated in terms of policy-learning as a process of problem redefinition. It is argued that the state government contains *pockets of learning*, with learning more or less complex depending on the context and such factors as a focus on problem definition. The state level is characterized by competing school violence problem definitions, as revealed in interviews and a reconstruction of the recent history of state policy actions in this area. We do not see a focus on problem definition in the state as a whole, nor in most decision-making locales. There is generally a focus on problem-*solving*, with the problem accepted as given: What should be done with expelled and suspended students? Even when deeper causes of the expulsion and suspension "problem" are considered, the central focus of most discussion and action remains on dealing with the results, with less focus on the prevention of violence and disruptive behavior, in effect removing the bad apples from the teacher's desk.

Trends in Violence and Crime in Colorado

A discussion of trends in violence allows us to place school violence problem definition and policy-learning in a realistic and more accurate context. The trends outlined below lay the foundation for a discussion of how, for example, upsurges in violence produced crisis-driven policy-making, and policies perhaps failed to take into account changes in overall violence levels, or ethnic and racial disparities in expulsion and suspension rates.

Colorado is a Western state with a relatively small population and several urban areas. In 1992, the state had a population of almost 3.5 million, almost a 6 percent increase from 1988. The percentage of youth in the population remained relatively constant during that same period, dropping just over 1 percent to about 14 percent in 1992.

Unemployment dropped from about 6.5 percent in 1988 to just under 6 percent in 1992. In terms of crime and violence, recent trends in Colorado are not terribly different from those in the United States as a whole. Violent crime declined in the latter half of the 1980s, rose again during the early 1990s, and has showed recent evidence of further decline.[2] However, juvenile crime statistics and school violence incidents are less encouraging.

Overall Crime and Violence in Colorado

Colorado's total homicide rates have consistently been below the national overall trends. While the national rate hovered around 8.7 per 100,000 after 1982, the Colorado rate dropped from about 6 per 100,000 to a low of 4.8. Both the national and Colorado rates rose again in 1991. However, while overall homicide rates have declined in the state, the homicide rate for juveniles aged fifteen to nineteen rose by almost 300 percent from 1987 to 1991. The percent of homicides that were committed by these young offenders increased by over 6 percent in 1987 to almost 24 percent in 1990.[3]

Several key trends have emerged in Colorado, trends not dissimilar from the national picture. Gang-related homicides have increased, but represent only a relatively small portion of the overall increase in homicides among youth. Homicides by fifteen- to nineteen-year-olds involving the use of a handgun have rapidly increased in number since the late 1980s. African Americans have committed a disproportionate amount of offenses relative to their overall representation in the population. While homicide rates in Colorado have generally been lower than the national rates, the rates of rape and suicide, the severest form of intrapersonal violence, have been higher. Aggravated and simple assault rates increased in the state between 1988 and 1992. They showed a small decline in 1993, as did the rape and suicide rates. Rates of child abuse showed a consistent and fairly strong increase in Colorado between 1988 and 1992, climbing from just over 200 per 100,000 to over 250 per 100,000.[4]

Longer term trends in violence (including rates of homicide, rape, robbery, assault, and overall violent crime) in Colorado show a gradual decline from 1980, with a small peak in 1986, and then a rise in the early 1990s. Gradual decline occurs again after 1992.[5]

Youth Crime and Violence in Colorado

More recent figures on youth crime show continued increases and
an overall dramatic rise in criminal charges brought against juveniles
and in youths in custody. While these figures may in part indicate
increased enforcement efforts, they also show consistency over the
past decade. Criminal filings against an estimated 17,500 juveniles in
the 1995 and 1996 tracking period represent a 41 percent increase
over 1993 and 1994, and a 100 percent increase since 1985 and
1986. An "average daily population" figure indicates the proportion
of youths held in any of Colorado's incarceration facilities, such as
jails and prisons, over an average day during a particular year. The
incarceration rate rose from about a 6 percent average daily
population in 1983 and 1984 to an estimated 13 percent in 1995 and
1996. That is, on an average day 13 percent of all youths in Colorado
were held in some kind of facility in the state. The state is facing
overcrowding in its juvenile facilities and more younger offenders.
According to a Denver deputy district attorney, the state is
experiencing youth crimes that are more "raw, violent and
frightening."[6] Controversy continues to surround proposals to build a
five-hundred-bed juvenile facility: towns with potential sites have done
all they can to prevent the facility from moving to their
neighborhood; and even the five hundred beds appear to be
inadequate, as projections for the necessary detention capacity to hold
the expected increase in youth offenders continue to rise.[7]

The 1995 Colorado Youth Risk Behavior Survey (YRBS) provides
self-reporting data from high school students and indicates
participation in violence and other "risk" behaviors among juveniles.
As part of the national Youth Risk Behavior Surveillance System
implemented by the Centers for Disease Control, it allows for interstate
and state-national comparison. For example, the three leading causes
of death for all U.S. teenagers are, in decreasing order of magnitude,
unintentional injuries, homicide, and suicide. In Colorado, teenagers
are also most likely to lose their lives to unintentional injuries, but
suicide is the number two cause of death, and homicide is number
three.[8]

The 1995 Colorado YRBS found that 32 percent of males in the
survey reported that they had carried a weapon, such as a gun, knife,
or club, at least once during the previous thirty days. Eleven percent
reported carrying a gun during that time period. An average of 10

percent of all students reported that they had been threatened or injured with a weapon on school property over the past year. During the past year, 42 percent of males and 26 percent of females had been in a physical fight at least once. An average of 4 percent of those involved in such fights had to be treated by a doctor. Gun carrying, weapon threatening, and physical fighting were most prevalent in the ninth and tenth grades. Limited comparisons to the 1990 Colorado YRBS show that the total number of students who had "fought with a friend" during their last physical fight over the past year remained constant, although the rate for males increased by 9 percent while the rate for females decreased by 9 percent.[9]

School Violence in Colorado

Focusing on the schools, it is difficult to accurately describe trends in Colorado school violence over time. Policy changes are strongly connected to counts of violent offenses in the schools. Prior to the 1994–1995 school year, the state did not even count suspensions and expulsions, themselves inaccurate measures of actual violent incidents and disruptions in the schools. Suspension and expulsion, according to one researcher at the Colorado Department of Education (CDE), was "not an issue." Responding to legislators' inquiries, CDE began counting and categorizing suspensions and expulsions, despite the fact that it is not mandated and no additional funding for the information gathering has been provided.[10]

An independent 1994 survey and report on the impact of 1993 school discipline legislation found that, in its sample of schools, almost half of principals reported zero expulsions during the 1993–1994 year. Just over 40 percent reported one to five expulsions. Thirty-four percent of the urban high school principals did report that more than five students were expelled, however. Over 59 percent of the principals surveyed reported no change or a decline in expulsions from the previous year. Some 17 percent reported fewer than twice as many. The largest increases in expulsions occurred in the middle and junior high schools and high schools and in urban and suburban schools. Over 16 percent of the urban high school principals surveyed (eighteen total in the survey) reported more than three times as many expulsions over the previous year. In terms of minority groups, only 5 percent of principals reported any changes in expulsions of minorities.[11]

The more recent CDE data is more detailed and comprehensive, covering all districts, suspensions, expulsions, and reasons for the disciplinary action. The total number of suspensions in the 1994–1995 school year was 47,072 students, a rate of 7.5 percent, and a strong jump from the just over 30,000 suspensions in the 1993–1994 year. In the 1995–1996 academic year, the number increased to 49,558, and a rate of 7.8 percent, a 4 percent increase in the suspension rate. Males consistently accounted for over 72 percent of suspensions in both years. About one-fourth of all suspended students were Hispanic. Just over half were white, and about 12 percent were black. About 10 percent of suspensions occurred in elementary school, and about 45 percent in middle or junior high school. These numbers remained fairly consistent over this time period.[12]

The suspension rate was higher in middle or junior high schools, at 15.6 percent; lowest in elementary schools, at 1.5 percent; and high in senior high schools, at 12.7 percent in the 1994–1995 year. The increase in the suspension rates occurred in elementary and middle/junior high schools, while the senior high school rate remained the same in the 1995–1996 year. In examining the reasons for suspensions and expulsions in 1995–1996, one sees that the overwhelming majority of suspensions occurred as a result of *behavior* at all three school levels, but this reason was much more predominate at the elementary level. "Other" reasons were more common at the higher school levels and included such factors as truancy and tardiness. Suspension for drug use also increased with school level.

Suspension is generally characterized as a short-term removal from school. Expulsion is considered a more serious, longer-term punishment that may last from one day to a full calendar year.[13] In-state research has found strong relationships between expulsion and a prior record of suspensions, and between expulsion and involvement with law enforcement and the juvenile justice system.[14] Less detailed information is available for past years, but there was a dramatic increase in expulsions and suspensions in the state in the 1994–1995 school year. The total number of expelled students grew from 548 in the 1992–1993 academic year, to 1411 in 1993–1994, and to 1,661 students in 1994–1995, an expulsion rate of 0.3 percent in that year.[15] In 1995–1996, the number increased to 1,873, but the overall rate remained at 0.3 percent. Males accounted for almost 80 percent of expulsions in the 1994–1995 school year. This proportion increased to over 83 percent of expulsions in 1995–1996. The percentages of expelled students by racial or ethnic group remained fairly constant. The percentage of elementary school expulsions decreased from just over 7 percent to 6 percent, while the expulsions that occurred in middle or junior high school decreased from 44 to 40 percent. Senior high school expulsions increased from 49 to 53 percent.[16]

The expulsion rate was higher in middle and junior and senior high schools, at 0.5 percent, and lowest in elementary schools in the 1994–1995 school year. An increase in the expulsion rates occurred in middle, junior high, and senior high schools, growing to 0.6 percent in each in 1995–1996. Weapons possession was the most common reason for expulsion of elementary students. However, there was controversy over the definition of a weapon, with some districts expelling students for a small closed pocket knife and others only expelling for knives with blades over three and a half inches long. Additionally, expulsions can vary considerably in length.[17] *Behavior* was a dominant reason for expulsion, and expulsion for drug use increased with school level.

As expulsions and suspensions have risen in the state, with disproportionate numbers of males and black and Hispanic students comprising the expelled and suspended population, state graduation rates have declined. Table 5 shows the demographic characteristics of various Colorado youth populations, illustrating the lack of parity in the rates of expulsions, suspensions, dropouts, detention, juvenile probation, and admissions to the Office of Youth Services between males and females and between minority groups and white students. While these numbers do not show causality, they do show that in terms of actual numbers, young males and minority group members are far more likely to be suspended, expelled, and involved in the juvenile justice system in Colorado. While there is closer parity between males and females in terms of the dropout rate, females show less of a tendency to criminally offend or to be suspended or expelled. This is an interesting pattern that needs further explanation. The overall pattern of racial disparity in these trends does not prove institutional bias, but other studies have shown that, even controlling for such factors as class and income, racial and ethnic bias can play a role in school disciplinary practices.[18]

Table 6 shows selected trends in expulsion parity over time. We see that as the number of expelled students has increased, the racial disparity between minority groups and white students has decreased.

Even though African American and Hispanic and Latino students were still more likely than whites to be expelled in disproportionate numbers in the 1995–1996 school year, the level of disparity was going down. In part, this may be due to the 1993 legislative changes described in this chapter. Additionally, we see that the disparity between expulsions in the Denver metro area and the nonmetro area increased over time. That is, in 1995–1996 students in the nonmetro area were more likely to be expelled.

Even with multiple causes, such as "irrelevancy" of the education process, the need or desire to work, and language and cultural impediments, identified as contributing to school dropouts and lower graduation rates, many in the state connected higher student expulsion and suspension rates to lower graduation rates. The state commissioner of education was quoted as saying, "These pieces of information are linked. . . . There is definite data to say that many kids who are suspended or expelled don't ever show up again. You get a downward spiral that affects more and more kids."[19] The overall state graduation rate, the rate at which entering members of a high school class graduate from high school, declined from 79.9 percent in 1993 to 78.8 percent in 1994 and to 77.4 percent in 1995. The rate rose slightly to 77.6 percent in 1996.[20] With graduation rates for minority groups and males lower than the average, there does seem to be an obvious association with higher suspension and expulsion rates for these groups, but the plain connection in the public mind-set perhaps ignores deeper causal factors underlying both trends.[21]

As mentioned above, the Colorado population has grown significantly in recent years. This trend has combined with several related and conflicting trends that impact education and crime in the state. The economy has boomed, as have state tax revenues. The criminal population has risen, creating the need for expanded prison space, with one estimate of four thousand new beds needed in the next seven years.[22] Additionally, the growing population has spurred the need for new school construction to accompany rapid housing development. At the same time, the state constitution limits the amount that government can spend in tax receipts, due in part to the 1992 Amendment 1, which limited the ability of the state to tax and spend without consulting voters. Tough sentencing laws in the state have boosted the need for prison space. The voters' decision to allocate lottery funds to conservation and park programs rather than education

has led to a need to direct current funds toward school building
maintenance and construction, as well as new prison expansion.[23]

Table 5

**Demographics of and Parity Ratios between Colorado Youth
Populations**

Population for 1994–95 School Year	Total Number	Male	Female	White Non-Hispanic	African Amer.	Hispanic Latino	Other
Students	640,521	51%	49%	74%	5%	17%	4%
Suspensions	47,072	2.6	–	–	3.3	1.9	0.6
Expulsions	1,616	3.8	–	–	2.4	2.5	1.7
Dropouts	13,077	1.2	–	–	2.5	2.6	1.4
Detention admissions	16,638	4.4	–	–	6.6	4.1	1.4
Juvenile Probation	7,182	4.7	–	–	2.9	2.3	1.7
Office of Youth Services admissions	606	11.3	–	–	5.2	3.1	2.4

Notes: Decimal numbers are parity ratios, which show the relative parity
between male and female percentages or between minority group and white
percentages. The closer to 1.0, the more parity, or equality, there is between
the groups. For males, a higher number indicates a greater likelihood of being
expelled, for example, than for females. For minority groups, higher scores
indicate a greater likelihood of expulsion, for example, than for white non-
Hispanics. "Other" category includes American Indians and Asians and Pacific
Islanders.
Source: Basic data from the Colorado Foundation for Families and Children.

Thus, Colorado is in the midst of a period of population growth
and change, with all its incumbent complications. Urban populations
have grown, as have migrations to rural and suburban areas of the
state.[24] Violence and crime problems have expanded from the Denver
metro core area as surrounding suburbs and cities have topped Denver
in a number of crime-rate categories.[25] In many respects, Colorado has
seen crime and violence, particularly the surge in youth violence, as a
new problem. Accompanied by fears of urbanization, fears that
include gangs and a wave, epidemic, or crisis of violence, this public

perception arose in the midst of returning economic prosperity.[26] It may be part of what one author calls an "obsession with crime" that "plagues the U.S.," but concerns for public safety and a focus on values such as education rose substantially in Colorado in recent years.[27] Such a rise in public concerns fuels, and is fueled by, the attention that has been paid to the issue by governors and state legislatures over time.[28]

Table 6

Trends over Time in Colorado Expulsion Disparities

	School Year		
Expelled Students	**1993–1994**	**1994–1995**	**1995–1996**
Number	1,452	1,661	1,873
Ethnicity			
African American	4.4	2.4	1.9
Hispanic/Latino	2.4	2.5	2.2
Other	0.7	1.7	1.0
Geographic Location			
Denver Metro Area	–	–	–
Nonmetro Area	1.1	1.5	1.9

Notes: Parity ratios are between minority groups and white students or between nonmetro-area expulsions and metro-area expulsions. See table 5 notes.

Source: Colorado Foundation for Families and Children.

In Colorado, the paradoxical relationship between risk and fear of crime was highlighted even during and immediately after Denver's so-called "summer of violence" in 1993.[29] During this period, reported crime in Colorado continued a decade-long decline, dropping almost 11 percent between 1992 and 1993. Murder dropped 19 percent during that period. While the local paper pointed out the contradictions in the public's understanding of the issue, it noted a local researcher's view that "despite statistical decreases, many Coloradans still don't feel safe." The exception to the decline in crime rates occurred in the area of juvenile crime, however, with juvenile homicide arrests climbing over 53 percent, and juvenile arrests for weapons charges rising 10 percent during the first nine months of 1993, as compared to the same period a year earlier.[30]

What happened was a rise in high-profile crimes in Denver and other parts of the state, crimes which were picked up by the media and given intense attention. On the same page that the *Denver Post* reported the aforementioned drop in crime rates, the paper printed an article about a high school student who was wounded by gunfire. Could the personal profile and detailed narrative of the violent incident, in the context of reporting on the school's "Students against Violence Day" reaction to it, have nullified the statistical message discussed immediately below it? The numbers were there, but the fact that "[the student] nearly died from gunshot wounds" when "[f]ive slugs ricocheted through [his] body, causing massive injuries and loss of blood" might have led readers to come to a different sort of conclusion.[31]

It would be these high-profile cases that would help drive extensive legislative and policy changes in the state from 1993 through 1996. There was the "massacre" of four people at a local pizza restaurant "in cold blood"; five-year-olds, three-week-olds, and six-month-olds who "were dumped by roadsides or smothered or beaten to death"; grandmothers "raked with gunfire as they stood in their kitchens"; the shooting of an eighteen-year-old on Halloween by a fourteen-year-old; and the wounding of a young boy at the zoo by an errant gang bullet. All of 1993's 130 homicide victims were listed at the beginning of 1994 by name and case description in a newspaper article that featured photographs of the diverse array of victims on the front page.[32] This article claimed to be "separat[ing] the facts from the fears," yet it sensationalized the deaths of the victims. It discussed the problems associated with the media driving public fears by focusing intensely on murder cases, but it nevertheless continued the practice itself, with vivid photographs, terrifying language and narratives, and over two full pages of crime stories. It valiantly attempted to illustrate "Murder by numbers," and instead illustrated the kind of media attention that would push the governor and the legislature "to do something," as one legislator put it in early 1994.[33]

State Legislative and Policy Actions

Colorado has enacted several key legislative and policy reforms in the areas of criminal justice, youth crime, and school violence in recent years. Key players have included the governor, the legislature, the state Department of Education, the state Board of Education, and a number of nongovernmental groups and individuals. The Department of Corrections, the Department of Social Services, and the Department of Public Health and Environment have played peripheral roles. The general story of Colorado's reaction to violence and disruptions in the schools is one of tough reactions to perceived dangers to school children. Legislators have tightened and clarified laws that govern how schools should handle violent or disruptive children, making it easier and, in fact, compulsory to remove dangerous or chronically unruly students from the classroom and the school building (see table 7).

In the broader context, Colorado took a number of steps at the state level to toughen juvenile crime laws while continuing to treat young offenders differently than adults. The state also lowered the age at which some offenders can be tried as adults and promoted crime prevention programs. In 1993, Colorado created a "Youth Offender System" for juveniles to offer an incarceration alternative between prison and juvenile hall. Violent youth are treated as adults but are sent to a special facility designed for them alone, rather than to an adult prison.[34] The state formed the Violence Prevention Advisory Committee, which met under the auspices of the Department of Public Health and Environment. This multidisciplinary, interagency group focuses on bringing various prevention and intervention specialists and stakeholders together to discuss strategies for state and local policy makers. For the most part it takes a public health approach to violence but does not have a major or direct policy impact.

Federal Legislative Influences

At the federal level, there were two key policy influences on school violence policy in Colorado: the Safe and Drug-Free Schools and Communities Act of 1994 (SDFSCA) and the Gun-Free Schools Act of 1994 (GFSA), both of which were part of the Improving America's Schools Act of 1994 (PL 103-382). The SDFSCA explicitly connected substance abuse and violence and focused on meeting the seventh National Education Goal. It noted the need for school-community and interagency collaboration and a comprehensive approach to prevention, and it revised the 1987 Drug-Free Schools and Communities Act. The SDFSCA provides federal assistance to states for grants to educational agencies for violence and drug prevention, intervention, rehabilitation, and education programs in the schools; grants to community, public, and nonprofit organizations for such programs; and activities involving training, program development, technical assistance, and coordination.[35]

In Colorado, the SDFSCA allowed the Colorado Department of Education (CDE) to manage and allocate funds for substance abuse and violence prevention programs that the state might not otherwise have had available. At the end of 1995, the CDE reviewed ninety-seven action plans that were submitted by local education agencies as part of the process of utilizing the federal money. These action plans discuss local goals, programs, accomplishments, and evaluation processes.[36] Thus, the federal government, through making funds available and mandating a basic framework through which these funds are allocated and used, has clearly fostered action in this area at the state level.

The GFSA required that states that received funds under the Elementary and Secondary Education Act of 1965 (ESEA) had to put into effect by October 20, 1995, a state law that mandated expulsion from school for at least one calendar year for any student caught bringing a weapon to school. The federal law upheld students' due process rights and required local school districts to enact policies in line with state laws. The GFSA held that state law must allow the "chief administering officer" of a school district to adapt the expulsion mandate on a case-by-case basis. It held that school districts had to be able to describe the specifics of each expulsion case and had to include as part of their policy a requirement that such expelled students be referred to the juvenile or criminal justice system. Finally, the federal law allowed states to include knives in their definition of weapons even though the federal definition did not.[37]

1993 State Legislative Actions

Colorado had a special legislative session on youth violence in 1993, one product of which was the aforementioned Youth Offender System. Another main accomplishment of this session was House Bill 93-1093 (C.R.S. 22-33-105 to 106), the so-called safe schools legislation. HB 93-1093, a revision to the School Attendance Act, required mandatory student expulsion from school for assault, the possession or use of weapons, and the accumulation of five or more "disruptions" by a student during the school year. This bill was

Table 7

Selected   Chronology   of   Federal   and   State   School   Violence Actions

Year	Action
1987	Federal passage of the Drug-Free Schools and Communities Act
1993	Colorado Special Legislative Session: Creation of the "Youth Offender System" Passage of HB 93-1093 (the "Safe Schools" legislation)
1993	Formation of Colorado's Violence Prevention Advisory Committee
1994	Federal passage of the Safe and Drug-Free Schools and Communities Act (SDFSCA) and the Gun-Free Schools Act (GFSA)
1994	Creation of governor's Expelled Student Task Force
1994	Formation of Metro Denver Project PACT
1994	King research report issued
1994	LARASA studies impact of 1993 legislation
1994	Formation of Colorado Lawyer's Committee's School Discipline Task Force
1994	Colorado Foundation for Families and Children begins study of discipline issues
1995	Governor's Task Force issues report
1995	LARASA issues report
1995	HB 95-1317, based on work of governor's task force, is defeated
1996	Passage of HB 96-1203 and SB 96-063, revising the 1993 legislation

intended to send a strong message to students, the public, and local and district school officials about the state's lack of tolerance for disruptive or dangerous behavior in school. Focusing attention on the issue, it directed districts to review and revise discipline policies, fostered the setting out of clear discipline practices and guidelines in the schools, and increased the ability of school administrators to remove students who were causing problems.[38] Colorado enacted its school weapons law in 1993, ahead of the federal requirement, making expulsion mandatory for students bringing weapons to school. Additionally, other school districts were allowed to refuse enrollment to students who had been expelled for the offense.[39]

HB 93-1093 toughened the state's posture toward disruptive students. It allowed principals or their assistants to suspend students for five days for minor infractions, and for ten additional days for serious offenses. It allowed a student to remain in school if the principal and teachers were willing to let a parent accompany the student to class. It allowed expulsion if a student committed a serious enough offense off campus, or if the student was thought to create a dangerous environment for other students, set a negative example, or proved to be a disruptive influence in class. HB 93-1093 provided for mandatory expulsion of up to one calendar year, as opposed to one school year, for students possessing or using a deadly weapon, students selling drugs, or students engaged in offenses that would be characterized as robbery or third-degree assault if committed by an adult. For the "habitually disruptive" student, the law required schools to create a remedial discipline plan before expulsion.[40]

For students diagnosed with special education needs, the law stipulated action under appropriate existing federal and state law, including the Individuals with Disabilities Education Act (IDEA, 20 U.S.C., 1400-1491o), Section 504 of the Vocational Rehabilitation Act of 1973, as amended (29 U.S.C., 794), and *Goss v. Lopez* (419 U.S. 565, 1975). These laws generally hold that dangerous or disruptive students who are diagnosed with disabilities may be removed from school for up to ten days. After that time a more formal meeting must take place, including parental notification, in order to discuss a change of placement for the child, whether the student's conduct resulted from his or her disability, whether it resulted from an inappropriate placement, or whether it resulted from an appropriate Individual Education Plan that was improperly implemented for the student. The relationship between special education students and disciplinary action continues to be worked out in the courts and the legislatures. Essentially, the state has complied with federal law requiring more extensive due process and alternative education procedures for students with disabilities, as defined in the law, even making it more complicated to expel such a student for possession of a weapon under the GFSA of 1994.[41]

The tension between protection of the rights and needs of special education students and the safety of others in schools has been the subject of public controversy, with the details of the law's requirements and allowances lost in the debate. In 1996, Colorado saw the forced removal and then resignation of a popular principal in the Boulder Valley School District. This was due in part to the public reaction to three special education students not being expelled after their handling a gun in school. This case illustrates the sensitive issues involved in working with students with disabilities and the impact of federal law on state law and local district and school actions.[42] Resolved differently across the state's school districts, this tension illustrates one of the ways in which district policies in the area of school violence and discipline continue to differ in their character and implementation. This occurred even after the 1993 legislative changes and became an impetus for further state-level action.[43]

Reactions to 1993: The Governor's Expelled Student Task Force

There were a number of reactions in various quarters of the state to the 1993 school discipline legislation. Several nongovernmental groups and individuals got involved in research and writing projects reflecting on the legal changes, and on the issue in general. Legislators continued working on additions and modifications to the law. School districts and schools began modifying their policies in accordance with the new mandates.

Governor Romer formed a task force to meet on the specific issue of school expulsion policies during the 1994–95 school year. The Education Commission of the States (ECS), a local, nationally known interstate compact, education policy and research group for which Governor Romer had served as chairman of the Board of Commissioners, supported the work of the governor's Expelled Student Task Force after it already had begun. ECS, under a grant from the Metropolitan Life Foundation, was in the midst of a five-state research and information-sharing project on school violence.[44] The task force formed in September 1994, when Governor Romer brought together an interagency group to examine issues surrounding expelled students. As a result of the 1993 state legislation, Colorado saw an increase in the number of expulsions and suspensions in the state in 1994. Governor Romer's task force was established by an executive order that expressed the concern in Colorado about the lack of alternative educational programs for expelled students. The group brought together representatives from the departments of Education and Human Services, the Office of State Planning and Budgeting, local community groups, schools, juvenile justice services, and higher education. The task force met approximately every three weeks over a one-hundred-day period.

The goal of the task force was to put together a state level program that looked at all aspects of the expulsion and alternative education issues. The group looked at state laws and regulations that were already in place and needed to be changed and at local expulsion and attendance policies. It examined the types and numbers of expelled students, programs in other states, and curricular and program models for disruptive students. It explored funding strategies and state and local services that could be integrated with a new program. In January 1995, the task force issued its report. Finding that expulsions had increased across the state while options for parents, communities, and expelled students remained limited, the task force concluded that:

> students who are expelled need to be supervised and, where possible, rehabilitated during the period of their expulsion. Students who do not have some form of remediation or education during the expulsion are less likely to return successfully to the school setting, more likely to be unsupervised during the day and prone to getting in trouble. Rather than abandoning the student who is expelled, the expulsion should serve as a turning point—an opportunity for the community to intervene in a troubled life, begin rehabilitation and head-off more serious problems with the law.[45]

The task force recommended local initiatives for providing alternatives for expelled students within a state-assisted framework. Among the principles that the task force advocated were prioritizing discipline in the classroom, educational alternatives for expelled students, high expectations for all students, community responsibility for expelled students, and local control. The task force recommended focusing first on students under sixteen, who must attend school under Colorado law, and making sure that violent and dangerous youth in particular are supervised and assisted. It suggested that schools provide follow-up help for returning expelled students and that agencies coordinate services and funding together. Finally, it recommended including members of local juvenile justice "hearing committees," previously established in 1994, to coordinate service delivery for expelled youth.[46] The task force's work was transformed into HB 95-1317, a bill that integrated many of the recommendations of the task force, but that was defeated on the last day of the 1995 legislative session.

The Colorado Lawyers Committee

For the most part, the focus of research, public discussion, and nongovernmental group activity remained on expulsion, and what to do with expelled and suspended students, between 1993 and 1996. Various groups took different approaches to this particular issue, but for the most part, the problem definition remained as given: In order to protect the majority of students and to maintain a disciplined learning environment, dangerous and disruptive students had to be removed from school; the issue now involved educating the expelled and suspended students and securing a fair process through which these students were removed from school. Prevention of suspension and expulsion, early intervention with suspended students to get them off of the path to expulsion, and rehabilitation and reintegration of suspended or expelled students into the classroom remained peripheral issues.

The Colorado Lawyers Committee (CLC) took a rights-oriented perspective. A lawyers' association interested in the rights of students and parents relating to free public education, the CLC took it upon itself to study the impact of the "safe schools" legislation.[47] It formed a School Discipline Task Force at the end of 1994. One member of the task force explained the impetus for the CLC's involvement this way:

> After the passage of the Safe Schools Act of '93, I . . . just started hearing immediately from a lot of parents, pretty much wherever I went, about a certain level of confusion and misunderstanding and uncertainty . . . And so it was enough of a reaction to raise some questions and make it look like an issue that needed to be watched . . . What we saw was not only the rise sort of across the board in the number of suspensions and expulsions, which everybody saw. But which was a particular concern to us, being . . . originally an alliance-based organization, was that *disparity between the*

> *number of minority kids and Anglo kids . . . That was why we initially*
> *started looking at this, was to see if there was a way to address the disparity*
> *issue.*

The CLC reacted to parent and community concerns, particularly the apparent disparities in suspension and expulsion rates among ethnic and racial groups. As another task force member put it,

> Colorado Lawyer's Committee itself tends not to take on issues that are individual, but rather systemic sorts of problems . . . particularly those that involve children, and particularly within that group, those that may show disparate treatment of minority children . . . and when the Lawyer's Committee decided to form this task force . . . *our initial focus was to be sure that the due process rights of children in schools were being safeguarded.*

The result of their work was a report designed to educate parents about school discipline issues and their rights, emphasizing the need for parents to get involved and to take responsibility for protecting themselves and their children's education.[48] The CLC lent "qualified support" to the aforementioned amending legislation to the 1993 law in 1995. This bill passed the Colorado House but died in the Senate Appropriations Committee due to a lack of available implementation funds. The CLC would go on to work closely with the same state legislator who carried that bill to craft changes to the 1993 legislation. It helped to draft a bill that would become HB 96-1203. It circulated fact sheets about the results of the 1993 law and justifications for the changes recommended in 1996.[49]

LARASA

The Latin American Research and Service Agency (LARASA) responded in similar fashion to HB 93-1093. A locally based research and advocacy organization for the Hispanic-Latino-Chicano community, LARASA undertook a study of the impact of the 1993 law in the summer of 1994, a study that was "in some ways informally commissioned by the Department of Education." LARASA questioned the fact that "School discipline initiatives often overlook the motives that led to the disruptive behavior and how that behavior could have been prevented." And it asked, "What are the consequences of the discipline action on the student, emotionally and academically, and what are the ramifications for the family members?" LARASA was explicitly concerned about the disproportionate numbers of ethnic and minority students who made up the suspended and expelled population in the state. It collected case studies of families with a suspended or expelled child. It interviewed students in focus groups and community leaders involved in education.[50]

In its interviews, LARASA discovered "two prevailing streams of thought" shared by parents and community leaders: HB 93-1093 allowed schools to remove disruptive students from school so that the rest of the students there could learn and schools did not have the resources to deal with students' behavioral problems versus the view that students could be "over-expelled," with no alternative education programs provided to them and with no concern for what happened to the students who were removed from school into the community. While parents and community leaders disagreed among themselves over the effectiveness of expulsion as a disciplinary action, most parents felt that their child should not have been removed from school. All the students thought that expulsions would have a more negative than positive impact on the student.[51]

It is noteworthy that both viewpoints identified by the LARASA research again focus on expulsion, its prevention, and the need for alternatives once it happens. This is the starting point for the research, perhaps due to the setting of the problem by the state legislation. However, LARASA takes on a more comprehensive perspective, concluding with recommendations for alternative disciplinary measures, counseling, and parent training. LARASA suggests early childhood education and violence prevention, multicultural training, and smaller classrooms, in addition to improved due process procedures and alternatives for expelled students.[52] As a LARASA administrator put it:

> We decided to go out into the community, find families whose children— sons or daughters—had been expelled and/or suspended from school, interview them to decide what kind of impact had the expulsion or suspension had not only on the student but also on the family, *because we were seeing it more in a holistic sense from a family perspective as opposed to an individual student being disciplined. Again the concern for me was raised in terms of the differentiation by race and ethnicity.*

Some of LARASA's recommendations would also help to shape the 1996 legislation.

The Colorado Foundation for Families and Children

A private, nonprofit research organization, the Colorado Foundation for Families and Children (CFFC) became actively involved in the school discipline issue after the passage of the 1993 legislation. With a prevention-oriented approach, CFFC received a grant from the Colorado Juvenile Justice and Delinquency Prevention Council, funded by the Office of Juvenile Justice and Delinquency Prevention at the U.S. Department of Justice. CFFC studied the costs of commitment of youth to the Colorado Office of Youth Services. It examined the expulsion issue through data collection and interviews with expelled students.[53]

CFFC played an information-gathering and sharing and advocacy role during the period between the passage of the 1993 and 1996 legislation. In addition to its research work, CFFC presented its results at state conferences. It provided information to school districts and educators about alternative expulsion programs in the state.[54] After the 1996 laws, CFFC collaborated with the Colorado Department of Education in hosting four meetings throughout the state to inform educators about the new laws, program models, the request-for-proposal (RFP) process, and suspension and expulsion in the state.[55]

Practitioner Groups

A number of practitioner-oriented, direct service provision groups have operated in the state for some time, often in partnership with government agencies. These groups have engaged in training, intervention, and information provision activities. For example, both the Colorado School Mediation Project (CSMP) and the Conflict Center have trained educators in mediation and conflict resolution techniques. CSMP has worked in the Colorado schools since 1986, with original funding from the Juvenile Justice Council of Colorado. It is a nonprofit organization that has developed, implemented, and evaluated conflict resolution programs for teachers, parents, and students. The organization hosts annual regional conferences on conflict resolution in the schools. It is currently participating in a four-city, controlled study of school conflict resolution programs.[56]

A cosponsor and cofounder of CSMP's annual conferences, the Conflict Center has the largest school conflict and anger management skills school program in Colorado. It has published papers on teaching these skills in schools and families. It works in many districts and individual schools in the state implementing and evaluating conflict resolution programs. CSMP and the Conflict Center have been two of the mainstays in promoting alternative school conflict resolution and a prevention-oriented approach in the state. A Conflict Center administrator, when asked what she would recommend in terms of school district action in the area of school violence, said,

> Well, I would like to see district-wide guidelines for the creation of violence-free zones in all schools, and the training that's necessary to make that happen, and consensus being built on what we can do as a community to prevent violence. I think every child needs to be taught conflict and anger management skills.

CSMP's 1996 conference included twenty-three cosponsors, from the National Association for Mediation in Education (NAME) to Kaiser Permanente, the largest HMO in the state, to Partners in Parenting, a state-funded substance-abuse prevention program based at Colorado State University.[57] This multigroup participation indicates the strength of the nongovernmental prevention network in the state.

Two other alternative initiatives, based more in the area of criminal justice and corrections, are the metro Denver project PACT (Pulling America's Communities Together) and project PAVE (Promoting Alternatives to Violence through Education). PACT was formed in 1994 through an agreement among the governor, the Denver U.S. representative, and the mayors of Denver and Aurora, a neighboring city. In 1995, PACT received federal funding through the Department of Justice and established the Colorado Consortium for Community Policing. With the goal of increasing partnerships between police agencies and officers and the community, PACT has sponsored grants for officers to conduct problem-solving activities with the community. It has engaged in training, marketing, and community mobilization. In 1996, PACT's consortium was the lead agency in a "Summer of Safety" initiative in metro Denver. It planned for future statewide expansion.[58]

Project PAVE focuses on the prevention and reduction of child abuse and domestic and teen violence, offering counseling and education programs to youth. Founded in 1986, PAVE works in the Denver metro-area schools and hosts counseling programs at its own facility. PAVE has received funding from a variety of foundations, including United Way, Youth Crime Prevention and Intervention, and Juvenile

Justice Delinquency Prevention sources. PAVE counsels both victims and perpetrators. It works closely with the Denver district attorney's office on many cases.[59] The PAVE and PACT programs illustrate some of the interagency and public-private partnerships that have been established in the state. With federal, state, and private funding, these groups have furthered many of the so-called alternative approaches to school and youth violence, working with juvenile justice and social service agencies, schools, and families on skills-building and violence prevention, intervention, and rehabilitation activities.

Academic Research

There has been little specific academic research conducted on school violence and the discipline legislation in the state. The Center for the Study and Prevention of Violence (CSPV), at the University of Colorado at Boulder, has conducted extensive research and information-gathering and sharing work in various areas of violence prevention, but only recently began a specific project to look at school violence issues across the country. The center's director recently coedited an excellent volume on the school violence problem nationally, based in large part on this research.[60] To my knowledge, while individuals at CSPV have been involved in discussions with state and district policy makers and have presented their research and recommendations at a number of conferences, trainings, and meetings, the center has not engaged in a full study of school violence and related legislation in Colorado. The most direct, and perhaps only, such study was conducted by a professor at the University of Northern Colorado.[61]

Originated by the researcher, due to his interest in school legislation, this study surveyed school principals in order to examine the implementation and effects of the 1993 legislation. Its survey was shown to the Colorado Department of Education, the Colorado Association of School Executives, and the Colorado Association of School Boards for comment, and possible funding assistance and support, before its administration. The study produced a number of recommendations for refinements of the legislation, some of which would impact the 1996 legislative changes. The study and the survey specifically focused on the 1993 legislation and on the process and impact of expulsions and suspension procedures from the viewpoint of school principals. Nevertheless, the report's final recommendation was that "There should be a concerted effort by state and local leaders of all agencies serving families and children to focus their collaboration efforts on the problems that underlie youth violence. In particular, we encourage educators and law enforcement agencies within communities to become partners in this struggle."[62]

1996 Legislation

In 1996, the state continued its expulsion approach through legislation. It simultaneously toughened and clarified its 1993 actions, but began to provide some measure of direction and support for both pre- and postsuspension and expulsion programs. Two major bills were passed and signed into law in 1996; they revised and expanded the 1993 school violence legislation, HB 96-1203 and SB 96-063.[63]

In what the Colorado Association of School Boards (CASB) described as "an annual rite of summer," the Colorado legislature in 1996 focused its discussion on the "needs of expelled students," avoided "a major overhaul" of the 1993 legislation, took "another look at the hard-line approach adopted in 1993," and sent two new messages: "expulsion should be the remedy of last resort and schools should cooperate with other community-based agencies to help kids." CASB noted that the fact that the changes were mostly "refinements to current policy and procedures . . . should be a relief to school officials" who had done significant work changing their discipline policies after the 1993 legislation.[64] CASB played a role in translating the policy changes for school boards. It sent out revised sample policies that superintendents could utilize as models.

Senate Bill 96-063: Support Services, Educational Alternatives, and Information Sharing

SB 96-063 had three main components: the identification of students at risk of suspension or expulsion and the provision of support services by the district to help them avoid removal from school (C.R.S. § 22-33-201; § 22-33-202); the provision of information about educational alternatives for expelled students to parents and encouragement for districts to participate in agreements with local government agencies to provide such alternatives (C.R.S. § 22-33-203; § 22-33-204); and the sharing of "discipline information" from a student's record between school districts, between school districts and courts, between principals and any teacher in the classroom or counselor in the school "who has direct contact with the student," and between the school district and parents [C.R.S. § 24-72-204 (3) (c); § 22-32-126 (5) (a, b); § 22-33-106.5 (1, 2)].

The law included in its definition of "at risk" students those students who had been or were likely to be declared "habitually truant" or "habitually disruptive." The law mandated that school districts work with parents to provide support services for these students. It allowed that districts could contract with local government agencies for these services. However, if the district failed to identify a student as at risk, or did not successfully change the student's behavior through a prevention program, the law explicitly disallowed failure from being used as a defense in an expulsion hearing or in preventing the district from expelling the student. Thus, the law recognized that expulsion "should be the last step taken" by districts that had tried in other ways to handle a student with discipline problems. SB 96-063 recognized that districts "should work with" parents, state agencies, and community-based nonprofit organizations in order to prevent at risk students from being expelled and to support those who were "unable to avoid mandatory expulsion." The law had moved toward mandating district prevention efforts as a result of the great increase in expulsions in the state after 1993.

Nevertheless, given the fact that large numbers of students were being and would still be expelled, SB 96-063 attempted to push districts into providing alternative education services. It did not, however, mandate how such services were to be provided, or that districts had to operate these programs at all, apart from saying that districts had to contribute an unspecified portion of their per pupil operating revenues for these services for each at risk or expelled student. Districts were required to provide information about alternative education, and, if requested, home-based curricula, to parents of expelled students. If the district chose to provide educational services, then the expelled student would be included in the district's pupil enrollment. The district was required to contact a student expelled for the remainder of the school year at least once every sixty days in order to check on the provision of educational services, unless the student was enrolled in another district or in an independent or parochial school, or was committed to the Department of Human Services or criminally sentenced. The law provided examples of the types of agencies and organizations with which the district could contract, and the types of services that the district and its partners could provide. Essentially, the law was fostering interagency cooperation but was not forcing districts to provide services on their own accord for suspended or expelled students.

The information-sharing portion of SB 96-063 was an ill-defined attempt to allow districts to communicate with one another regarding students with discipline problems. It would force districts to share with principals, and principals to share with teachers and paraprofessionals, that same information. This was a provision that teachers adamantly favored, fearing for their own and their classroom's safety. The Colorado Education Association (CEA) stressed this particular portion of the bill in its lobbying efforts, arguing that "SB 63 addresses various problems resulting from the implementation of student discipline bills passed in the 1993 session. . . . Educators wish to reach all students. Information and communication is essential to their ability to do so."[65] The main problem with the information-sharing process here was that the term "discipline information" was nowhere defined in the legislation. So, as the bill sought safeguards by mandating that discipline information shared with teachers must also be shared with parents, it created confusion by not stipulating exactly what the state meant to be included in that category. CASB came up with its own definition that it recommended to school boards and superintendents but noted that "Understanding what constitutes 'disciplinary information' is critical because the new law requires that the district give parents/guardians an opportunity to challenge the content of whatever is communicated regarding their child."[66]

House Bill 96-1203: Expulsion and Suspension Revisions and Alternative Programs

HB 96-1203 was more comprehensive and specific than its Senate counterpart and more directly addressed revisions to the 1993 legislation. The two 1996 bills were compatible and complementary, but they also showed duplication of effort and a lack of coordinated planning. Nevertheless, they shared the same definition of the problem and a similar focus of action. HB 96-1203 had two main elements: fixing problems arising from 1993 and creating education alternatives for suspended and expelled students. The problem was still school discipline, as yet undefined, and the need to remove disruptive and dangerous students from the mainstream population.

But added to this were the goals of keeping students in school and furthering the education of suspended and expelled students.

HB 96-1203 made a number of key changes that were intended to improve the implementation and enforcement of the 1993 legislation: the total period of a suspension was capped at twenty-five days; the meeting between school and parents before readmittance of a suspended student to school was required to address the potential need for a remedial discipline plan to prevent further problems; suspended students were required to have an informal meeting with the principal, or his or her designee, prior to their removal, except in an emergency case; students suspended for longer than ten days could request a review before the school district; schools were required to do their best to meet with the parent/guardian of a suspended student but were not allowed to extend a period of suspension due to their failure to meet with that parent/guardian; schools were required to allow students an opportunity to make up school work during their suspension in order to facilitate their reintegration into the academic program of the school [C.R.S. § 22-33-102; § 22-33-105 (2) (b), (3)]. All of these changes clarified and attempted to further standardize the suspension process. They required districts to protect certain rights of students and parents. They prevented periods of indefinite suspension.[67]

HB 96-1203 made expulsion for third-degree assault no longer mandatory. Rather, the school district would meet to determine if the offense warranted expulsion or an alternate education program [C.R.S. § 22-33-105 (5) (a), (b)]. One of the most noteworthy changes in the legislation was the redefinition of an "habitually disruptive" student. This was designed again to standardize definitions and suspension and expulsion processes across districts. This change made three suspensions that resulted from "material and substantial" disruptions during the school year the basis for designating a student as habitually disruptive, rather than five general disruptions. While the number of disruptions was lowered, the standard for counting a disruption toward the total leading to expulsion was raised to only include material and substantial disruptions resulting in a suspension [C.R.S. § 22-33-106 (1) (c.5)]. Thus, not all suspensions even counted toward the habitually disruptive designation. However, the intention of this change was not clear to many educators.

Additionally, the bill required that parents/guardians would be notified in writing of each suspension that counted toward the habitually disruptive designation. The bill required the development of a remedial discipline plan for the student, stressing the goals of addressing the disruptive behavior, meeting the student's educational needs, and "keeping the child in school," now after the first "material and substantial" suspension. The district was required to engage parents in developing this remedial plan [C.R.S. § 22-33-106 (1) (c.5)]. This specifically forced districts and schools to engage in intervention procedures with the student immediately after the student began displaying highly disruptive behavior. It is clearly complementary to the intentions of SB 96-063's focus on at-risk students. This early implementation of a remedial plan has already produced negative reactions from administrators upset about the amount of work they must now put in with suspended students. A Colorado Lawyers' Committee member mentioned that at one post-1996 expulsion information meeting,

> One administrator was really not pleased with having to develop remedial plans. And she was talking about how many children were suspended in her school district and how overwhelming it was to do that many remedial plans and that's certainly true. *On the other hand, the whole point of this is to stop the number of suspensions [from increasing].*

Clarifying another problem apparent after 1993, HB 96-1203 redefined mandatory weapons expulsion. It would result from the possession, bringing, carrying, or use of a "dangerous weapon" rather than a "deadly weapon." The bill clearly defined a dangerous weapon in an inclusive manner, limiting knives to those with blades longer than three inches for fixed blades or three and one-half inches for folding blades [C.R.S. § 22-33-106 (1) (d)]. Changing from a definition based on criminal law to one based on school law, this section also allowed districts to expel or not expel based on a student's intent or lack thereof to use a weapon. The issue of intent was one that arose in previous expulsion hearings and was unclear in the criminal law definition.[68] Finally, in terms of clarification, the bill required another plan to be developed by school districts for "habitually truant" children. These plans would stress "the goal of assisting the child to remain in school." They would hopefully be developed in conjunction with the parent/guardian [C.R.S. § 22-33-107 (3) (b)]. Thus, while the senate bill urged schools to intervene with students who were at risk for suspension or expulsion, the house bill was much more specific in stipulating the plans and procedures that schools and districts would need to create and follow.

Perhaps the two most radical changes in the house bill were the two separate acts intended to provide alternative intervention and education programs for suspended and expelled students. The first, the In-School Suspension Act, was intended

> To encourage the development of creative and innovative approaches to the management of suspended students, with the hope that the programs developed as a result of these grants might serve as models for addressing the needs of, as well as the problems created by, suspended students.[69]

This act created a grant program for public schools and their public or private partners to create in-home, in-school, and transitional programs for suspended students, programs focused on education, supervision, discipline, and the prevention of further disruptive behavior and suspensions and expulsion. Schools would apply for two-year, renewable grants of up to twenty-five thousand dollars for these programs, which were encouraged to include "new instructional, counseling, or disciplinary concepts," current staff, parental involvement, individualized and technology-assisted instruction, and "behavioral or anger management techniques." Programs were to be evaluated to determine their effectiveness. Provisions were to be made for the dissemination of program results to the state Board of Education, the district, the school, parents, and the public. Fairly specific data-reporting requirements were put into place, including the ethnic and racial composition of program participants, recidivism rates, and costs (C.R.S. § 22-37-101-107).

Here again the house bill specified more clearly and made provisions for the kinds of intervention programs and support services that the senate bill encouraged. It appropriated just over five hundred thousand dollars for the grant program. Like the senate bill, the house bill aimed for early action to prevent expulsion, yet called for intervention only after a suspension had taken place. Identification of students in need of assistance came only after their first suspension. The focus in both was on the individual's behavior in school and how to change that behavior in the future in order to avoid expulsion and remain in the mainstream student body. Parental participation and involvement was encouraged, but root causes of student behavior were not explicitly discussed.

The second separate act in HB 96-1203 was the Colorado Pilot Schools Act. It was intended to "support and encourage diverse approaches to working with expelled and 'at risk' middle school age students, and provide expelled students with the opportunity to further their education."[70] The act clearly states the legislature's goals: providing education opportunities to all students who care to take advantage of them and maintaining discipline, which sometimes required expulsion of students in public schools. The act recognized some of the available research, stating, "Students who are expelled from public schools are much more likely than their former classmates to fail to obtain a high school education and to have early contacts with the criminal justice system." The state argued that giving sixth- through ninth-grade students the chance to continue their education in "a proper setting" would improve the likelihood of their continuing their education and meeting another of the state's goals, that of becoming "productive members of society." The state called for early intervention with the student, by which it meant in middle school. The state recognized the conundrum of expelled students belonging to no particular school district. It used this to justify state action in this area (C.R.S. § 22-38-101, 102).

The act then authorized the creation of four pilot schools, two residential and two nonresidential. It advised that they be located in four separate geographical regions of the state. These schools would be granted five-year-renewable contracts by the state board. They would be evaluated in similar, but more extensive, fashion to the suspension prevention programs described above. The schools could request waivers from state and local policies and regulations. They would operate on a year-round, extended-day basis. The nonresidential schools would serve sixth- through ninth-grade students, while the residential programs would preferably serve only expelled eight- and ninth-grade students. Each school would serve at least sixty students, two-thirds of whom had been expelled and one-third of whom were at risk. Here, the house bill defined "at risk" differently and more explicitly than the senate bill, meaning " a student who is in the sixth, seventh, eighth, or ninth grade, who is under seventeen years of age, and who has been the subject of at least one suspension in the past year" [C.R.S. § 22-38-103 (1)].

Thus, the general population of expelled and at-risk students in the middle grades would now have a place to go. The minimum total population of the schools, at 240, would not serve one-quarter of the expelled student population, and no money was asked for or appropriated for these pilot schools in 1996. But the state had finally authorized separate education for expelled students. The state Board of Education was granted authority to oversee these programs and passed the administration of the grants and the programs to the Colorado Department of Education.[71] The state had increased its involvement in the area of school violence. It had attempted to correct for some of the problems arising out of its 1993 actions. As a representative of the Colorado Education Association explained,

> In the past, if we come in and somebody says, well, this and this has happened, they'll say, well, that's only here in the metro area. Well, now, you can't really say that, see, because it's spread outside the metro area, and . . . the people in the rural areas have the same concerns about safety that the people in the urban areas have. And the suburban areas. So, it's not just isolated in one spot, it's all over . . . *I think it's a reason for greater state involvement, is that they're beginning to see that this is not only happening, say, right here, but it's happening all over, and we need to do something to deal with it.*

The state had fostered district flexibility and discretion in some areas, such as program innovation and weapons expulsion, but had mandated district and school actions in others, such as the initiation of remedial discipline plans and parental involvement.

Future State Policy Actions

Several state actions remained on the agenda during the 1997 and future legislative sessions and agency calendars. However, the overwhelming sense in the state at the end of 1996 and the beginning of 1997 was one of wait and see. Given the amount of change initiated since 1993, interviewees spoke of giving the legislation time to work. When asked about whether changes in school violence and discipline legislation were on the agenda for 1997, one interviewee responded, "No, unless . . . we start running into some problems with some of this and then we'll have to look at going back and amending, or whatever it takes to take care of those problems." Nevertheless, elements of the prior legislation need to be completed. The first of these is funding for the four pilot schools authorized in 1996. It was anticipated that $4 million would be needed and appropriated for these schools. Applicants were encouraged to seek additional revenue sources. It remains to be seen how much funding the legislature will actually produce.[72] The governor was apparently seeking only $2 million for these schools in 1997, as compared to $2.7 million for improvements of educational achievement assessments, $4.5 million in college financial aid increases, $58.6 million more for colleges and universities, a 3 percent increase in school funds to cover inflation, $57.7 million for building and capital construction programs, and $395 million for prisons and more state patrol officers.[73]

Second, the evaluations stipulated for the pilot schools and the suspension prevention programs will need to be conducted. The state board and the state Department of Education will eventually need to react to these evaluations and make further decisions regarding contracts, funding, and effective programs. Will this produce learning?

Extent of Learning: Causes of State Responses to School Violence

The main determinants of the changes in the state's approach to school violence and its overall learning have included public outrage and media attention, national legal changes, individual elite influence, interest group study and involvement, and state agency actions. The school violence problem gained a place on the state's agenda, beginning in 1993, due to these factors, as key policy entrepreneurs took advantage of a window of opportunity.[74] The issue would remain on the agenda. Policy changes would be made as a direct reaction to the 1993 legislative action. Overall, the state has experienced relatively simple learning, which I have assessed as a change in problem definition along only one or a few of Lasswell's problem orientation categories (goals, trends, conditions, projections, and alternatives).[75] Learning has occurred in pockets but has not extended to encompass the state's fragmented system. The overall problem definition generally has not been based on accurate assumptions or information about the school violence problem.

Causes of State Policy Changes

Fear and Crisis: The "Summer of Violence"

Fear was the dominant impetus for state action in the areas of school and youth violence in 1993 and 1994. Perceptions of huge increases in violent crime, particularly among juveniles, and reactions to a "summer of violence" in the metro-Denver area drove the legislature to act, act toughly, and focus on the safety of the majority. As one legislator put it,

> It was all the violence that summer. People were really frightened . . . The governor was very much a leader. He had a committee . . . I think he's certainly shown leadership when we needed it, and he showed it then, by calling the legislature into session; and they realized that if they didn't do something, the public was just, maybe, going to throw them out of here. There was a public outcry. A fear, almost a panic in Denver. People, women were afraid to drive around at night, anywhere in the city, not just in the area where there were gang fights. And there was a rumor, you know, that the initiation for a gang member was to shoot a white person somewhere, so, you know, *it was sort of a panicky situation.*

A flood of articles appeared in the media, talking about causes of crime, possible solutions, and myriad personal tragedies. Boot camps, curfew plans, juvenile gun laws, and new youth-offender agencies were debated and enacted. Yet comprehensive information about the problem was seen as scarce.[76]

The legislature's special session on youth violence, called by the governor in 1993, was a very public reaction to the perceived increase in crime. But this session, rather than making the problem more comprehensible for the public and the government, seemed to complicate matters. According to some in the legislature and the juvenile corrections system, it seemed to have "fractured" the juvenile corrections area "rather than bringing it together." The director of Youth Services said, "If I were to try to describe this as a system, I would really struggle because I don't think it's systematic." A legislator called the system "fragmented" and argued that the legislature had fragmented and "screwed up" the system even more. A journalist concluded that agencies were "baffled" and that their roles were "muddled."[77] The session seemed to be rushed and reactionary, a palliative to the public's rising fear.

One must go back before 1993 in order to find media evidence for the public and legislative mind-set. One of the best and most well-remembered stories was aired on *Primetime Live*, November 19, 1992. It was a national news story, one that claimed to be based on a six-month tour of fifty schools around the country. But it focused in on two schools in particular: Martin Luther King Middle School in Denver and East Junior High in Colorado Springs. While Diane Sawyer admitted that *Primetime* had seen well-behaved classrooms and schools, the footage *Primetime* showed, and the stories it told, were of "pandemonium," "confusion, chaos and bedlam in American schools." They had hidden cameras showing fights, gun sales, gang members bragging, out-of-control classrooms, aggression, unfeeling youth, a convicted killer, and stunned parent, teacher, and administrator reactions to the tapes.[78]

The *Primetime* story was a shocking revelation to many in Denver, Colorado Springs, and Colorado as a whole. Many interviewees in this study recalled four years later, with mixed feelings of resentment, regret, disbelief, humor, and resignation, this broadcast and its subsequent effects. Some remembered only that such a show had been aired, but could not remember the details. Others knew about the schools in each city, but forgot the program. The *Primetime* show seems to have crystallized sentiments among many in the state. It helped foster the climate of crisis that led the state to seek solutions in a special legislative session. A Denver School Board member clearly remembered the show and its effects:

> I think *Primetime* went in and filmed a classroom at MLK Middle School that was totally out of control, and that's actually what stirred the writing of the law on disruptive kids, you know, kick them out . . . Actually, they focused on two schools. One was in Colorado Springs, and one was Martin Luther King Middle School. *And both schools were—the classroom was out of control. I think a lot of laws are usually a reaction to an incident.*

Policy Entrepreneurs

Individual legislative initiative played a role in policy change in Colorado. The governor was a key force in calling the special session, and in following it with the Expelled Student Task Force. Several legislators with long-term interest in issues related to school violence and discipline were the main sponsors of the 1993 and 1996 legislation. These individuals were constrained by several factors, however, including the composition of the legislature, the state's political culture, and resource limitations.

Partisan Politics

The Republican-dominated legislature and Democratic-controlled executive branch have made compromise essential in Colorado. That perhaps has limited the consideration of "alternative" prevention-oriented approaches at the legislative level. These kinds of activities have occurred within the Department of Education, for example, but have been largely absent from legislative debate. Instead, the legislature and the governor have agreed on the tough, expulsion-oriented, zero-tolerance approaches to violence and discipline. In the legislature, a bill's future was seen to be determined by its sponsor's party membership and individual reputation. A state lobbyist described the informal rules of the game:

> See, bills die, bills live and die, depending on . . . who brings up the idea. And there's been one of our bleeding heart Boulder liberals . . . who is a retired school teacher, and she is the quintessential liberal on anything, and she is the quintessential bleeding heart, and environmentalist . . . She's always bringing this bill on corporal punishment; it's institutional abuse. You know, oh, woe is me, the immorality of it. And most of these other Republican legislators—if you hadn't noticed, ours is Republican controlled—look at her and say, ugh, local control, I vote no, kill the bill . . . If some freshman flake, from anywhere, brings a bill that has massive changes in tax policy, they're going to look at him and think, you don't know, you can't spell mill levy, kiddo. You don't know what you're talking about. If the majority leader of either house brings some bill that's got all subtleties about property tax and things, most people will take him, you know, if you say it's cool, it's cool. I'm an "aye" voter. Oh yeah. *Who sponsors has everything to do with it, has more to do with it than the idea itself.*

Political Culture and Ethnic Diversity

Additionally, the state political culture of individual responsibility and limited state action has restrained state interference in teaching "values." It has had a focus on the individual student's own behavior as problematic. Moralistic overtones about setting clear guidelines about what is right and wrong have contributed to strict prescriptions against "bad" behavior.[79] Concerns about racial and ethnic fairness have been addressed through a focus on due process rights, but were belatedly included in the law in 1996, perhaps as a result of a lack of legislative organizational strength at the state level on the part of minority ethnic groups.[80] Even after LARASA's research on expulsion and suspension issues discussed the disparities between white and particularly Latino groups in the system, minority concerns received only minor attention in 1996.

Budgetary Constraints and Unfunded Mandates

The lack of financial resources available in the state has played a role in how the state addressed the school violence issue. More precisely, one should say the lack of ability to raise and spend those resources has, since 1992, made it more difficult for the state to consider and develop new programs and even to direct money toward problems it has identified and addressed. For example, the 1995 legislation on expulsion that failed to pass died in the Senate Appropriations Committee due to a lack of implementation funds.[81] A school board member in Colorado Springs emphasized the importance of local control and the need to avoid unfunded state, and federal, mandates:

> The one thing I did notice is that the state legislature, in the last five years, would oftentimes have proposals before it to require school districts to set up programs, and then they wouldn't put any money into it . . . Most of things died, but [Rep.] Jeanne Adkins in particular was, she was making lots of proposals that were very *micro-managing*. You know, well-intentioned; but she was just going to cost school districts a lot of money is . . . what I thought . . . So *they put in rules, but they don't follow it with money.* And some of the states where education is higher on the priority list maybe . . . the district might get state funding . . . I sat on the legislative committee for the Colorado Association of School Boards, so I used to see all these proposals, and we used to pretty much try to put the kibosh on a lot of them, because, number one, they were getting into *local control,* but, secondly, they would end up *costing us money* . . . We were particularly resistant here, because we weren't being funded very equitably, and so we didn't feel very good about more requirements from them. But, of course, the federal government is far more of a problem than the state government is. I mean, the state government of Colorado, actually, is pretty, pretty good. They really are. I mean, Jeanne Adkins might be *proposing these very specific prescriptive laws, but they wouldn't pass. They didn't pass. So, there is a wisdom up there in government.*

Overall, opposition to HB 95-1317, the governor's Expelled Student Task Force's bill, according to a representative from the Governor's Office, centered on three issues: the availability of money for the alternative education funding, money that would cover costs above the seventy-five percent of the student's home district's per pupil operating revenue that would follow the student into the alternative program; concern, by people on behalf of the juvenile services committees, that expelled students were a school, not a community responsibility, and that these committees should not be involved in providing alternative education services; and the sense that the state did not need legislation to accomplish what it could already do by administrative or executive order.

Problems with the Status Quo, and Information from Interest Groups and Constituents

The work of the Expelled Student Task Force illustrated the complexities of the expulsion issue and the necessity for adequate consideration of the educational needs of expelled students. Clearly, the status quo, expulsion without alternative education, supervision, or remediation, was not acceptable to many communities in Colorado. Financial and political difficulties in legislating solutions were plentiful, however. The defeat of the proposed bill indicated the difficulties involved in fostering a more comprehensive approach to this problem and in engineering interagency cooperation. The task force did accomplish a great deal in providing a picture of expulsion and expelled students in Colorado, thereby detailing the extent of that problem. It focused on educational alternatives and the realities of expelled students and their families. It identified the need for the state to provide direction and assistance to local communities and school districts that were handling increasing numbers of expelled students.

It would take another year for the state to act on recommendations from the governor's task force, the Colorado Lawyers Committee, LARASA, Professor King, the Colorado Association of School Boards, the Colorado Association of School Executives, and the Colorado Education Association due to both funding difficulties and the time it took for information about the problems of expelled students to impact the legislature. However, these groups did eventually impact state policy, representing an advocacy coalition, or a broader issue network on this issue. But overall agreement about this issue does not exist in the state. There is not a clear community of experts to provide a definitive assessment and definition of this problem, or a paradigm, for the state overall, even though the dominant problem definition centers on expulsion and what to do about expelled students' behavior.[82] There is disagreement over the nature of this problem, as shown by such groups as the Colorado School Mediation Project or project PAVE. Yet, within the legislative apparatus, agreement began to emerge on the state's direction in 1996. The dominant advocacy coalition fostering the dominant problem definition has not questioned that definition in depth. It has sought to solve the problem as given, with minor tinkering around the edges.

National Influences

Finally, national legislation and policy have impacted state action. Laws concerning guns in schools, special education, and grants for drug and violence prevention programs have caused the state to continue its zero-tolerance approach to weapons in schools, protect the due process rights of students with disabilities, and administer a prevention grant program.[83] For example, an administrator described the importance of federal grants in providing specific prevention programs in Colorado:

> First of all, from the state perspective . . . *unless we're funded through a grant, we don't target specific issues* . . . The closest we would come to this is Safe and Drug-Free Schools. And at the state level, the way that generally works is there's a process where the local districts come up with a plan and they submit that plan to us, and if we feel it falls within the parameters of Safe and Drug-Free Schools, we approve the plan, and then the school actually carries out the services based on their need.

Extent of Learning in the State: Pockets of Problem Redefinition

As a whole, the state has not redefined the school violence problem in a way that is comprehensive, accurate, and integrative. Thus it has not experienced complex learning. There have been *pockets of learning*, where individuals or groups have examined the problem in a broader sense. But as a whole, and looking particularly at state legislative and policy actions, the learning process looks fairly simple. For example, there has not been a real discussion or definition of the concept of "discipline." The accepted definition implies classroom control, student obedience to authority, the removal of troublemakers, and punishment for student misbehavior. To illustrate this further, alternative conceptions of discipline might include student empowerment through personal development, internal control, hard work, or a structured learning environment with well-known expectations for performance and consequences for breaking rules.

A pocket of learning is a portion of a policy system, a portion that has relevant involvement with the policy problem at hand and which is learning on a more complex level than other actors or institutions in its surrounding environment. It may be an agency within the government or a department within a particular agency. It may be a nongovernmental organization that influences or is involved in policy making. It may be an individual who has direct responsibility for or involvement in the policy decision process within an office or organization. Thus, the state Department of Education could be a pocket of learning in relation to the state governmental system. Additionally, the sole occupant of an office that administers a particular grant program within a school district could represent a pocket of learning.

Individuals in Colorado have experienced complex learning and a comprehensive redefinition of the school violence problem. Their problem definitions have taken into account broader and more accurate assessments of the school violence problems. Occupying assorted public, research, and advocacy positions, these individuals have to some extent influenced institutional learning. However, the best characterization of policy-learning in the state is one of pockets of learning. While learning has occurred in various agencies and in parts of the legislature, the overall process of defining and redefining the school violence problem in the state has been fragmented and static. It has lacked a focus on problem setting, as opposed to problem-solving, and the dominant expulsion-oriented problem definition has been tacitly accepted as given.

This definition associates the goals of furthering learning and protecting the majority of "good" students from "bad" students with trends that indicate increasing student violence and disruption and causal narratives attributing school violence to a small percentage of bad students raised and supervised poorly by their parents. In this definition, expectations are for increasing suspensions and expulsions but also for improved learning and less violence and disruption in schools in the long term as students and parents "get the message" and are deterred from problem behavior. The dominant policy solutions are compulsory expulsion and suspension for misbehavior, "get 'em outta here," resulting in an after-the-fact search for separate educational environments in which to place students who are removed from mainstream schools.

The overall process of learning in the state has been one of hand-wringing and reactive attempts to handle the burgeoning population of expelled and suspended students, in addition to the rising population of juveniles involved in the justice system. The sharp trend upwards in suspension and expulsion has caused decision makers to consider how to keep students in school. It has caused them to think about what to do with these students once removed from school, but it has not caused a reconsideration of the overall definition of the problem or a reassessment of the primary alternative chosen to deal with it. Goals have remained consistent in various groups, and evaluation of selected alternatives, consideration of alternatives from other states, and a comprehensive attempt to forecast future trends resulting from the expulsion selection have been limited.

Thus, more or less complex learning has occurred in pockets that are more or less isolated but has not happened in a collaborative, comprehensive, statewide manner. It seems that stories about learning successes are less numerous than those about learning failures. Where complex learning has succeeded in a pocket, that success has not then been integrated or expanded to encompass the rest of the system.

For example, researchers at LARASA found anecdotal evidence of bias in expulsion and suspension outcomes and procedures after the 1993 legislation. Their goal of racial and ethnic equality and due process remained stable. Their interview-based study produced for them, or at least reinforced, a fairly comprehensive redefinition of the school violence problem. This definition encompassed a causal understanding of the problem which included "unacceptable behavior, difficulty in resolving conflict, combined with poor communication between parents and schools," in addition to limited education alternatives after expulsion, parental perceptions of unfair treatment, and a lack of parental knowledge or ability to prevent their child's expulsion or suspension through resolving existing problems. LARASA forecast a long-term future without potential doctors, teachers, and scientists if students' basic problems were not addressed. LARASA's selection of alternatives included an acceptance of the dominant, "conservative" approach, expulsion. However, it stressed the provision of alternatives for expelled students, including a recognition that low-income families could need help in educating their children and making sure they were ready to return to school academically prepared and current with their work. LARASA added to its alternatives list concerns about due process and recommended in-school discipline choices and early prevention measures. It suggested multicultural training, changing classroom size and structure, and conflict resolution training and counseling.[84]

Thus, LARASA arrived at a more comprehensive definition of the problem, taking into account additional goals, causes, future forecasts, and alternative solutions. It did not find or show adequate quantitative data proving an increase or decrease in minority expulsion or suspension disparity over time, or since the passage of the 1993 legislation, but that data was not readily available. LARASA learned at a fairly complex level about this problem. And it is apparent that the organization's research found its way into other arenas through such means as presentations at the Colorado School Mediation Project's annual meeting and contacts with some legislators. The 1996 legislation would reflect a certain amount of understanding about the issues LARASA was raising, but not enough to show a real attempt or result on the part of the legislature to learn about or revise its definition of the problem. Thus, LARASA represents a pocket of learning in the state, with its own problem definition process informing, but not fully penetrating, into the realm of the decision-making authorities in this area.[85]

Given the dominance of the expulsion-oriented problem definition as institutionalized through state legislation, it is apparent that a reflective process needs to occur whereby complex learning that may occur outside of the state system is reintroduced into the state. The same is true for pockets of complex learning within some state institutions. For this learning and comprehensive problem redefinition to have broad effect, it must be institutionalized in such a way as to supplant the existing problem definition.

To say that complex learning occurred across a system, such as a state or school district, one would need to see the active linking of pockets of complex learning. Then, at the broader level, one would identify the redefinition of a complex policy problem in a manner that is comprehensive in expanding the scope and understanding of the problem, accurate in its assessment of the actual state of the problem, and integrative in its explicit joining of segmented pieces of the problem.

Conclusions and the Context for District Actions

The state of Colorado reveals dominant and competing problem definitions in the area of school violence. The dominant problem definition focuses on school safety, order, and security, with the main issues being disruption, suspension, and expulsion. Causes of the problem are individual actions by students, regardless of their deeper conditioning factors. The primary solutions to the problem are suspension and expulsion, with secondary solutions being the prevention of those disciplinary actions and the placing of students after they have occurred. As one legislator described the legislative process in Colorado, "As a problem gets worse, we try to define it, provide the tools to correct it, often cause new problems, and then readjust to that. That's what the legislative process is all about." This legislator noted that the Legislative Council and various state legislative staffs looked to other states to build on what they had done well. Yet the overwhelming impression of state action in the area of school violence is one of reaction to public fear, a lack of real problem setting, and a general "tinkering," incremental approach to the problem. Again, while we cannot expect perfect rationality from our legislative institutions, we can and should expect more than a "muddling through" approach that may never produce complex learning and more accurate and comprehensive definitions of complex social policy problems.

In my interview survey sample of decision makers, I found strong support for educational, preventative strategies to deal with school violence. Table 8 shows summary survey responses for state-level, Denver Public Schools, and Colorado Springs District 11 respondents. The statements that received the most consistent and strong support across the state and school districts were numbers 5 and 9, both advocating prevention-oriented alternatives. Expulsion for weapons carrying also found support (1), although the effects of expulsion (2, 3) were less clear. There was general agreement that a strong school disciplinary structure is important in limiting violence (7), and that public authorities were able to control school and societal violence. This survey is not extensive enough to produce a complete understanding of school violence problem definitions in the state. It was not intended to serve that purpose. However, it does indicate that there is general agreement on education, expulsion, and order approaches to the problem across the state and the two school districts.

A competing problem definition in the state views the school violence problem as a systemic social issue, associating poverty, racism, child neglect and abuse, the failure of schools to be meaningful to all children, and a broader culture of violence with student behavior. Solutions derived from this definition focus on cooperation between government agencies and between these agencies and the community, restructuring of the schools, multicultural curricular reforms, and early childhood education and intervention programs.

Another problem definition focuses on the lack of alternatives to violent conflict resolution which students possess. Here, students have been taught nothing but fight or flight reactions to conflicts, have easy access to weapons, and do not know how to manage their emotions. This problem definition focuses on teaching students skills for dealing with conflict and attempts to create a broader culture of peace in the schools.

Table 8

School Violence Survey Results

Statement	Total	Col.	Den.	Col. Spr.
1. Principals should expel any student who is caught with a weapon.	2.93 N=44	1.78 N=9	3.14 N=28	3.57 N=7
2. Expelling a student who is caught with a gun will not change that student's behavior.	0.32 N=44	1.00 N=9	−0.18 N=28	1.43 N=7
3. Mandatory student expulsion will act as a deterrent towards future student gun possession in school.	1.43 N=44	0.44 N=9	1.46 N=28	2.57 N=7
4. The school system needs alternatives to suspending and expelling teens who get caught with guns and knives.	2.12 N=43	3.33 N=9	1.30 N=27	3.71 N=7
5. Conflict resolution programs that teach students how to solve problems amicably should be implemented at all school levels.	3.77 N=44	2.67 N=9	4.04 N=28	4.14 N=7
6. Violence prevention curricula are not helpful in reducing aggressive behavior by high school students.	−1.69 N=42	−0.75 N=8	−2.22 N=27	−0.71 N=7
7. The lack of a strong school disciplinary structure contributes to student violence.	2.23 N=43	0.89 N=9	2.48 N=27	3.00 N=7
8. Disruptive students should be sent to separate education programs within the district.	0.45 N=42	−1.56 N=9	0.81 N=26	1.71 N=7
9. Students should be trained as "peer mediators" to help their classmates solve problems.	3.45 N=44	3.33 N=9	3.43 N=28	3.71 N=7
10. Public authorities are unable to control violence in our society or our schools.	−1.30 N=43	−1.56 N=9	−1.11 N=27	−1.71 N=7

Note: Respondents were asked to respond to the statements by circling a number from -5 ("I disagree strongly") to +5 ("I agree strongly"), with 0 indicating neutrality or no opinion. Score reported is mean score.

These problem definitions are not unique to Colorado. They can be found across the country. In Colorado, the dominant problem definition has become institutionalized through legislation at the state level and in the public mind-set. Alternative problem definitions are marginalized and are not given widespread acknowledgment. It is the dominant problem definition that has most strongly set the context for district and school action in the state. The state has experienced the classic conflict between demands for local control versus state standardization. In the area of school violence, state action is now considered essential. While local district and school administrators have argued for more flexibility, they have simultaneously made the plea for state support in ridding their schools of disruptive, problem students. The result has been flexibility in the ways in which schools pursue prevention and education programs and mandates as to the ways in which suspension and expulsion policies must be implemented. Coupled with funding priorities, this has led the latter to be enacted and the former to be neglected.

Changing the tough mandates in the 1993 legislation, though perceived as desirable by some, was also seen as impossible. The groups involved in the legislative process, such as the Colorado Lawyers Committee and LARASA, sought to alter the law, add to its basic structure, and make it more comprehensive. Once the overall public outrage died down, changes quietly were made to address, for example, concerns over ethnic and racial equity. A compromise problem definition has begun to evolve in the state, at least under the surface. For example, CASE and CASB, two political organizations generally identified as part of the educational establishment, supported the legislative changes in 1996, much to the surprise of one participant in the process:

> But I think we came out with a strong unanimity on the need for some steps, and that's embodied in last year's House Bill 1292. That was our baby. It got ultimately approbation from the Colorado Association of School Executives, who made a few suggestions to it. It got support from the Colorado Association of School Boards. It got a lot of support from the Federation of Teachers . . . To be truthful with you, *we didn't expect to have any of that kind of support.* We didn't have active support from the Colorado Education Association, which is the large teacher's union. But I didn't expect it.

So, perhaps there is an emerging agreement on a common problem definition at this point in the state, a sort of community of practitioner-experts.

Yet expulsion, or the "get 'em outta here" approach, as it was often referred to, remains a division. Not everyone agreed with the notion of removing kids from school. It was evident that this approach had resulted not from extensive study and reflection, but from perceived political need:

> Well, it's not going to correct it; I mean, punishment, at this level, is not really solving the problem. The problems are . . . really in early childhood success. And I think the family centers is going at the problem the right way. Looking at whole families that are in trouble, and trying to address some of the real problems, which might be daddy's an alcoholic, or he might be violent, or any number of other things . . . Well, we're going in both [the punitive and preventive] directions at once, but not enough in the preventive direction. You know, we do have fifteen family centers, and those are . . . partially state funded. And there's some local children's centers. But we aren't doing enough of that. *We aren't seeing these people whole, and the reason we're doing that is it's easier, and it's cheaper.*

The overall climate of resource limitations has impacted learning in the state by limiting the ability of schools, districts, and the state to adequately pilot, evaluate, and potentially replicate promising programs. Even with grant money from such sources as the Safe and Drug-Free Schools and Communities program, districts and schools are, as one CDE administrator noted, largely unable to truly assess their efforts:

> Well, you'd hope that [schools] look at it on a local level in terms of, you'd hope that they'd want to run their programs as based from what they've assessed was going on in their district, or whatever success rate they had with a program if they did implement one. When we say the drop in funding, these people can't afford it, when you think that . . . the smallest district we have here gets $138. What would you do with that? . . . I don't expect them to do a whole lot of evaluation with that kind of money. Now, there are districts, obviously, that get a lot more money than that. *To do an evaluation though, of any size and depth, and not spend every dime that they had, I mean, they are certainly clamoring for other things with that money.*

This is a matter of money as well as time, and there are not enough staff made available to reflect on this issue and its possible definitions and solutions:

> I'd like to see something go on for longer than twelve months, just so we could . . . stop racing after trying to inform people and just see something

tested that's got some time behind it. Because I don't trust any of the statistics that I see any more . . . *Our programs barely get up and running, and then . . . we're on to the next thing, and the next change, and these folks can't get time to plan.* It takes a year to do good planning; it takes at least one to two years to implement and start measuring; and it takes another couple of years to get results. I don't see how you can do anything in less than five. And we ask for five-year, or for three-year plans in the school districts, but again then we jerk around their funding, so, just 'cause I told you you've got three years and take your time and develop a good plan, but, oh, by the way, I can't tell you a bit about how much money you're going to get. I mean, how would you plan for that?

School violence is a complex problem, but uncertainty has not necessarily led to learning, or to a search for experts who know what to do. Moreover, a community of experts as such, with a well-established and accepted paradigm for this problem, does not exist, so there is no easy answer.[86] Competing expert communities exist, roughly structured on the prevention-punishment debate fault line, while a middle path that merges both problem definitions has not been fully taken. Uncertainty in the state has led to inaction in the area of prevention and reaction in the area of immediate safety and security in the schools. There has not been much interstate learning, at least at the overall level. Learning has happened in pockets and among individuals who are members of national organizations, but the state has been relatively isolated in its attempts to deal with this issue.

Simultaneously, Colorado was perceived by some as an innovator and a leader in this area. This was true for both the expulsion and prevention approaches. One legislator involved with the state discipline legislation discussed receiving requests for copies of the Colorado bill when at a national conference. A CDE prevention administrator talked about how Colorado was out in front of national moves toward coordinated, comprehensive prevention efforts, arguing that CDE had begun connecting safety and drug use before the federal government had explicitly linked the two in its grant program.

The existence of pockets of learning leads to the notion that these pockets need to be connected in a better, more public way. The fragmentation of the policy-making system in this area has limited overall learning. Alternative ideas have been sidelined, and even task forces and commissions do not seem to have impacted the overall policy process in a meaningful way. Personal experience and assumptions, coupled with grassroots appeals, strongly impacted state action. These factors led in 1993 to imperfect legislation that would later need to be revised. As one legislator said, "You can't expect to start out with legislation put together at a kitchen table and have it work perfectly." The special legislative session confirmed preexisting notions of how to get tough. Later ideas about how to restructure state action were dismissed, failed to be implemented, or were forced to conform to the established course.

Finally, school violence is not seen as a priority issue by everyone. At least it is not picked up as such by those in traditional decision-making positions, even though the public outcry is loud and continuous. Public concern is downplayed or even criticized by the media, which in effect has wondered aloud why, if the problem is not so bad, the public is so worried about it.[87] Simultaneously, the media has graphically and personally portrayed the problem as one worth caring about. The main education issues in the state are standards, funding, and literacy. Violence and discipline are only important as they impact learning. Thus violence itself, its causes, its nature, and its role in society are pushed off the agenda. The window of opportunity for policy action in this area at the state level appears to have opened and shut. The policies that resulted from the established problem definition during the period of time that the window was open are imperfect and incomplete. The question is, Will learning continue and improve, as allowed for in limited fashion in state legislation, or will two tracks of students created by mainstream and "alternative" schools and programs widen while the state rests on its assumption that the expulsion problem has been solved. Furthermore, will the Columbine incident drive a reexamination of school violence policies and problem definitions in Colorado and the rest of the country?

Chapter 4
The Denver Public Schools
Learning about School Violence at the District and School Levels

The School District

School districts are middle-level decision-making institutions under the ultimate control of the state but exercising authority over local schools. The current wave of governance reforms in education has put districts in a paradoxical position, as states have assumed stronger roles in such areas as standards and discipline, while districts have begun simultaneously to decentralize toward community and parental involvement and forms of site-based management.[1] Districts, however, are seen as the primary locus of decision-making and institutional authority in kindergarten through twelfth-grade education. This is true even as individual principals and teachers remain the key implementors of policy and important shapers of school change.[2] School districts raise and distribute the large majority of school funds. They play essential roles in curricular, staff, management, and organizational issues. An elected district school board and an appointed superintendent and staff are primarily responsible for district policy.

This chapter discusses learning and problem definition in Denver Public School District 1. District trends in violence are summarized, as are district policy changes over time. Sources of these policy changes are discussed. The guiding hypotheses of this study are considered and evaluated in relation to the school violence problem in Denver. These issues are then discussed in relation to three high schools and three middle schools in the district. It is argued that the district has been prompted to change largely by the state. The state's dominant problem definition has shaped the district's approach to school violence. However, like the state, the district reveals certain pockets of learning, with more or less complex learning depending on the particular circumstances. Similarly, there are in place formal learning processes which have not led to more complex learning in the district. At the school level, the principal is vital in the direction that the school takes in school violence policy. The schools show a dynamic that is related to that of the district and the state. Both the schools and the district desire discretion, but they also want tough mandates and enforcement authority from above. The district shows competing problem definitions, as revealed in interviews and district policy action. Again, problem-solving focused on expulsion and suspension is dominant. Examining and defining the school violence problem as a whole does not have a priority position on the district's policy agenda.

Trends in Violence and Crime in Denver and the Denver Public Schools

Long-term trends in violence in the city and county of Denver, a contiguous entity, mirror those in the state of Colorado as a whole. After 1980, rates of violence declined, increased somewhat in 1986, increased more dramatically in the early 1990s, and then declined again after 1992.[3] Juvenile arrests followed a similar pattern, with peaks in 1987, 1991, and 1993.[4] The total population in the city and county increased through 1987, declined to 1992, and has since been rising, reaching its early 1980's level again in 1994. The Denver pattern for the first six months of 1996 fits with national trends which saw no change in overall crime rates in cities of 500,000 to 1 million people, and declines of 1 percent to 4 percent in smaller cities.[5] Between 1988 and 1992, the proportion of youth in the Denver population rose from almost 12 percent to over 13 percent, a 14 percent increase.[6] Thus, the context for the Denver Public Schools (DPS) has been a recent rise in violent crime rates and juvenile arrests, followed by a more recent decline.

DPS enrollment grew from 64,358 in the 1995–96 school year to 66,534 in 1996–97, its largest number since 1978, and an increase over a low of 58,312 in 1989. Hispanics accounted for some 47 percent of the student population in the 1996–97 school year.[7] Violent incidents in the schools are difficult to track over time, as until recently, the district did not make a serious effort to gather information on these offenses. Even in 1996, close to full and consistent reporting had not been achieved. Thus, comparisons between recent and past years are almost impossible to make. In a balancing act between scaring the public and justifying the need for increased "security" in the schools, DPS has been careful about the information that it has released, as discussed below. However, in November of 1996, DPS released information on 225 "security incidents" that had occurred to that date in and around the schools. That compared to a total of 451 incidents in the 1995–96 school year, and 341 incidents in 1994–95. Through November 7, 1996, nine firearms were confiscated in Denver schools. Sixty-five assaults and nine aggravated assaults were reported. Seventeen incidences of drug possession, three sex offenses, and one robbery were reported.

Much of the increase in incidents occurred as a result of additional officers, more vigilance by principals, and better reporting, according to the DPS security chief. However, the chief operating officer of the school district and the security chief both warned of an increase in security needs, predicting over 1,000 incidents for the 1996–97 school year and requesting additional funds from the school board for more security officers.[8] Thus, reported incidents have risen due to increased attention to the issue on the part of the district, schools, and the public, a stronger district emphasis on accurate and consistent reporting on the part of schools, and a greater security presence. However, it is difficult to ascertain whether actual incidents have increased. Given the overall trends in adult and juvenile violence in the city and state, this is certainly plausible.

A student conduct and discipline survey was issued by the superintendent to the student, faculty, parent, and administrative members of the Collaborative Decision-Making Committee (CDM) of each school at the end of 1994.[9] While primarily focusing on policies and procedures, this survey found that 89 percent of respondents agreed or strongly agreed that their "school rules and expectations have been effective in helping to create a school environment that is safe and orderly." No high schools disagreed with this statement, but nine elementary schools (12 percent) and three middle schools (19 percent) did disagree.[10] Thus, the great majority of CDMs responding to the survey indicated that their schools had a "safe and orderly" environment.

A survey of all bus drivers in the system by the bus drivers' union in 1994 found that 60 percent perceived "a significant problem with student discipline or student misbehavior" on their bus, and 41 percent perceived significant problems at the schools that they served. The most common problems identified on the bus were "abusive or profane language" used by students against other students, threats of violence against students, vandalism, and failure to obey safety laws. However, 41 percent identified language directed at them as a problem. Forty percent mentioned assault on students, and 27 percent mentioned threats of physical violence against the driver. Four percent said that a student was assaulted by another student with a deadly weapon on their bus, and 47 percent said a student was assaulted without a weapon. Six percent had been assaulted by a student, and 5 percent by a nonstudent. A majority of those surveyed indicated that violence had become more of a problem and that most problems came from the middle school students.[11]

A more recent survey by LARASA of the predominately lower-income North Denver community found that the "biggest problem" facing that community was "youth gangs and crime." Parents asked for stricter discipline at Horace Mann Middle School. They wanted to be notified right away if there was a problem with their child at school.[12]

A "school safety assessment" conducted by the National School Safety Center in 1996 similarly found that "students and faculty members alike did not express any serious concerns for their safety." This assessment identified a small group of students as causing most school disruptions. It mentioned graffiti and gang sign "tagging" as having "contributed to a climate of intimidation and fear." Moreover, one of the report's key recommendations was the improvement of the "school crime reporting data base," due to the "significant gap" between reported crimes and actual circumstances in the schools.[13]

Once again, suspension and expulsion counts are one of the only concrete ways of measuring violence in the schools. Changes in suspensions and expulsions could also occur as a result of the same increases in vigilance and security which drive incident reporting. Looking at the number and rates of suspensions in DPS over time, one sees an increase in both even before the 1993 safe-schools legislation, a sharp increase after the passage of that law, and then consistently high levels since then. There were some 5,500 total suspensions in the 1986–87 school year, a rate of 9.0 per 100 students. These figures rose steadily to over 10,000 suspensions and a rate of 16.8 per 100 students in 1992–93. We then see a jump to over 13,000 suspensions and a rate of 21.5 in 1993–94. In the 1995–96 school year, the number had leveled off to about 12,000 suspensions and a rate of 18.9.

Table 9 shows a doubling in both expulsions and expulsion rates in DPS between the 1991–92 school year and 1995–96. While the rates overall are fairly low, the pattern is similar to that in the state as a whole. Males, blacks, and Hispanics make up the large majority of those expelled, and the proportion of expelled Hispanic students increases sharply over time.

Table 9

Expulsions, Rates, and Percentages in the Denver Public Schools over Time

School Year	Total Number of Expulsions	Male (%)	Female (%)	American Indian (%)	Black (%)	Asian (%)	Hispanic (%)	White (%)	Expulsion Rate
1991–92	37	81.1	18.9	2.7	64.9	0.0	27.0	5.4	0.06
1992–93	37	91.9	8.1	2.7	37.8	0.0	43.2	16.2	0.06
1993–94	65	75.4	24.6	0.0	58.5	4.6	30.8	6.2	0.10
1994–95	75	68.0	32.0	1.3	40.0	2.7	52.0	4.0	0.12
1995–96	78	76.9	23.1	0.0	29.5	3.8	52.6	14.1	0.12

Isolating this disciplinary trend, we can look at minority suspensions as a percentage of total suspensions in the district over a ten-year period. While the percentage of white, American Indian, and Asian suspensions has decreased somewhat or remained fairly constant, the percentages of black and Hispanic suspensions has fluctuated. However, in years when the black percentage decreased, the Hispanic percentage increased, and vice versa. Thus, these two minority groups together continued to account for a consistently high percentage, about 8 to 90 percent, of suspensions in the district.

Table 10 identifies the top ten reasons for suspensions in the district over a five-year period, as reported by schools and collected by the district. It is possible to see consistent patterns over time, even though reporting categories changed in 1994. Violence as a basis for suspension is indicated by the number of suspensions for fighting, assault, weapons, serious threats, gang-related causes, and theft. However, defiance and willful disobedience, neither of which is clearly defined in district policy, account for a large number of suspensions, as do truancy, disruption and educational interference, and alcohol and drugs.[14] It is worth noting that such publicly prominent offenses as weapons, gang involvement, and harassment make it onto this top ten list, but represent a relatively small proportion of overall suspension-related offenses.

Table 10

Denver Public Schools: Top Ten Suspension Reasons over Time

School Year	1991–92	1992–93	1993–94	1994–95	1995–96
#1 Reason Suspensions	Fighting 2,492	Fighting 3,124	Defiance 3,811	Fighting 3,201	Fighting 3,402
#2 Reason Suspensions	Defiance 1,802	Defiance 2,654	Fighting 3,087	Willful disobedience 3,104	Willful disobedience 2,667
#3 Reason Suspensions	Truancy 788	Assault 744	Truancy 1,010	Other detrimental behavior 1,716	Other detrimental behavior 1,895
#4 Reason Suspensions	Assault 651	Weapons 549	Disruption 770	Educational interference 819	Obscenities 898
#5 Reason Suspensions	Disruption 561	Alcohol/ drugs 473	Assault 720	Obscenities 720	Educational interference 794
#6 Reason Suspensions	Obscenities 450	Obscenities 453	Obscenities 597	Alcohol/ drugs 519	Alcohol/ drugs 608
#7 Reason Suspensions	Weapons 408	Disruption 415	Alcohol/ drugs 532	Harassment 300	Harassment 423
#8 Reason Suspensions	Alcohol/ drugs 331	Truancy 376	Weapons 501	Theft 274	Gang related 292
#9 Reason Suspensions	Verbal abuse 241	Willful tardiness 240	Serious threat 363	Weapons 258	Theft 275
#10 Reason Suspensions	Theft 211	Serious threat 237	Gang related 316	Gang related 225	Weapons 246

Note: For the 1994–95 school year, the classification scheme for reporting suspension reasons was changed to reflect new laws. Other detrimental behavior does *not* include detrimental behavior categorized as disruptive appearance, use of obscenities, destruction of property, harassment, fighting, theft, use of tobacco, use of slurs, or unapproved organizations.

Source: Department of Planning, Research, and Program Evaluation, Denver Public Schools, Denver, CO, 1996, unpublished data.

Table 11

Denver Public Schools: Total Expulsion Reasons over Time

School Year	1991–92	1992–93	1993–94	1994–95	1995–96
Reason Expulsions	Weapons 18	Weapons 31	Weapons 29	Weapons 23	Weapons 30
Reason Expulsions	Disruption 13	Assault 5	Assault 9	Defiance 13	Robbery/ assault 15
Reason Expulsions	Assault 3	Drugs 1	Serious threat 7	Robbery/ assault 12	Defiance 11
Reason Expulsions	Defiance 1	Serious threat 1	Gang related 6	Detrimental behavior 11	Detrimental behavior 10
Reason Expulsions	Gang related 1		Defiance 5	Gang activity 11	Gang activity 6
Reason Expulsions	Drugs 1		Obscenities 2	Offense against staff 2	Sale of drugs 3
Reason Expulsions			Disruption 2	Sale of drugs 1	Substance abuse 2
Reason Expulsions			Obscenities 2	Educational interference 1	Toy gun 1
Reason Expulsions			Fighting 1	Destruction of school property 1	
Reason Expulsions			Theft 1		
Reason Expulsions			Verbal abuse 1		
Reason Expulsions			Harassment 1		
Reason Expulsions			Arson/fire 1		
Total	37	38	67	75	78

Source: Department of Planning, Research, and Program Evaluation, Denver Public Schools, Denver, CO, 1996, unpublished data.

Table 11 shows all of the reported reasons for and numbers of expulsions over a five-year period in the district. Weapons offenses top the list consistently, with assault, defiance, and disruption of the educational process following behind. Gang activity as an identified cause of expulsion shows increases over time. The total number of expulsions increased over time, particularly during and after the 1993–1994 school year, the year the state's safe-schools bill was passed. As with suspensions, black and Hispanic pupils represent a disproportionate number of those expelled.[15] This is to be expected, considering the relationship between a record of prior suspensions and eventual expulsion.

District Policy and Administrative Actions

Denver's approach to school violence at the district policy level is mostly limited to following state and federal laws and setting tough parameters for school-level administrators. The district problem definition mirrors the state's expulsion-oriented definition. Denver has had little choice but to create policies that conform to state mandates. Denver has a number of programs outside of the realm of discipline, security, and student removal from school, but these are generally not considered as part of the district's "discipline policy" approach to school violence by many in the district. Furthermore, the district has not set mandates or evaluated schools in the area of prevention as it has in the security area. This is related to the district's notion of itself as a site-based decision-making system, although there is a clear contrast in terms of setting direction in the area of discipline versus the realm of violence education and so forth, in part due to the state legal mandates.

Discipline, Safety, Security, Suspension, Expulsion, Drugs

The main school violence approach of the Denver Public Schools is contained in the district's "Student Conduct and Discipline Policy." The basic emphases of this policy are on the safety of students, the security of the schools, proscribed student behaviors and their consequences, and disciplinary practices complying with and conforming to state law. The district expresses a central discipline goal that echoes the problem of learning disruptions identified in National Education Goal Seven. "A school environment that is safe, conducive to the learning process, and free from unnecessary disruption is essential to achieving the district's mission and is the joint responsibility of students, staff, parents, and the community." DPS goes on to describe the broad structure of its policy:

> The Denver Public Schools seeks to achieve self-discipline on the part of every student by communicating student conduct rules, teaching and reinforcing appropriate behavior, and holding students accountable for their actions. Prevention will be emphasized and problems addressed immediately. A positive school climate is a necessary component of an effective disciplinary program. Discipline procedures shall afford due process, be consistently and equally applied, and help to create an atmosphere conducive to learning in each school and classroom.[16]

We will see that while prevention is emphasized here, prevention in the form of educational programs, for example, is not addressed in any significant way in other parts of the policy or district program. The dominant model here is structure, consequences, order, and control. One outside observer described her view of the district's approach:

> Well, I'm finding it a little on the *militaristic side*. There was a leaning toward more police officers at secondary levels, expulsion/suspension, *get 'em outta here*. Last year there was a huge suspension policy in place, and for middle school no alternative middle school in place. Now, that's silly. Suspend them to the streets? I mean, we aren't looking at any long-term solutions; it's just kind of a NIMBY thing, of not in my back yard, you know, get them out of my hair. But what was going to happen; put them out on the street, and no education, I mean . . . we'd be paying as a society a long time, because *we might as well just put them in prison*.

A district security officer reflected this view: "So that's what we try to do with our security staff, and discipline, is to remove those people who are being disruptive to the education, so those who want the education can get it. Are we successful? I would say for the most part, yes." A district administrator illustrated this point further:

> Well, I think that we have to first of all have adequate security in our buildings. What form that takes, that can vary. I think that in Denver, currently, we're probably understaffed in that area, and *we probably need to beef up our security*, and probably need to beef up our ability to react quickly and to communicate quickly . . . So I think that we have to be proactive, and not wait until the worst happens and then say, OK, we better beef up security. I think you need to do it before, and be prepared. So that,

> hopefully, those things don't happen, or that things get out of control. *You've got to keep a tight lid on things. You can't wait until they're out of control and then try to reel it back in.* That's really hard to do.

This conception of a "proactive" approach to violence, based on increased security and vigilance, was often expressed by those who worked in safety and security and by those in high-level school or district administrative positions. It is an interesting contrast to more educational notions of prevention and proactivity. It represents a clear peacekeeping posture. It illustrates that an individual's problem definition of an issue influences the meaning he or she ascribes to particular language and symbols.

The Student Conduct and Discipline Policy

The DPS "Student Conduct and Discipline Policy" prohibits eighteen specific behaviors, including those that are "detrimental to the welfare or safety" of those in the school, such as interfering with learning, having a weapon defined as such, engaging in gang-related activities, fighting, and so forth. The policy explicitly prescribes due process considerations for suspension, behaviors that trigger mandatory expulsion proceedings, grounds for suspension and expulsion, and grounds for denial of admission.[17] The DPS policy clearly follows state and federal law. It goes on to discuss disciplinary procedures, staff responsibilities, and communication of disciplinary information. It mentions disciplinary action, the district's disciplinary referral ladder, the remedial discipline plan or behavior contract, substance abuse, and implementation of the policy throughout the district. Schools are required to "annually review their school climate" and submit in written form information pertaining to intervention and prevention strategies, disciplinary referrals, suspensions, expulsions, and consistent application of this and related policies. Schools are required to develop education and intervention programs for substance abuse and gang activity.[18] Again, the state legislative changes are represented by additions and revisions to the DPS policy.

Overall, the "Student Conduct and Discipline Policy" clearly sets out goals, expectations, proscribed behaviors, rights and responsibilities, and consequences. It carefully adheres to state and federal law, but does not go beyond it. Prevention mandates in this policy are limited. The overall tone and content reflect an order-expulsion perspective. Even prevention and intervention programs seem to be oriented toward suspension and expulsion and not, in a broader sense, toward the needs of the individual or the school.

Site-Based Management and Discipline

Formally, DPS is a district that has decentralized to a form of site-based management. Each school has a CDM that is responsible for establishing "instructional programs, schedules and structures that will promote the achievement of District outcomes by students in that school."[19] Within a framework of goals and standards set by the district, the CDMs have the authority, among other things, to "Develop school procedures and policies, including a review of discipline and safety issues at the school; incorporate as a part of that review, an analysis of data on verbal threats and physical harm to teachers, students and community members."[20] Local school control in this area is emphasized in the development of a building discipline plan by the CDM. Such plans include discussion of the conditions under which students will be referred to the school administrator and when and how they will be returned to class. The referrals are to emphasize the rights of the majority of students to a safe learning environment, the due process rights of parents and individual students to fair disciplinary action, and consistency of application among teachers in a school.[21]

Decentralization, Consistency, and Due Process

This concern for consistency was a key issue for many in the district and is analogous to the concerns in the state for consistency across districts. One principal thought the district's policy was appropriate and put it this way:

> I think it works very well in the sense that, if you know what the policy is saying, and you're able to use your *blueprint* to get the message across to all of those who have to see to it that the policy is in adherence, students are informed, parents are informed, and the processing of the policy, as it is interfered with, is consistent, and fair, then there is very little difficulty you run into. And I feel the district has been very up on the equity, fairness, and the dissemination of understanding of the policy.

So, in the midst of an ostensibly decentralized system, principals, district administrators, nongovernmental organizations, and security officials all identified consistency as essential for the working of an effective discipline policy. These individuals added to this a more or less strict view on the role of consistency and expectations in holding students accountable to a firm notion of order and administrative control in the schools.

CDM and school policies are designed to fit within a district structure, but the district does have the power and responsibility to set goals, standards, and policy guidelines. It is apparent that the district problem definition has significant power in this respect, even in a decentralized context. Yet the importance of the school principal in setting the problem definition in each school and interpreting and implementing district and state mandates cannot be overstated. One principal, for example, strongly indicated this:

> The district has a full-blown, spelled-out, discipline code of conduct that all schools follow, OK, so we're all alike that way. *Whether you follow it or not is strictly within the building* . . . In my experience in schools, and I've been both at the high school and at the middle school level, it really rests with the school. The district could have five bazillion policies, but that doesn't mean anything's going to change within the school. It just means there are certain steps you go through to do certain things . . . It's just procedures. There's not a philosophy necessarily that says, like we do, we're here to have you learn to read and write and compute, and our whole emphasis is on learning, not on discipline, because if we're teaching you right, and you're learning what we want you to learn, the discipline problems are not there to the same extent. To be respectful of learning and of the people who work with you in that is another part of it . . . You can't really dictate that stuff. That's stuff that really grows out of each school on its own. You can't legislate that stuff 'cause that's really values. That's morals . . . That's got to come from the adults in the building. I've never found that you could legislate it. *And, in fact, usually a lot of the legislation is more detrimental than it is helpful. It just puts another layer that you have to go through, you know, to help solve some of the problems.*

The level of decentralization in DPS can be measured by the following criteria: the presence and level of voluntary intra-district public school choice programs for students, charter schools in the district, and deregulation through waivers from district rules and localization of education codes; and the presence and extent of school-based management, localized budgeting responsibility, and shared decision-making among local administrators, teachers, and parents.[22] Considering these factors, DPS shows a moderate degree of decentralization, with schools responsible for a variety of matters and with parents allowed a modicum of choice. However, some elements of a decentralized system are still in the process of being implemented, and interviewees tended to affirm the continuing dominance of the central office.

Alternative Education

The district has several alternative educational options for students who are expelled or suspended, but it does not have an extensive program to deal with this population. In addition to homebound schooling, where the district provides a teacher in the home, and homeschooling, where parents request that they be allowed to provide for their children's education at home, the district has piloted an alternative middle school and begun an alternative high school.[23] Not all of the students enrolled in these options are necessarily suspended or expelled. The alternative middle school began operation in the 1995–1996 school year and served forty-two students that year. The population was mainly referred to the school due to behavioral difficulties and was disproportionately comprised of black students (62 percent). The program was given a fair grade in an initial evaluation, but further evaluations, greater resource support, consistency across classes, and a clearer focus on program purpose were recommended. Additionally, the evaluation noted that there was no security officer at the school, although one had initially been in the budget, and that the program manager felt that no security staff was needed.[24]

The program itself was difficult to establish, as one school board member indicated:

> And we tried to put an alternative middle school over at Byers, which was a half-empty building . . . and the neighborhood just became unglued and said, no way. They didn't like the alternative high school that was there. They didn't in any way want middle schoolers there . . . I think it's an ongoing issue. It's not a policy issue. *We have the policy, but if people don't know how to proceed, don't have procedures to follow the policy, then you're going to continue to have problems.*

The NIMBY issues were combined with funding problems, as one paraprofessional noted:

> Well, we looked at last year an alternative middle school, but it . . . wasn't quite just for those kinds of kids. It was for a lot of different issues, and didn't have the money. And I think that in order to get some money, you're going to have to tell the, convince the public, who votes on the mill levy increases, or the legislature, that it is such a huge issue that we have no

choice. And you know, they'll have to find more money, however they do that.

Another administrator, alluding to the superintendent's learning more about the problem after his arrival, pointed out the importance of alternative education to the district:

> When Superintendent Moskowitz came in three years ago, he really didn't want to have much alternative ed. He was looking much more at addressing the core curriculum in the high schools and middle schools and that kind of thing. And we had in the works at that time an alternative high school, building a building and all that kind of stuff, and he shut it down. Absolutely not. *Well, it didn't take him too long to realize that when you shut down alternative ed, you shut a lot of kids out in an inner city.* We have lots and lots of kids in Denver who just are not going to make it in a high school with a thousand to fifteen hundred kids.

Denver continues to struggle with implementing more alternative programs, including a new push for "in-school suspension" and "school within a school"–type programs. State law now attempts to foster these kinds of approaches, and Denver applied for and received a grant through the state's 1996 request for proposals to fund such a program, as one special education administrator described:

> We've got kids that any teacher in Denver Public Schools could tell you from the time they're in kindergarten where they're going to end up. And are we doing anything with those kids? Are we doing anything proactive? DPS just got one of the grants that the state put out . . . and it's dealing with elementary age children who are being suspended, feeling if we intervene then, then we can stop it from being so bad by the time they get to middle and high school. When a kid gets suspended in elementary school, that's really pretty serious, and we have thousands of them a year being suspended in elementary school. And, it's getting younger and younger. Well, when you have that kind of thing happening in a kindergarten and first-grade kid, you know what's going to happen, and particularly once you meet the parent . . . .We're going to . . . use trained people to try and intervene with those families. We're going to try and get social services involved earlier with those families, if appropriate. That kind of thing happening. *Will it do any good? I don't know, but certainly it's something that you have to try. And twenty-five thousand, you know, doesn't even hire a body. It's a drop in the bucket.*

That same administrator also discussed the Alternative Transition School, a new program set up specifically to educate youths involved in the juvenile justice system:

Our alternative programs have really grown lately. You know, we even opened a collaborative school this year with Denver Juvenile Court. All sixty kids have to be on probation. They have a full-time probation officer. We have a task worker who is a drug and alcohol person there from juvenile court; that's full-time. We have a mental health person. DPS provides the building and the teachers and the paraprofessionals, and these are kids that the [probation officers] were saying to us, you know, they go into school and they just don't make it. They aren't welcomed; they don't feel welcomed; they don't want to be there. *It's obvious the school doesn't want them there. They've got ankle bracelets on.*

Thus, Denver has implemented some alternative programs for suspended and expelled students. It educates a number of them through home- or homebound schooling. Yet these programs lack funding, as well as broad support, due to their extremely high cost per pupil. The district has left it up to schools in many instances to try to contain their disciplinary problems.

In terms of *policy*, the district has taken a firm line established by the state, but in terms of *procedures* and *programs*, the district has established some alternatives and tried to retain students in school. A district administrator noted:

The district, our response to discipline, really has changed radically, partly driven by internal policy changes and philosophy, partly driven by the state of Colorado law and mandates as regards mandatory expulsion proceedings and suspension proceedings. And, so, as a result, our expulsion proceedings have increased a great deal. The rate of expulsion probably has increased only a very little. We still, we have a very low rate of expulsion per capita in Denver compared to other school districts, suburban or urban. And we're very proud of that. *Part of the philosophy in Denver is that we do want to intervene.* We want to intervene successfully, we want to intervene at . . . the earliest indicator as to when we should intervene, but we want to be able to provide kids with alternatives to it, which we've been doing a good job of for many years in Denver now. Hence the much lower rate of expulsions despite the high number of proceedings that are mandated by law. *We intervene at many levels.* We certainly look at the school level, we look at community interventions. We look at district-level interventions, and we look at outside agency and purchase service interventions in some cases.

Nevertheless, behind the scenes, students are being pushed out, dropped out, and transferred throughout the district, from school to school or out of school altogether. It is a process that seems like educational musical chairs. Principals "trade" students among schools. A common form of disciplinary action and a solution to a student's misbehavior in one school is to find a more "appropriate" setting for that student. There is plain disagreement between some, like the above administrator, who stress the district's efforts to retain students, and others who stress the district's continuing hard-line on getting students "outta here." There is little available in the way of numbers in terms of tracking students who are pushed out, essentially told to leave or they will be expelled, or those who are transferred. Students generally seem to go through no district due-process proceedings when they are moved without an expulsion hearing. While some principals saw the avoidance of an expulsion hearing and possible expulsion as a benefit for the student, since that student could then enroll in another school without being prohibited from doing so because of the expulsion, it is unclear whether those students would not be better off receiving a fair hearing and possible additional intervention measures resulting from that process.

Education, Prevention, Treatment

Regarding its environmental and safety program, the district policy manual states that the "practice of safety also shall be considered a facet of the instructional program of the district schools." It specifically states that accident and fire prevention; emergency procedures; traffic, bicycle, and pedestrian safety; and driver education "shall be provided in the appropriate grades and classes."[25] Violence prevention, however, does not make the list. Again, CDMs are given a role in instructional development. It appears that district- and school-level administrators alike view violence-prevention educational programs as a school-level decision. However, schools work within the context of district standards and goals. The district has departments and individuals that work from a more systemic, comprehensive, education-oriented perspective, but this type of approach does not receive much public attention. It seems distinct from the disciplinary and safety and security perspectives.

Prevention: District or School Responsibility?

There are models for district action and guidance through specific educational, preventative, instructionally based programs in the areas of drugs and alcohol and HIV/AIDS. Following state and federal law, including the amended Drug-Free Schools and Communities Act of

1986, the district notes that it "shall provide age-appropriate, developmentally based drug and alcohol education and prevention programs from early childhood (preschool) through grade 12." The board describes a comprehensive approach to drugs and alcohol and multiple objectives involved in reducing their use and abuse. These objectives "are rooted in the Board's belief that prevention requires education and that the most important aspect of the policies and guidelines of the district should be the education of each individual to the dangers of drugs, alcohol and tobacco." Furthermore, the district explicitly assumes a high degree of central responsibility in this area. "The curriculum, instructional materials and strategies used in this program shall be recommended by the superintendent and approved by the Board."[26]

The district is similarly explicit about "Family Life/Sex Education" and HIV/AIDS education. It points to HIV/AIDS as a "public health crisis" requiring public education as "society's most effective weapon against this deadly disease." The board recommends integration of HIV/AIDS education into "a comprehensive health education program," ongoing in-service training for staff, and student and parent involvement in program planning.[27] Models and precedents exist for district policy, curricular, and program involvement in sensitive, value-laden, controversial, safety-oriented, and public health-related areas. Yet the district does not seem to have taken similarly strong action in the area of violence prevention, conflict education, or peace education, for example, at this level. Rather, it has largely left the initiative in this area to the schools and a few district programs.

Safe and Drug Free Schools and Communities (SDFSC)

The district's Safe and Drug-Free Schools and Communities coordinator is responsible for implementing and overseeing the use of federal SDFSC grants within the district. This is one location of an alternative problem definition within the district. This office, for example, recently sponsored a three-day conference, mainly for teachers, that offered "the opportunity to enhance resiliency skills, to move beyond deficit thinking into building assets and to promote self concept and self confidence."[28] Given the structure of the federal program that funds this office and sets its mission, and the background of the individual who is the coordinator for the district, this is a primary location within the district for an alternative problem definition (see chapter three). The definition is comprehensive, research-based, and prevention-oriented:

> [There are a] wide [variety of] reasons for violence. And I think that we look at it from a menu of things. And so I think when we look at how we can help our students nurture and strengthen relationships, then we take a look at it from a different *paradigm*. I mean, we look at it from what kinds of things are kids bringing to us in the schools that help them succeed, not only academically, but emotionally and socially. And I think what we'd like to look at is, [to] assess what strengths our kids are coming with, what assets . . . The Search Institute has done some nice work with that, in terms of the developmental assets, so we've been gearing our programs to match assessments and measures and interviews and program development around those forty developmental assets.

This individual is conscious of the different paradigms used to approach violence, indicating an awareness of problem definition as influential in the ways that different people address the issues involved. Furthermore, points of view based on academic or analytical orientations lead directly to solution choices, which are seen as more or less effective:

> I think, because violence in the teen population is something we're still trying to grasp a hold of, in terms of studying it more carefully, I think lots of experts have their point of view about it . . . So I think that what we know in terms of the research behind it is still being done, still coming out . . . [We are] really looking at *a bio-psycho-social model in terms of how we can ensure that we are covering our bases.* And I think the more success we have, it is because we have looked at this approach of resiliency, trying to get people to understand that we've got to start building on students' strengths and assets, both in their family and community, and in the world that they live in, and that takes a much bigger involvement than just the school system.

Here the perspective is strikingly similar to the approach recommended by the National Research Council (see chapter one). One of the particular programs, recently implemented with SDFSC grant money, which reflects this problem definition is the Community and School Assistance Teams (CSAT) approach, described in more detail by the same administrator:

> I think what we've done is we've embraced all the schools to look at what we call Community and School Assistance Teams. They're a cadre of professionals to serve as a team to take on referrals for kids that are having

difficulties. And these teams are frontline folks, psych, social work, nursing, special ed teachers, Title 1, regular ed teachers, administrators, so on and so forth. And I think that what is real helpful around this is that *each person has a role to fulfill in that team.*

Such a multidisciplinary approach, one that many people in the district were aware of, seems based on a more complex understanding of the violence problem, one that is perhaps the result of a basic prevention, psychological, or public health approach. The official continues, "I think in prevention, you look at the problem, you assess it, and meet people with where they're at."

Student Services and Safety and Security: Personal Experience and Institutional Roles

An individual's training, background, and role in the district influence his or her definition of the problem, and thus the approach to dealing with it. This is illustrated by the contrast between treatment-oriented and security-oriented departments. The district's offices of Student Services and Special Education offer alternative methods of handling students with behavioral and related problems. A Student Services administrator noted that through the CSAT approach, they

have trained most of our schools in that resource and process of looking at broad-based and holistic needs of kids and trying to develop an array of interventions, including within and outside of school resources . . . and teach the schools about the resources to intervene effectively with kids in discipline problems, and we have great hopes that that will be an infrastructure which will positively influence kids' lives. Cut down on the discipline problems and really beef up the effective interventions.

Again, the alternative paradigm is evident. But personal training and one's individual and departmental role in the district are dominant factors, as one person in the Student Services Department noted:

There's so much pain involved with these young people's lives, and they're really messed up because of violence . . . On the other hand, I can't think of a school in Denver that I walk into and feel any personal fear at all . . . but . . . we had a meeting this week around these kinds of issues, and clearly Safety and Security . . . I mean, I guess there's already been three gun incidents this year that have been pretty frightening, that I don't think have necessarily made the paper. I haven't seen them. But had the potential for something pretty scary, and they feel, but you have to understand that *they're from a military background, so they're gearing up for war no matter what* [laughs]. But . . . they feel that we're one step away always from something fairly serious that could involve hostages, or something around violence. So, clearly the awareness that those kinds of things could happen within the district are there, and some real planning's being done around just how to contain and how to respond to a critical incident that might include violence.

Another contrast is evident in the ways in which individuals within these two departments perceived and implemented changes in the security procedures at the district offices. These changes involved a gradual increase in visitor identification, surveillance monitoring, signing in, a desk guard, and so on. At Safety and Security, there was an awareness that these steps had to be taken gradually, given the "culture" shift in the district which they represented:

Well, [the board] always knew [security] was a problem, I think . . . *what they lacked was a concerted battle plan*, if you want to call it that, or a strategic plan to deal with security issues. Throwing money at something without a plan is bullshit. So, we went in and said, here's how we'd like to approach it. And so we're ramping up based on this approach. You know the superintendent, Mr. Moskowitz, came from California, so he's seen what can happen to your schools if you don't deal with the security issues. He also came from Cleveland Heights. So he's been in urban environments. I came from an urban environment . . . so, you know, I've dealt with a lot of this, but you got to go in there and say, well, if you give us resources, here's where we're going to spend it and why it's important for the schools . . . They didn't have a program before. They didn't have anybody down there that knew how to develop a program. When you walked into this building you're seeing changes that are going to be occurring. You had to sign in. That's a first . . . I just started phasing that in. I've had somebody sitting down there, just to look at people, and then we started signing in. Within a month, we're going to have people, the whole front changed, and you'll get a visitor pass, and I'll know where you're going, and people are going to be calling. But I've got to phase that in, because it's a *culture change*.

Thus, there is an acknowledgment of the scale of changes involved in the district, what, over the course of a number of interviews, almost sounded like a coming of age for Denver as an urban center, a city with all its companion problems and realities. Safety and Security has explicitly not taken an "armed camp" approach, in its own mind, but has tried to "beef up," professionalize, and better organize its system and its staff. Yet this department has encountered resistance in terms of funding constraints, a school that didn't want a security officer "pawned off" on it because of the message that it would send, and district resistance to open publicity about violence problems.

At Student Services, the change in district office security procedures was perceived this way:

> If you look at district policies, I mean, I don't know what all the factors were that went into this decision, but this building has changed between last year and this year. We now have a security guard down at the bottom of the elevators. We never had that. We had . . . kind of a reception area down there, and we had a fellow from security that was manning a counter, but I think his role was mainly to answer questions . . . Now, we've got badges and all of that; it's really changed the way that we think about coming to work . . . It's inconvenient [laughs]. And all those other factors. You know . . . I see something like that, I walk in at the beginning of the year without knowing that they were going to implement this policy, and I see guards, gate-keeping into the organization, and I immediately begin wondering why. You know, what are they fearing . . . were there specific incidents triggering this? And I wonder if they know something that I don't.

It was acknowledged that most public agencies are implementing similar changes in the way they screen visitors and identify employees, but individuals at Student Services noted the psychological effects such security measures had on staff at the district office and in the schools, regardless of their necessity.

The Crisis Team: Innovation and Rediscovery

An interesting, and somewhat ironic, twist associated with the implementation of one program innovation illustrates the district's initial lack of learning and then potential learning from experience. The Department of Student Services began using a crisis team originally in order to intervene in schools when a tragedy, such as a death by an accident occurred, but the nature of the crisis team's work changed over time. It seemed to one team member

> that when the district crisis team gets called out, it's around issues of violence, much more than it ever used to be. And we had to kind of regroup and understand how to deal with kids around gang and violence issues, because that was not the use that the crisis team was put to . . . But now, it almost always is around violence, so clearly increasingly there's that concern in the schools, and I also know that there's been enough that teachers really feel the strain of it.

The team was formed by district treatment professionals, based on their experience, and represents a proactive, problem-setting approach. Yet, this team member explained, at one point the crisis team disbanded, for reasons of funding, overwork, decentralization, and initial lack of support:

> So, anyway, we put that together several years ago, and *we spent quite a bit of time planning around traumatic events*, and how we wanted to look, and how we wanted to define what a crisis was, and so, it had been all through the years, nurses, social workers, and psychologists . . . and so, it was one from each discipline on call for a week at a time, and then just a rotation, so we had three. And then we went up to five teams a year after the Carl Banks shooting case. We were getting so many calls that we were getting, we were in crisis, actually, the crisis team was, so . . . then, two years ago, we did . . . a retreat, and we did put together some protocols for everything we could think about. Some of the things that the district now is thinking about, which is natural disasters, violence in the neighborhood, those kinds of things . . . and then we did some training with all of our staff and asked the principals to develop in-building crisis teams. Some schools did and some didn't, but that's always true in a big district, certainly in DPS.

As more responsibility for the crisis teams was given to the schools, central calls decreased, and the district negotiated a new contract with its mental health care provider, which insisted that it could provide the necessary crisis intervention for the district. But original team members disagreed:

> So we've had some extensive talks with them, because we didn't feel that they knew the school system well enough, and they're not for students, they're for employees, and how would that [work]. Well, they were sure that they could do that and, in fact, were really kind of casual about it, so we went out of existence, disbanded the team. *Well, the superintendent found out about that and said, uh, uh. So, we're back in business, as soon as we can pull it back together.*

Members of the team were learning about how to deal with violence, even as more of the crisis intervention work became more school based. One team member noted:

> We learned that after a gang incident you don't bring kids together in an auditorium. We learned that you had to have a nice ethnic [and] cultural mix on the team, because I'll tell you that African American students in crisis do not feel that Anglos have much to offer in the way of support or understanding. That became a real important issue . . . [We learned] that we needed to know more about violence and about gang-related crises, because

we didn't have a good base of knowledge so that we felt competent. We didn't have good words of wisdom for either faculty or kids when it first exploded the way it did.

Another member added:

It's continuing, too, because we did get some information. We had speakers that came and spoke to our group, psychologists, nurses, social workers. We did learn more about the whole violence dynamic, but it's still an ongoing need. We need to know more. We need information to help us in our practice. Just in my tenure here with Denver Public Schools, too, crises have really changed . . . Now, it seems like most of the calls we get are involved with some sort of violence. I got a call right at the end of last year for an incident where a father took his wife hostage and then shot her, shot himself. Dealing with their children, who were in my school. And it did bring it right into the school for the staff, for the kids, who began thinking, you know, gosh, this is a nice neighborhood. If this is happening with Jimmy and Billy's father over here, what can happen to me. So I think it's made it more immediate in that sense.

The learning was almost stifled. Yet, meanwhile, the Department of Safety and Security had learned from its members' own experiences, as well as a high-level school safety review conducted by an outside organization, that a central crisis team was an essential element of a good school safety plan. A district official indicated this:

We will open our crisis command center in January down here. We've already rehabbed the facility. We're bringing in all our telephones and alarms and everything into one command center. Next door we have a crisis center. We've also started the work on the crisis team, that has a very defined chain of command, and we've already started identifying different types of activities, or different types of situations, and the response that we will give to those situations, and who's to do what, who needs to be in charge. We've already had two meetings on that . . . *It's a multi-disciplinary team, that includes crisis management type folks, psychological behavior, plus the normal things, like security, and environmental.*

While the "normal things" might be defined differently in the two departments, they had both arrived at the same conclusion from different perspectives: that a central crisis team was a key component in dealing with this problem. The two perspectives are complementary. They have led to a more comprehensive approach in this area. The crisis team is an example of successful learning in the district. It shows the need for cooperation between different district offices with varied backgrounds and expertise, as well as the need for key leadership to bring these institutional fragments together. This example is not a great model for future learning, but it shows the potential benefits of integrating partial problem definitions within institutions.

The Prevention Resource Guide: Information and Loss Thereof

The Department of Student Services conducted a survey of all schools in the district during the 1993–94 academic year in order to put together a resource guide for prevention and intervention programs in the district and the city. The survey shows many different programs in use at all school levels, most through the school social worker or psychologist. Some outside agencies, such as project PAVE, the Colorado School Mediation Project, the Conflict Center, the Denver Police Department, and the Safe and Drug-Free Schools and Communities Office at CDE, are listed as being primarily responsible for the programs.[29] According to one interviewee, this resource guide project was intended to be continued on an annual basis but was "put on hold" indefinitely. It has not since been repeated. The board and the superintendent do not appear to have used this report to inform their decision-making on school violence. Here is an example of a failed opportunity for learning, where resources were not dedicated to information gathering and where a useful idea was abandoned without due consideration.

At-Risk, Community Involvement, and Academic Achievement

More generally, DPS recently decided to put a large portion of state money for at-risk students directly in the hands of elementary schools, based on how many students at each school qualified for free or reduced-price lunch. DPS emphasized its literacy goal by stipulating that the money be used to improve verbal and textual language skills. The state money, used along with federal Title 1 funds, for example, is designed to compensate for the additional stress of neighborhood poverty on children's educational potential.[30] In this example, the definition of "at risk" shows the district's emphasis on the primary goal of learning, the same goal it connects to violence and disruption. The district has more directly connected the state and particular schools, but has restricted the schools' use of these funds to basic academic pursuits.

Another prevention area is the fostering of parent and community involvement in the schools. There has been some district action and focus in this area, in addition to the creation of the CDMs. For example, the district's Black Education Advisory Council (BEAC) identified school, parent, and community partnerships as its primary goal in a 1996 report on improving the education of African American students. BEAC members connected recent progress in lowering the African American dropout rate and share of the total number of district suspensions and expulsions to increased black parental involvement.[31] The goal of parental and community involvement has also been used to justify the district's return to neighborhood schools. However, as some have noted, neighborhood attendance areas do not guarantee increased involvement. Many neighborhood schools had problems with discipline, academic success, and community support prior to the imposition of court-ordered desegregation.[32] One principal speculated on the change to neighborhood high schools next year in this way:

> I think, on the one hand, it will allow the schools, if they let us, to speak better with each other, in other words, to communicate better, because now I'll have three schools feed in here, rather than fifty-three. OK, our kids then will go to one high school, rather than five. So that should, that should help . . . *But, in the old days, when we were all neighborhoods that never happened*, so maybe it won't happen this time either, because I was around then, too, when all this conversion took place, so it's interesting for me to see this conversion twenty-five years later, back to how it was. *To me there is no reason for an all-black school not to be a wonderful school with the same expectations as an all-white school would be, but it lies with the leadership and the teachers.* That's exactly where it lies.

Ad Hoc Discipline Committee

In 1994, DPS revised its student conduct and discipline policy to conform with state law and to make a number of divergent and disparate policies more coherent. "The policy was designed to be broad enough in scope to allow each site the flexibility to develop its own school code of conduct."[33] In response to a heightened level of concern about discipline issues in the district and community, the superintendent surveyed CDMs as described above. A discipline committee, made up of members of the community, students, and school and district staff, was formed to analyze the responses and report recommendations to the school board. The Ad Hoc Discipline Committee held four meetings.

This survey and committee represent the clearest formal attempt by the school district to understand the scope and nature of the school discipline problem. The focus, however, was limited to the established problem definition and policies. Its request for input centered on set survey statements and was very solution-oriented. This was a restricted search for information. Nonetheless, the survey and its recommendations illustrate the diversity of school responses to violence, the conflicts among school definitions of the problem, and the fairly limited district reaction to school input on the problem, input that could conceivably have motivated learning. The committee agreed that the discipline policy at that time was "adequate and effective as written." Among the committee's recommendations were a district forum for discipline issues, reviews and revisions of school codes of conduct, and additional resources for interventions, especially at the elementary level. The committee suggested district-wide training on the new policy, development of site and district communications plans, and principal initiative in explaining and fairly implementing the school policy.[34]

It is unclear where the statements for the survey originated, but it is likely that they came from the Planning, Research, and Program Evaluation Department at the behest of the superintendent. The survey statements are clearly suspension, expulsion, and discipline focused. They generally produced conflicting results and comments among those surveyed. For example, 42 percent disagreed or strongly disagreed and 58 percent agreed or strongly agreed with this statement: "Additional staff training in classroom management techniques would improve the effectiveness of the disciplinary program in our school."[35] The main indication of a disconnection between the district problem definition, as represented in the survey, and the problem definitions in at least some schools presents itself in response to the survey request for "practices that have been effective in improving discipline at your school." While focused on solutions, the breadth of responses shows clear contrasts between schools, although not all of the alternatives mentioned would be mutually exclusive in any one school. For example, the summary of responses lists such practices as clear expectations, everyone promoting strong discipline, and hall sweeps, as well as conflict resolution training, positive reinforcement, and peer mediation.[36] These practices indicate conflicting problem definitions, some of which are broader than others. They also show the extent to which the district has left the determination of specific disciplinary practices up to the schools, within the framework of district limits as prescribed by state law.

The results of the ad hoc discipline survey and committee process appear to be rather limited. District training sessions on new discipline policies did take place. Opportunities for discussions among school-level administrators continued, but without a focus on discipline. The ad hoc committee itself fizzled out, particularly as one of the key district administrators involved in its formation and continuation left the district. Meetings held by the district for school administrators at each school level occur monthly. They serve as a source of feedback for the district as well as a forum for discussion and sharing and a place for the district to introduce information and best practice materials. New district directions and support for alternative practices, or a resource book for schools, did not appear out of the committee's work. Increased funding for elementary-level interventions did not happen. Essentially, the main conclusions of the committee's meetings and survey were that the district's policies as written were fine but that their implementation and consistency across schools needed to be improved.

Interrelationships and Programs with the City and County of Denver: Successful Learning Processes

DPS shares a number of coordinated programs and initiatives with the city and county of Denver and its agencies. Informally, DPS students and families can take advantage of additional programs administered by the city. For example, the City-Schools Coordinating Commission, a twenty-year-old body that was recently reestablished, consists of DPS and Denver leaders who meet monthly to "share information and coordinate services."[37] "Club Denver" was created in September 1996 to sponsor after-school clubs oriented around six themes in all DPS middle schools. Sponsored by teachers in partnership with city departments and funded mainly by private money, the clubs focus on the Platte River, medicine, and "21st Century Teachers," for example. Denver has funded two minority consultants to help DPS recruit twenty new minority teachers.[38]

The mayor's office has also been involved in youth violence reduction in the city. It responded to real and perceived increases in youth violence with the "Safe City Summit" in 1993 and created the Safe City Office in 1994. Touting a "triad solution to violence" comprised of "zero-tolerance" law enforcement, prevention education, and community involvement, the city has created police impact units. It has implemented a nuisance abatement team, community policing, and the SafeNite Curfew Program. It has promoted various after-school and summer youth programs, the mayor's Youth Job Program, and the sheriff's Work Program. The mayor's office claims that youth crime has decreased as a result of these efforts and that the school grades and behavior of many of the Youth Job Program participants have shown improvement.[39]

Initially, it appears that decentralization in the district hindered the city's attempts to work with the schools, due to the fact that the city was not able to go to one identifiable contact source at the district level in order to implement its programs. At the mayor's office, one person put it this way:

> Well, I think one of the barriers . . . that we first addressed is we have an independent, elected school board, then we have CDMs . . . so [in] the coordination . . . when we were tying to set up various programs, or deal with various issues, not only did we have to work with the school board, but we had to go individually to the various respective schools to sell them to help us to change some of the ideas. And, in a sense, while that's really helped strengthen [our coordination], initially, when you're trying to deal with some issues right away . . . for the short term, you need to be able to implement programs and have one source [of contact] at that time . . . Some of the positives that I've been able to see . . . is the very fact that the school board came on board, 'cause they realized that they needed some assistance, and so the fact that we were able to go in, and just actually within . . . two or three months, place different activities in the schools. And I think one of the initial barriers that we saw was being able to use school buildings in the evenings, and look at costs, where they could accept some of the responsibility, and where we could actually put things into the school buildings.

Thus, decentralization made quick action between the city and the schools difficult, but over time the district administration joined with the city. Equally important, the city was able to develop more substantial and meaningful relationships with various school sites, as this same city official noted:

Well, initially, in the short term, that [coordination] was very difficult. As it's come about in the long term, it's turned into more of a positive situation because we've been able to develop a closer relationship with the individual players in the respective schools. *So that's forced, given us an opportunity, and I won't use the word "force." That's really given us an opportunity where we sit down, and we can hear the different views and why people feel the way they do* . . . [We work with] school principals and help to look at their particular issues and help them address them on an individual basis, because, and what's good about that is, by decentralization, we've actually been able to identify, by respective areas, what those issues really are, because . . . people [usually only] see the broad range of education . . . And so, individually, it will be based upon that respective community. We'll be able to address the needs individually, and I think that's what the positive piece of it is. And understand or welcome the differences and reward the accomplishments, based upon those individual needs.

Denver and DPS have worked together on truancy programs. Denver and DPS were both part of the mayor's "Great Kids Initiative," which funds community development projects and supports the recent change back to neighborhood attendance zones. The city has sponsored health clinics in thirteen DPS schools. In interviews, members of both the school district and the city emphasized the importance of regular meetings between the city, the district, and schools in fostering better cooperation and coordination. These institutionalized interactions have been important in fostering and furthering successful and more complex learning among city and school officials.

Several additional efforts at city-school cooperation exist. The Denver Police Department (DPD) operates seventy-one Drug Abuse Resistance and Education (DARE) programs and sixteen anti-gang programs in the schools.[40] The Denver Police are also working with DPS Safety and Security to coordinate officer training, patrolling, and general school security issues. DPD has stationed one police officer in Lake Middle School as a pilot program. It deemed the effort successful, but expensive. DPD has not supported the creation of a DPS police department, although it has backed increased training and professionalization for DPS security staff.[41] DPS and DPD formed a joint task force in April 1995 to address youth issues, improve cooperation and coordination, and accomplish specific objectives in such areas as improving the management of school security personnel, reporting incidents, and providing students with identification cards.[42]

The DPS Truancy Reduction Project has attempted to connect schools, parents, students, and community representatives on the

Student Attendance Board in hopes of diverting students from the juvenile court system. Truancy has been linked by the district and the city to elevated dropout rates and increased crime by and among youth who are not in school. The program was piloted in two middle schools in the 1995–1996 school year, and was expanded to two additional schools in 1996–1997 in part due to success in increasing attendance rates at the first two schools.[43] The story of the cooperation between the city and the schools around this particular violence-related issue, as told by a district administrator, illustrates some of the benefits associated with collaborating on dealing with a systemic problem:

> When a new superintendent came on board two years ago, he invited me to this meeting that he had been invited to at the juvenile court, with the juvenile court judge. There was this . . . committee that had been meeting for about a year . . . with other superintendents, and they had been talking about the truancy problem. They had discussed a whole bunch of things, and I was really surprised when I got to this meeting because the director of social services was there, the juvenile court judge was there, the director of probation . . . What had emerged out of that meeting is called the Geraldine Thompson Committee, and there's an attorney from social services who sort of convened this because social services, they get a lot of referrals of kids who are not making it. *I think they began to feel that they needed to get collaboration going here to address a problem that was affecting so many systems.* They had a good handle on it, they had all the right people there and I was so impressed, and just imagine a social worker who has been totally tuned into this whole problem for all these years and this would be what needed to happen. If somebody would've said [to me], What do you think we need to do here? This is exactly what I would've said: *We need to get all the people involved at the higher levels of administration around the same table to talk about it and come up with this. But it just happened; it was already there.*

Here we see the importance of leadership in getting the district involved in this ongoing meeting process. The social worker who is speaking is describing a logical reaction to the need for collaboration on a problem that affects multiple institutions. This person was seeking an outlet for coordination but needed the proper institutional channel through which to become involved:

> It was needs-driven. Everybody was feeling the pressure of the problem and felt that if the kids were in school, that was the best place for them . . . *It gave us a chance to ventilate about our frustration with social services.* When we would call in a neglect case, parents were not getting the kids to

school and we would visit with the family and we'd visit with the parents, and either they would not do anything about it or they could not do anything about it, so we had no support from anywhere. Sometimes we would refer a student to social services and they would say, that's a school problem. *So here I am in the middle of this group of people where I could say to the director of social services, we don't believe it's just a school problem.* It was wonderful.

This meeting forum allowed representatives of different institutions to confront their counterparts' impressions and potentially contrasting problem definitions. Here, conflict between problem definitions served as a source of learning because the conflict was structured through a communications process that promoted the assessment of the whole problem as a shared problem. A multifaceted solution was produced through adding action-oriented discussion. This same social worker continued,

What the superintendent told me to do was to think about this and to *come up with a model* in order to begin to do what this big committee had been talking about. So . . . we have a full-time social worker, . . . a . . . catch-up class, where the kids get mentoring, tutoring, whatever they need, academic help, a staff person within the building with a place to work . . . with the teachers referring the kids that aren't there to the social worker. The social worker is doing what they need to do, which sometimes is a home contact, trying to find out what the problem is. If they are not successful, referral to the truant officer. Truant officer goes out to the home and brings the kid back to school; talks him into it because we don't force the kids to come to school because the philosophy is that we need them in a positive frame of mind. And what we want to do is bring them back to school and help them readjust and change their attitude about school so that they will stay and won't walk out the back door . . . Now we're working on . . . community-school assistance teams . . . Meanwhile, the school social worker is coordinating this whole thing. If we have done everything that we can, brought the kid back to school, talked to him, counseled him, tutored him, put him back in the classroom, and he still isn't there, and we've tried everything that we can try, then we make a referral to what we call the Student Attendance Review Board. We have established two now, we have one per two schools. This is a group of people from the community, these are not school people . . . The director of social services is the chair of this board. He has assigned a social worker from the Department of Social Services to be at those meetings . . . [and a] district attorney representative and a police officer, and we meet at the District 4 office. So, when we have a meeting once a month, and the social worker does the workup, the kid has not made it, we have been through all of this. It's time to make a referral. The social worker does the referral, presents to this group at District 4, the kid and his parents are there, and then they just sort of have a conference

about what can we do with this student? What is missing here? So, if
something comes up . . . then all of these people . . . [are] there and they
want to be able to come up with a way to help this family so that the kid can
come back to school.

Another important piece in this learning process is the
continuation of a problem-setting perspective. Once the problem has
been addressed, it is not forgotten as having been solved. Rather,
continuing work is done to refine and expand the problem definition
as new issues are raised in practice. A district administrator illustrated
this:

> I'll tell you what the problem is. *Confidentiality issues.* Sharing
> information about other kids . . . The Family Educational Rights of Privacy
> Act . . . states that you can only share information with school employees.
> So the nurse, psychologist, teachers, principals, all of these can sit around
> and talk about a kid. But, the rest of these people, we have to have parent
> permission unless it's a health and safety issue. So, it's kind of sticky. We
> haven't figured a way around it yet . . . Under the compulsory attendance
> [law] and as a part of the Geraldine Thompson group that I described, the
> judge is very, very hard on these kids that we refer to him then through this
> whole process. There's just no more excuses . . . They've tried everything.
> So now we have another committee that's meeting that's called the *Creative
> Options Committee* where we're trying to help the judge come up with
> creative ways of making these kids comply with the orders. So that's kind
> of what we're doing on attendance and this is what can happen. *O.K. a
> problem is identified, it becomes a priority, there's a lot of interest,
> somebody says do it.* Or, we sneak up on them sometimes.

City-school coordination and interagency cooperation are key
elements of the district's approach to school violence. One of the
most important benefits of such work is its role in broadening
individual and institutional problem definitions. Through working
with one another, individuals are exposed to contrasting views. They
may integrate new information in order to learn more about the
problem. One DPS administrator explicitly connected this to changes
in the district's approach to school violence:

> I think that there was a fairly easy attitude among schools and school
> administrators toward just sending kids away from their building, and
> kicking them out for periods of time. And I think that's become a lot less
> prevalent than it was, and I think part of it does have to do with our attitude
> towards young people generally now has been changing a lot in the DPS for
> the last few years, and I think that our agency partners, the social service
> people, and the police, and the courts, in working with us, have helped us

also to *embrace this problem from their perspective,* and realizing that it doesn't do anybody any good just simply to have the young person out of school . . . That's the other thing which has been changing in the last few years is *far more effective partnerships with other city and district and county agencies, like the courts and police, and social services.* We do a much better job of providing each other with information, understanding processes . . . effectively utilizing them, knowing what people can and can't do, and having realistic expectations about that. And then, communicating that to schools . . . That helps the agencies to understand what our needs are. It helps us to understand what their limitations are, and it helps principals and other people to realize that there may not be good alternatives out there for young people and that we have to increasingly develop those within our buildings.

Both the need to use limited funds wisely and the search for more effective solutions to the problem were identified by district administrators as contributing to the increase in both informal networking and formal coordination in terms of memorandums of understanding, committees, and programs.

I'd say that all of this started [with] . . . first of all, probably that spike in *violent crime* that I perceive happened probably in the early nineties, and then . . . *budget crises* have driven everyone to look to finding more effective ways of, efficient ways of working together. Motivation, certainly. We've got some *well-motivated leaders* in Denver, including our superintendent, and also the mayor, and our school board, and many of the city council members. So, I think, budget and motivation, desire to do what's right for young people, and then certainly the needs that the young people have presented to us have become a little more dramatic . . . Everyone realized that it wasn't doing any good just to kick 'em out of school, and the kids basically told us that we weren't meeting their needs by their behavior.

Thus, the district, in coordination with the city, seems to be learning from experience and from its formal and informal exposure to different ideas and perspectives held by others in its environment.

National School Safety Center Assessment

In the major example of proactive lesson-drawing in the district, DPS reached out to the National School Safety Center (NSSC) in 1995 for a review of its school safety situation. While the report included mention of educational and student-centered forms of violence prevention, it focused on environmental and administrative methods of improving district safety and security. The report was requested with the dominant problem definition in mind, reaffirmed that definition, and was interpreted and acted upon with the same mind-set.

The NSSC report represents a comprehensive definition of the school violence problem if taken in its entirety. It includes discussion and recommendations in such areas as crime prevention through environmental design, crime reporting and tracking, student leadership and involvement, and a curriculum focused on "pro-social skills and conflict resolution." The report is based on a review of DPS and its policies and a more in-depth examination of fifteen schools. However, the report includes significant portions that are evidently based on prior NSSC research and experience. The NSSC makes a number of specific recommendations for Denver, some of which are discussed below in terms of the changes that DPS has made in response. One of the main recommendations, the development of a district-wide, comprehensive "safe school plan," includes myriad safety and security practices, violence prevention programs, community and parent involvement strategies, and recommendations for ongoing assessments of district, school, and community goals and evaluations of practices.[44]

One district administrator placed the NSSC review in the context of work on improving safety and security, work which was already underway, including the joint task force between DPS and the Denver Police Department:

> That was a strategy to move forward . . . These are the things that I felt were important to us in working with the task force people. These are things we came up with. I had the National School Safety Center come in here because I wanted *a national view of this thing* . . . *They're very well respected* in looking at school security issues, in conjunction with the Justice Department. I asked them to come up and do not a detailed but a high-level review of some of the things. They had the information, where we're headed. Hey, we're on target with a lot of things, and there are things we can't get done, and others, but we've moved this district, in a year and a half, to where we are now.

The district has acted in many of the areas identified in the NSSC report, some of which had already been identified by district administrators prior to the review. The NSSC represents a national "expert" organization, to which the district turned to help solve a complex problem. Yet the district is constrained in its response to the review by the decentralized structure of the district as well as personal and institutional problem definitions that as of yet do not include a truly comprehensive, district-wide, safe-school plan.

Future District Policy Actions

At the time of this research, DPS had no plans to revise its student conduct and discipline policy, as it underwent extensive revision in 1994 and 1996. DPS is contemplating few other specific actions in the area of school violence at the district level. Some of the plans in progress or under discussion include redesigning school lunchrooms to make closed campuses, a voluntary school decision, more palatable for students and principals. Surveillance equipment will be piloted in some schools. The district plans to continue to train, increase, and restructure the school security force and crisis command center. DPS hopes to foster cooperation and understanding through the Community and School Assistance Teams and to continue to improve incident reporting.

A related issue that the district is facing is the end of school desegregation busing efforts and the subsequent reorganization of the district to neighborhood attendance areas. As discussed below, this will affect a number of neighborhoods and schools in such ways as increasing minority and lower-income population concentrations, moving magnet schools, integrating various gangs into the same school, and changing funding provisions. Interviewees mentioned the potential for these changes to affect levels of conflict and violence in the schools. One board member weighed the benefits and drawbacks of the change:

> The structure of our schools, and returning to neighborhood schools . . .
> hopefully . . . community and parental involvement in our schools will
> [improve] . . . More of a sense of community in the schools . . . I hope, will
> enhance that. [There are schools] that have potential for greater violence
> because you're returning to neighborhood schools. Manual High School,
> for example, as I understand it, has five different gangs—as opposed to kids
> going to different places, will now be in the same place . . . There are
> science experiments that say that you don't want to do that. But, that's the
> situation we have, and so I know that there are efforts underway with Manual
> to try to figure out . . . what are we going to do . . . I think there are some
> areas, with the return to neighborhood schools, that will be more
> problematic. I think, basically, it will enhance or make better our potential
> for less violence and less discipline problems in the district, but there are
> also places where we're going to have to be ever vigilant.

Another board member was similarly aware of the dangers:

Now, as part of [reorganizing], we're concerned about a possible effect of our new boundaries, of bringing rival gangs together. I mean, we're aware of those things, and we're dealing with that . . . What's going to happen in Manual High School when you have two or possibly three rival gangs all in the same school? We don't want that to even happen, but how would we deal with that? And we talk with the city a lot about cooperative efforts that we can make in the schools and with the police department.

And another board member recognized that just having a neighborhood school would not guarantee community and parent involvement:

One of the . . . things that I've heard from predominately minority communities, the Latino communities in particular, but also the African American community, they've said, While our kids are off across town, we don't know what they're doing. We're not able to go there when they have a problem, and so, if they were closer to home . . . there'd be more people who know them and who care about them . . . So then it would be easier for somebody to go in and intervene . . . and *they would feel more ownership*, that this is their community, this is their community school, and that it's their responsibility to make it work and to make it good. That's, I think, what is the hope . . . And I don't think anybody knows if that will happen or not . . . There have been neighborhood schools where that hasn't happened. So, I don't know. But that's the theory.

Extent of Learning: District Responses to School Violence

The approaches of the Denver Public Schools to school violence have been for the most part reactive to state initiatives. Institutionally, the district is in a paradoxical position. It is driven by state mandates and an increasing state role in such areas as academic standards and suspension and expulsion policies. Yet the district has also decentralized to the point where it defers action in many areas to the school level, preferring to set district policies that are broad and flexible enough to allow for school-level diversity. DPS continues to be perceived by the public, and to perceive itself, as playing a central policy-making role. It continues to act in like manner. However, the actions the district has taken indicate its definition of the school violence problem, its priorities, and the main determinants of district policy in this area. The district has not experienced complex learning overall about school violence due to its preoccupation with state laws, school-based management, resource limitations, and, overall, the dominant problem definition institutionalized by state legislation and individual district administrators. As in the state, pockets of learning exist in the district. Numerous alternative programs underneath the surface belie the tough public image of the district, but an overall comprehensive, integrative, and accurate problem redefinition has not occurred in this area.

Causes of District Policy Changes

District policy and learning has been driven by a number of factors, some of which are similar to the state conditions described in chapter three. These factors include state legal changes, fear arising from some key violent incidents, and key personnel changes. Research reports, dissatisfaction at the school level with current policies, and the institutional configuration of the district also have impacted policy and change. The most dominant of these have been the state's actions in 1993 and 1996.

State Legal Mandates

As discussed above, the state's legislative agenda, beginning in 1993, increased the role of the state in school discipline and violence policy at the school and district level. Less room was allowed for flexibility in approach and interpretation of meaning. Districts and schools were required to comply with standard state dictates. The state spurred district and school action in discipline planning and suspensions and expulsions for infractions ranging from disruptive behavior to drug use and weapons possession. Where the state required action, the district complied. Where it recommended action, the district was less cooperative. Again, the prevention and education components of a school violence approach were underutilized.

In 1996, when the state revised its legislation, the district followed suit. Here, there was more of a reflective process between state and district as district feedback contributed to the state modifications, which in turn caused the district to revise its policies. Thus, when the state specified the "material and substantial" three-suspension requirement, the district wrote that into its policy manual. When the state mandated that the district try to identify students at risk of suspension or expulsion and intervene to prevent such action at an early stage, the district added language to its policy stating "The disciplinary referral ladder is used to identify and provide students with support so as to avoid future disciplinary action."[45] The district made provisions for suspended students to make up work, for the district to share student disciplinary information as specified in the law, and for a behavior contract, or remedial discipline plan, to be implemented with suspended students. These revisions to the discipline policy were approved unanimously in 1996.[46]

In terms of non-mandatory actions, the state also influenced the district, but not on an overall level. As mentioned, one district administrator took it upon herself to apply for one of the state's alternatives-to-suspension grants. It is clear that the most obvious influence on district policy was the state.

Crisis, Fear, and Public Incidents

The NSSC report represents both a forward-looking review of safety and security procedures in the schools and a reaction to school and community fears of an increase in youth violence. As the introduction to the report states,

> Although Denver Public Schools is not facing any particular crisis, school officials determined that it would be prudent to proactively review school safety operations within the District. This decision was influenced by increasing concerns associated with juvenile crime in the Denver area.[47]

The NSSC study grew out of personnel changes that fueled a more professional and serious approach to safety and security issues in the district. The study itself produced some modifications and improvements in the way that the district handled these issues, such as increased attention to building structures and the physical school environment and the identification of students. Other changes occurred with open and closed campuses, crisis response ability, and the professionalization and reorganization of the Safety and Security Department.

Isolated discipline-related incidents in the district also contributed to the district's assessment of its school violence and discipline problem. One such incident involved public and district outrage over a disciplinary action taken by a particular assistant principal. Ruben Perez, an assistant principal at Horace Mann Middle School, tried to simultaneously suspend ninety-seven students for a variety of reasons in 1994. Receiving notoriety for "his strict brand of discipline,"

Perez was disciplined by DPS for not following established discipline procedures.[48] A number of participants in the study perceived the so-called "Perez incident" as a source of conflict and a cause of district introspection. Most in the district administration perceived the situation as a misapplication of policy rather than a policy failure. Perez himself received much community and state support and attention for his tough stance. A DPS board member reflected on the incident this way:

> I think that the irony with . . . that whole Ruben Perez thing, if you remember that, he said it was the policy, but *it wasn't about policy*. The policy that we had was fine. He misapplied it, and he even misapplied the one that he had written for his own school . . . I mean, that was what I found was so amazing. He had helped write the Horace Mann discipline policy in conformance with the district discipline policy, and he didn't implement it. But . . . *it wasn't a problem with the policy. It was his actions that were the problem*, so, because there wasn't anything in the policy, well, the policy did say you can't expel a kid for chewing gum. It didn't prohibit him from acting to correct the behavior of those annoying kids.

Similarly, a district administrator noted that the problem here was with process, not policy, touching on issues of consistency in the district, the formation of the Ad Hoc Discipline Committee, and the basic support of that committee for the policy as it stood:

> Last year we had a situation occur. I don't know if you remember hearing about the Ruben Perez issue, and that really was a discipline issue because that involved an individual who attempted to *bypass the process* and kind of make a statement and make an example, and make a media event of discipline. After that occurred last year, the superintendent put together a representative group of central administrators, site teachers, administrators, parents, community people, and a little bit of everything to look at the issue of discipline in Denver. And, basically, what the committee came up with . . . is that they didn't feel that there were huge problems, or that the district was failing to deal with problems appropriately. So there really [weren't] . . . problems, at all, and so that was kind of interesting in itself, is that, basically, people were saying, we feel that things have gone pretty well. So there wasn't a lot of meat that came out of that.

The public's reaction was more vitriolic, according to one administrator:

> I also see society is telling us, get tougher on these kids. I mean, just look at the society's reaction to Ruben Perez, when he was at Horace Mann. They

thought he walked on water. They thought he was wonderful. They thought he should be able to suspend a hundred kids in one day. Why not get rid of those disruptive kids? Those kids are going to . . . ruin my kid's education, *get 'em outta there*, you know, nothing about the rights of those kids or anything else. So, you know, I do see society getting much tougher on kids.

The result of the Perez incident was media and public attention, the formation of the Ad Hoc Discipline Committee, and a basic reaffirmation of established district policy. Why an ad hoc committee and not more extensive program evaluation? A district researcher put it this way:

Because it needed to be a big, huge, community-input kind of situation. That's not what [the Program Evaluation Office does]. [It's] just two people that just gather data and sit in classrooms, . . . like an investigative team, and this is different. No, this was; it needed a lot of community input, and . . . there's a discipline committee that's very politically correct . . . All the ethnicities are represented, all the private interest groups that make up the public education system. *Everybody has a chance to be represented.* Elementary school, middle school, high school, comprehensive in representation . . . [Disciplinary policy] is not a program.

It seems that the discipline committee was very much a reaction to public sentiment, a reaction to an incident or crisis, and did not produce much learning. But it did serve to publicly show that the district was taking action to deal with the problem.

A second major incident occurred at Thomas Jefferson High School at the end of the 1995–96 academic year when police officers from Denver and the metro area beat and pepper-sprayed students after a dance at the school. Students and parents raised allegations of police brutality, racism, and overreactions to a student fight.[49] The incident touched off and continued debate in the city about race relations between police, citizens, and students; the relationship between the police and the schools; and the ability of the police and the city to investigate and discipline themselves. In early 1997, legal and administrative debate surrounding the case continued.[50] One board member mentioned the attention the incident had received by the city and the schools:

The latest discussion . . . on the City-Schools Coordinating Committee is the response . . . of the police to this dance that occurred. And it was actually an over-response . . . and *it all goes back to this notion that we've got a bunch of hooligans in our schools.* And actually we don't, and it's really a misperception in many ways. So, the kids at this dance really took the brunt of it, which is why I'm a little bit alarmed by this whole incident. Because then the city is like, well, it was four hundred African American, mostly African American students, in a predominately Anglo community. Is that why you had sixty-five policemen show up from three different jurisdictions when they had a minor fight in the parking lot? If there had been four hundred white students . . . how many police would have shown up? *And we really haven't gotten to the bottom of that . . . They don't want to [explain it].*

The Thomas Jefferson incident raised public interest in the issues of race, policing, and school violence. It contributed to the district's ongoing work coordinating school security and police officer responsibilities and actions. It also illustrates the continuing need for that effort to take place, given the miscommunication and mistrust between segments of the school district, police department, city, and community.

Key Personnel Changes

In 1993 DPS hired a new superintendent. He came from Los Angeles County and established a focus on literacy in the district. In conjunction with the Chamber of Commerce, the district commissioned a study of DPS operations by Arthur Andersen and Company in 1994. The study focused mainly on physical operations, facilities management, district organization, and division of responsibilities for policy and procedure development. One of its recommendations was the hiring of a chief operating officer (COO) to serve under the superintendent and to be responsible for Information Technology, Finance and Accounting, Budgeting, and Operations and Logistics, which includes Safety and Security.[51] DPS went ahead and hired a COO the next year, who proceeded to bring military and organizational experience to the district. The COO commissioned the NSSC study and hired a former police officer to direct the Department of Safety and Security. These two personnel changes fostered further organizational and procedural changes, as their security, safety, enforcement, and control orientation led them to institute a stringent approach to school violence.

The focus of these efforts was on the operations side, as these individuals are not responsible for education-oriented decisions. Thus, as discussed earlier, district role and organizational structure influence individual problem definitions. An operations officer focuses on security, safety, and organizational decisions, for example, while a

Student Services social worker focuses on effective interventions with individual students.

While the new individuals filling both old and new offices brought with them problem definitions that shaped the district approach to school violence, some in the district were critical of the reorganization process represented by the Andersen study. Members of the Chicano-Latino community, upset over the demotions of a number of Hispanic administrators in the 1993–1994 school year, argued that the result of such study and reorganization was both a cause and a symptom of poor district leadership:

> The District has been reorganized at least five times in the last four years. The recently completed Andersen Study conducted with the assistance of the Denver Chamber of Commerce to measure the management effectiveness and efficiency of the District will once again show what many in the Chicano/Latino community already know. Constant change in organization and leadership roles creates confusion, impedes accountability, and generally creates a negative impact on school services. The new reorganization is a product of ineffective management and reflective of poor decision-making at DPS. In demoting Hispanic administrators, the superintendent did not follow the tenets of collaborative decision-making or the strategic plan.[52]

Members of this community were arguing that reorganization produces chaos, not learning, although clearly they were upset in particular about the direction and extent of the reorganization at hand, arguing that "No subject is more important to providing quality education for Chicanos/Latinos than the restructuring of schools."[53] Under a new superintendent, efforts at reorganization continue. These efforts still raise questions about the roles and authority of the central administration and CDMs, with recent announcements that schools and administrators will be held accountable and subject to "a jarring wakeup call," according to a reporter, or "redesigning," according to the superintendent. In essence, schools that consistently do not perform to expectations will be subject to restaffing.[54]

Extent of Learning in the Denver Public School District

As a *district*, DPS has not experienced complex learning. Its policy mainly focuses on discipline, following state mandates. In its actions, the district pursues many different objectives, all of which taken together could represent a comprehensive but insufficiently integrated problem definition that is evolving over time. However, due to the fragmented nature of the district's institutions, the pockets that are learning, each in their own respective areas, are not joining to create an easily recognizable, public, cohesive, concerted approach to school violence. Thus, we could say that the district as a whole is achieving simple learning.

For example, as further evidence that the NSSC report served to confirm what DPS administrators already believed, the DPS-DPD Joint Task Force report described above, which was written some eight months prior to the NSSC beginning its study, recommends action in a number of areas that the NSSC also highlights. Action taken by the district after the NSSC report was issued continued to focus predominately in these areas. Thus, action was taken in a way that emulates the search for a group of experts to provide help in handling a complex problem. However, it appears that complex learning did not take place, even though the NSSC report allowed for a more comprehensive problem definition by doing some of the work necessary to integrate partial problem definitions. In fact, the NSSC report was not publicly released or even acknowledged until late 1996, when DPS officials provided a news reporter with data on incidents in schools as a way to justify their request for additional security officers.[55] It took almost two months for me as a researcher to get the district to release the report, after I found out about it serendipitously in an interview. Clearly, DPS was not following the advice of the NSSC to include community members and students in a comprehensive review of school safety.

Problem Definition and Policy-Learning at the School Level

I examined six Denver schools, three middle schools and three high schools, in more detail in order to assess the relationship between the district and the schools concerning problem definition and policy-learning. As expected, it was apparent that individual principals and administrators matter a great deal at the school level, even in a system with CDMs. Given the flexibility that the district allows in terms of approaches to school violence within the constraints of district and state laws and regulations, principals and their staff serve to set the tone and define the school violence problem in their schools. School policies and environments clearly reflected the approach indicated through interviews with school administrators and examination of school data.

Schools and School Policies

Schools were selected at the middle and high school levels due to the predominance of the school violence problem at those levels.[56] Appropriate schools and school administrators were identified through interviews with district administrators and consideration of district records. Criteria for school selection included ethnic and/or racial composition, geographic location, school violence and discipline policy actions, and variance between schools. The six schools differed in approaches to school violence, levels of violence, and individual perspectives.

Table 12 shows data on student membership at the six schools chosen for more detailed study and at the middle school and high school levels overall. One can see that Hispanic students dominate the district population, constituting almost half of all middle and high school students. White and black student populations are closer in terms of their percentage of the overall student population, with white students making up a bit larger proportion of the district's students. Asian and American Indian student populations are considerably smaller. The six schools chosen for study represent a fairly good approximation of the district's demographic composition, varying in terms of the proportions of students at each school. In retrospect, it should be noted that at the high school level, it would have been more appropriate to have selected a school with a larger proportion of Hispanic students and/or one located in the northwest part of the city, such as North High School.

Formal school policies conformed with district policy, as principals and CDMs are required to implement a school discipline policy in line with the district's interpretation of state law. Administrators, and their procedures and practices, however, differed in terms of their approach to the problem and their emphasis in different areas. One principal described the district-school policy relationship in very structured terms when asked about making sure that what she was doing at the school level fit with what the district, or the state, was prescribing:

> Very specific. No modifications. No, it's cut and dry . . . because state laws
> and district policies are going hand in hand. There is an alignment there,

and with that alignment, there is no way that one can deviate from . . . being in compliance, and districts know good and well they're not going to take lightly what state statutes are out there . . . There's a very close adherence, as to am I in the right direction . . . State makes the statutes. Districts make the policies based upon their interpretation of the statutes, and once a district has interpreted the statute by its legal members, then they have to put it into the common language that is going to be readily understood for that district.

Table 12

Ethnic and Racial Composition of Students at Six Denver Schools and Two Levels, 1996–97

School and School Level	Total Number of Students	Hispanic (%)	White (%)	Black (%)	Asian (%)	American Indian (%)
Cole M. S.	669	22.3	23.6	52.5	1.5	0.2
Gove M. S.	424	11.6	17.5	68.9	1.2	0.9
Hamilton M. S.	996	45.7	32.5	18.6	2.8	0.4
All M. S. Total	13,627	47.7	25.6	21.4	4.1	1.2
East H. S.	1,613	10.0	43.7	43.3	1.9	1.2
Manual H. S.	986	14.0	42.4	42.4	0.7	0.5
Thomas Jefferson H. S.	946	15.6	46.8	34.1	3.0	0.4
All H. S. Total	15,746	41.7	30.0	22.9	4.3	1.2

Note: Figures may not add to 100 percent due to rounding.
Source: Department of Planning, Research and Program Evaluation, "Report of 1996–1997 Student Membership by School, Grade, Gender, and Ethnicity," Denver Public Schools, Denver, CO, 1996.

Yet a district administrator noted that principals, and teachers, were essential in setting individual schools' policies and acting on them:

I think sometimes principals don't set the tone; they don't review the policy . . . What we have found is that everybody thinks that their school is pretty good. It's all the other schools that are bad. So, within each school there are many teachers that haven't ever seen the district policy, or at least that's what they say. And the individual school policy is supposed to mirror or at least support the district policy . . . There were a lot of teachers that enforced whatever the school policy was, and there were teachers that flat out ignored it . . . . Sometimes the principals aren't making it known what [the policy] is. Each school, I think, is individual, an individual case. I think you have the state law, and you have the district policy, which

> basically sets the parameters for the district. And within that, each school is supposed to develop a code of conduct and their own discipline procedures that are in accordance with the policy but can be varied a little bit to fit the circumstances of their school. But what we've found is many times *that hasn't been communicated through the principal to the faculty. Or it hasn't become a priority or isn't an issue until there's a disaster.*

The individual tone, style, or culture of each school was different, and each school had its own approach to violence within the parameters of the district policy. Schools are free to make various programmatic, curricular, personnel, and procedural decisions. This has led individuals within schools to institutionalize differing problem definitions through both formal and informal practices. Often, particular school approaches are fostered through grant funding and requirements.

Thus, schools chose a variety of programs and approaches. One school implemented a Student Support Center that tries to comprehensively intervene with a student to avoid suspension and expulsions, promote alternative disciplinary practices, and help students' academic achievement. Another school completely adopted the Carnegie School model that promotes a comprehensive approach to student success and community involvement. One school created a Leadership Institute involved in mediation and conflict resolution training, student support, and a school-within-a-school approach for students who are having difficulty succeeding in the regular school environment. Another fostered a peer mediation program and an intensive effort to intervene early and effectively with students by analyzing student records at the beginning of the year and meeting with at-risk students and their parents.

School policies were consistent, in that they all were within the district's "parameters," as many people referred to the policy framework that the district created. Yet the programs that schools adopted varied, due to multiple factors. Individual administrative experience and preference strongly impacted a school's direction. Programs followed grant opportunities from foundations like Carnegie and the local Piton Foundation. Pilot opportunities such as the Colorado School Mediation Project's program at East High School created avenues through which schools could experiment. District pilots, such as the installation of surveillance cameras or the placement of a magnet program like the International Baccalaureate Program, provided funds and ideas for schools. Finally, an individual school's physical and cultural environment led to program adoption in one or another area. The flexibility of the district's school-based governance structure allowed for creativity at the site level in terms of addressing the particular needs of schools. All the schools expressed a similar approach to discipline policy, referring to the bottom-line following of rules, high expectations, clear communication between administration, staff, and students, and firm consequences for stepping out of line. In other words, the dominant state and district problem definition was clearly shared in the schools, and then each school expanded that definition in alternative directions depending on the factors mentioned above.

Lessons from the School Level

A number of important lessons can be learned from looking at the school level in the context of the state and district study. At this street-level institution, there is little time for learning. An individual's predilection for research seems particularly important in this regard. Administrators feared innovation. They shunned the sharing of best practices, even when given the opportunity by the district. Individual leadership was essential in setting the tone, style, and direction in a school. Grant and other funding opportunities were critical in fostering program adoption. The lessons overall for decentralization as a vehicle for district-wide learning are not positive, given the impediments to complex learning at the school level.

Lack of Time and Resources for Learning
Time and resources were scarce at the school level in terms of the ability of administrators to discover, implement, and evaluate effective programs. One principal described the process of shopping for programs in order to do something about the problem: "Some are out there saying that it's been 100 percent here, and this has reduced since this has been implemented. And you can't sit back and don't do anything, so you go out there, and you research and check with colleagues, and you're given leads, and so those kinds of interventions are readily available out there for you." Some of the information about these programs was provided by the district, through in-service training programs and seminars, summary sheets provided by the Department of Student Services, and at regular, monthly, district-wide administrator meetings. But when asked whether they researched,

evaluated, and shared programs, administrators indicated that they had little time to do so:

> We evaluate them when I get our numbers, for instance. I get the numbers of students suspended and what the causes are, and then the discipline committee looks at that and says, "Do you think we need more of this, or what do you think of this, or this is good." . . . Unfortunately, we don't have the time [to talk to other people in the district about what works and what doesn't]. I hate to say that we don't want to. We like each other, but we meet once a month, and we have to talk about not only curricular issues, but *issues that the district is focusing in on, for instance literacy* . . . We don't really have time . . . We don't have the chance to chitchat . . . *Even if we wanted to meet after school, we don't, because we have meetings, or supervising a game.* So, when do we have the chance to sit down and say, "You know, I tried this," and we might, sometimes we do, if something we think is working really well, and we do it real quick at the meeting. "Hey, you know," someone will say, "well, I have this," and we'll say, "OK." Because we meet at seven o'clock for breakfast, and for one hour we just— that's when our chitchat time about, you know, vacation, or whatever. And they'll say, "Did you see that in the newspaper? I had so-and-so," and they'll say, "I tried this," and that's when we'll do that. And we love that, when we can say, "Oh yeah, did that work?" And they'll say, "Yeah, that's cool," and then we'll write it down and we'll take it on our way. But, other than that, *we don't have time. It's really unfortunate.*

Another administrator noted how difficult it was to adequately assess the school violence problem: "I've never really sat down, and, I mean, my day is so busy I *don't have time to reflect on it.* I mean, I got in here at, what, before seven, and I'll tell you, it just flew. It's just been so busy."

The state's School Improvement and Accountability Committee (SIAC) system, which sets mandates for district and school accountability committees that report on standards, results, and so forth, creates a framework for evaluation and information sharing in addition to the requisite CDM reports that schools release. However, as one district administrator pointed out, even the SIAC process has not produced great results in this area:

> The state has each accountability committee reporting on expulsions and suspensions and trends, and also interventions. And as a matter of compliance schools do it. I'd like to see it move out of the arena of compliance to where people are really, because they're having that conversation, taking a look at the causes. And then design programs around it. I think some schools are doing that. *As far as affecting policy and getting feedback, I think that's really a good issue. I don't think we do it.*

And I think that's the lack of a strong accountability, central accountability system. I think if . . . the district really took accountability seriously, they'd be taking a look at those reports and seeing where some of the problems are, not just . . . coming into the one office and, yeah, we report it, but do we really share it with the board and with the policy makers and implementors?

Moving out of the realm of compliance, it was apparent that individual administrators in the schools made their own choice to read research materials, reports, and journals, either because of academic training, membership in state or national organizations, such as the Colorado Association of School Executives or the National Association of Secondary School Principals, or just personal interest. Many of them said that they read this material on their own time in order to increase their knowledge base and apply lessons to their school.

Fear of Innovating and Reluctance to Share Information

A second key lesson from the schools relates to and helps explain this sort of private research. School administrators noted their disdain for implementing untested programs. Some expressed their own and others' reluctance to share information about practices with other administrators, as did this principal:

You always go on a resource of someone who has used something and tried to apply it. You're kind of *putting yourself out there on a limb if you're going to try something that has not been tried before*. Not saying that it's wrong. Somebody has to be the first to try something. Come on. It stands to reason; someone has to, but you always don't want to wait to find out if it's going to give you a result. It's like anything else. Someone tells you about a good restaurant, and you'd much rather go there and spend your money than to go find out this wasn't what I had thought it was going to be. So you always try to go to a resource that can validate . . . Resources are probably coming from a district resource of programs that they've heard of, because we each in the district have liaison people who deal with those types of programs and who will refer them to you and say, "You know, we have some good reports on this type of a program." And you maybe have a workshop on the program, or something of that nature, and that tends to be a sell for you.

Then, in contrast to the statement above about sharing at breakfast meetings, another administrator argued that the peer culture of teachers and administrators seemed to mitigate against a principal sharing program success or failure with others, even though programs that worked could be transferred between schools. But how much sharing was happening? The administrator noted,

> None. And I can't tell you why, but I can give you one point of view, because I used work with the central office as well, with middle schools. *No school really wants to know what goes on in another school.* They really don't . . . Part of it may be how teachers and stuff were brought up . . . all of us were taught in college . . . that what you did was your own business. You went in, you shut that door, and you were in your class. And thank God that has changed to some extent over the years I've been involved as an educator, because you can't do that anymore. *You must be able to communicate with others.* Your colleagues, parents, kids . . . Life isn't the same as it was then, but we still have that old mentality of I really don't want to hear, I really don't care what goes on in other schools. I'm only interested in what goes on in mine, and so that sharing—sometimes we do share, and no one really wants to because you're put down, especially if it's good stuff, you know, then *you're put down by your colleagues,* whether it's other principals or whatever. [Other principals might] be derogatory, feel jealous, say, "Oh, you know, that only applies to that school, that it wouldn't apply to our school." And what I'm saying in all this is, in being a principal of two completely different middle schools, the same thing applies . . . It did . . . And the same results were there. Yeah . . . You bet [things can be transferable], more so than they want to admit . . . *I just know what works, and that it can be replicated, but, at high schools especially, they never want to change.* They're still doing business like they did fifty years ago, a hundred years ago. Nothing has changed.

Personnel Change and Administrative Influence

Principals and assistant principals approached school violence at their school largely based on personal experience, combined with a respect for the district's policy parameters. In many instances, administrators described their entering the school, assessing its situation in various ways, and then implementing a plan or program that fit with their goals and expectations, their problem definition. Parallel to the district level, personnel change has been key in affecting individual school direction. Some principals utilized their CDM and special planning teams to assess the school, steering this more inclusive process to result in a plan that was already in their own mind. Some principals stuck closely to the district's framework as they slowly moved their school in what they thought was the right direction. Administrators had differing priorities, such as academic achievement, options and choices, expectations and consequences, parent involvement, or communication, which they would connect to the school violence and discipline problem and which they would emphasize as the central theme of their school. A broader problem definition brought in by a new principal or assistant principal would structure learning, or problem redefinition, in the area of school violence to align with that overall perspective to form a consistent message.

Grants and Funding Incentives

Finally, the schools illustrate the central role that grant and other funding incentives play in directing program adoption and policy change. Administrators followed funds to programs. They matched programs to needs they identified in their school. This was true in the case of federal Safe and Drug-Free Schools and Communities money administered through the state and the district coordinators, Department of Student Services recommendations, Department of Safety and Security offers, and national and local foundation opportunities. As one school administrator pointed out,

> [Information sharing and providing program resources is] site-based. We get a certain amount of money and that's all we get . . . This is your allocation . . . We're lucky, because we have a pretty good business-community partnership, so we have a lot of businesses that will donate money to us. And we . . . have a great faculty, and they're pretty bright, and we have a grant-writing committee, so when I get the grant-writing packet every month, the district sends that out, you know, I circle things and say, "Hey, could we look at this?" . . . Then our grant-writing committee will narrow it down, and then they write grants . . . That's how we got our conflict resolution money. And we use some of our drug money that we got from the district, we don't get very much. We get about fifteen hundred dollars, but we use that money then for guest speakers or those kinds of things. So, what the school does is *identify the problems* that they want to, are our *school goals*, and then we talk about what we need to focus in on and how much money we need for this or that. And that's how we get the money. *But if you don't scrounge around for money, the district doesn't have any extra money to give you for innovative programs . . . First we look for resources*, because I hate to start something that we can't finish. So we look for resources first, and then the committee will say, "OK, we can do this." . . . For instance, if it's discipline, they'll meet with them and say, "OK, what areas are we focused on? What do we need? Do you see a conflict resolution class? How about if we bring in a guest speaker? Maybe we can do a combination. Maybe we can work with the police department, because the police department has some things that they'll do for us for free."

Schools appear mainly to learn from experience, in both an institutional sense and in the sense of key administrators learning over time and bringing their experience into a school. Lesson-drawing across space occurs through program adoption, but the outward sharing of good practices and the extensive evaluation of programs in more than just a monitoring or data-gathering sense is rather limited. There is a great deal of reinventing the violence wheel, in part due to the reduction in the central office's willingness and ability to assist in program and policy adoption, evaluation, and dissemination, as discussed further below.

Conclusions

In terms of a general assessment of the district, Denver resembles the state. DPS consists of pockets of learning in the schools, in particular offices, among some individuals. These pockets reveal contrasting problem definitions that, taken together, represent a more comprehensive definition of the school violence problem than does any one of them alone. Thus, these definitions are largely complementary and are not necessarily contradictory. An emphasis on safety and security in the schools can coexist with and supplement a focus on early intervention with families and children, or a zero-tolerance approach to guns in schools, or strict rules, high expectations, firm consequences, and maintenance of order. These problem definitions and approaches rarely are recognized and integrated by individuals in the district, although examples of such attempts do exist. The district as a whole does not promote or publicly represent this definition of the problem to or with the community.

The learning that is taking place in the district, the redefinition of the problem along more integrative, comprehensive lines, is stymied by the lack of time and funds for evaluation, the lack of time for reflection on the problem, and a district culture that mitigates against research, evaluation, and sharing among peers and institutional levels. Thus, the accuracy of the problem definition or definitions is called into question. And, significantly, continuing specialization, fragmentation, and compartmentalization of the district's departments and services hinders the learning process. The learning that is occurring in pockets does not seem to spread to other parts of the district or to inform decision-making in those various areas. It is necessary to have particular offices that are responsible for different policy and program areas. Yet it is also important to establish an overall district mission and broader problem definition in this area, and a deeper ethic of sharing across district offices, between the district and schools, and among the schools themselves in order to integrate the various problem definition pieces into a more complex learning process.

Chapter 5
The Colorado Springs School District
Similar Patterns of Learning in a Different Cultural and Environmental Context

Colorado Springs District 11

I examined Colorado Springs School District 11 as a comparative case to the Denver Public Schools. Seven interviews were conducted in District 11, and policy data were collected to further examine school violence problem definition and policy-learning issues in a similar district in the same state. Given the same state legal and cultural context, what differences would we see in another urban district? Although studied in less detail, the Colorado Springs district confirms many of the same tendencies witnessed in Denver. It raises some of the same concerns about the history, willingness, and ability of a school district to learn over time about the school violence problem.

There are some key similarities between the two school districts. First of all, the state legal and institutional structure was dominant in both. District 11 has had to respond to state discipline mandates in the same manner as Denver. District 11, like Denver, has focused on discipline policy in alignment with state law and on safety and security at the central district level. And, like Denver, it has support services at the district level but has left experimentation and implementation of alternative violence prevention programs up to the local schools. This is despite the fact that District 11 is not formally site-based. Still, schools there have flexibility in terms of programs, tone, and style, and the principal was similarly noted as a dominant figure in creating school direction and culture. As in Denver, principals and their schools were fused in people's minds, so that when someone discussed what a school was doing, they often referred to the fact that so and so was doing this or that at this school. Overall, Colorado Springs confirms the notion that the district's role is eroding while state dominance and local school autonomy increase, at least in most areas.

Examining this second district also illustrates a few contrasts that point to the importance of key factors that affect problem definition, learning, and policy. First, while the state influence was crucial in the district, the district had to respond to the district's political culture, community environment, and demographics. Some different dynamics were operating in this less urban, smaller, and more politically conservative district. This played out in a number of ways. There was a sense that Colorado Springs was tougher than Denver and that, overall, fewer attempts were being made to reroute expulsions and to channel kids into alternative programs. This did happen, but seemed more conflictual. Second, there was more of an emphasis on local control in Colorado Springs, mostly in reaction to state actions. This occurred in two directions when it went against the district or individual problem definition. The state was perceived by some as being too tough and by others as engaging in too much micromanaging through legislative mandates.

This chapter briefly describes trends in community and school violence in El Paso County, its major city, Colorado Springs, and District 11. This sets the context for the discussion of school violence policy there and shows the similarity in trends in both school districts. It then discusses the district's school violence approach, comparing and contrasting it to that evidenced in Denver. Key similarities and differences are noted. The chapter concludes with further reflection on the conclusions offered in chapter four, given the additional weight added by the study of a second district.

Trends in Violence and Crime in El Paso County, Colorado Springs, and District 11 Schools

Longer-term trends in violence in Colorado Springs are similar to those in Denver and the state. As elsewhere, District 11 evidences some decrease in crime rates but some alarming juvenile violence figures that have sparked calls for tough action against violence. Colorado Springs is the largest city in El Paso County, accounting for almost all of the violence reported there. Violence rates in El Paso County declined after 1981, one year later than in Denver or the state as a whole, peaked slightly in 1986, declined again, rose in the early 1990s, and began to gradually decline after 1992. However, there is less consistency in the El Paso County figures. The forcible rape and aggravated assault rates increased through the late 1980s, and the aggravated assault rate rose again in 1994. The total number of juvenile arrests rose consistently from 1980 to 1994, with a dramatic increase in that year. Meanwhile, the total population of El Paso County similarly rose during that period, approaching that of the city and county of Denver by 1994.[1]

District 11 is the fourth largest school district in Colorado and had an enrollment of 32,923 students in the 1996–97 school year. In 1996–97, District 11's enrollment was 73 percent Caucasian, 13 percent Hispanic, 10 percent black, 2 percent Asian/Pacific, and 1 percent Native American. The district has sixty schools.[2] Thus, the Colorado Springs school district is about half the size of the Denver district, and has significantly fewer ethnic and racial minority students than does Denver.

Table 13

Responses to Two-Year Safety Survey in District 11

	1994 (%)	1995 (%)
Are student gangs a problem in the local schools?		
Big problem	15	23
Somewhat of a problem	63	65
Not a problem	8	4
Don't know/missing	14	8
When your child is at school, what is your level of concern for his/her physical safety from violent activity?		
Very concerned	13	11
Somewhat concerned	47	45
Not a concern	31	29
Not applicable/missing	9	15
When your child is at school, what is your level of concern for his/her safety from accidental injury?		
Very concerned	6	5
Somewhat concerned	39	34
Not a concern	48	48
Not applicable/missing	8	14

Note: Figures may not add to 100 percent due to rounding.
Source: A.V. Kraetzer, "Fall 1995 Budget Priorities Survey Comparison with Fall 1994 Results," Department of Planning, Evaluation, and Measurement, Colorado Springs Public Schools, Colorado Springs, CO, 1996, p. A-7.

Nevertheless, District 11 is considered the inner-city school district in Colorado Springs. It shares similar urban problems with the Denver

Public Schools. School violence statistical reporting is as problematic there as it is in Denver. Again, the best data is that on suspensions and expulsions. A survey administered by the District Accountability and Advisory Committee's Budget Review Committee and distributed to the members of the district's fifty-three Building Accountability Advisory Committees did include a section on safety issues.[3] This survey found increased concerns regarding gangs and children's safety in the schools. Respondents were more concerned about the risks of violent activity than the dangers of accidental injury (see table 13).

Table 14

District 11 Suspension Referrals: Total and by School Level over Time

School Year	Total Suspension Referrals	Elementary School	Middle and Junior High School	High School
1988–89	234	32	106	96
1989–90	225	21	124	80
1990–91	196	22	109	65
1991–92	238	31	148	59
1992–93	236	30	139	67
1993–94	220	8	103	109
1994–95	**266**	21	149	96
1995–96 (to 5/22/96)	**447**	57	204	186
1996–97 (to 11/6/96)	95	5	36	54

Source: Office of Student Discipline Services, "Suspension Referral and Discipline Reports," Colorado Springs Public Schools, Colorado Springs, CO, 1988–1996.

Table 14 shows the trends in suspension referrals over time in Colorado Springs. While constant through the 1993–94 school year, suspension referrals rose somewhat in 1994–95 and sharply in 1995–96. The suspension referral numbers include multiple referrals for the same student and referrals that resulted in expulsions, dropouts, administrative placements, treatment, tutoring, and so forth. The majority of the suspension referrals tended to result in administrative placements, home schooling, and tutoring through the 1992–93 school year, but expulsions rose significantly during and after the 1993–94 school year (see table 15). Some suspension referrals led to more than one result.

In terms of racial parity, more white students were suspended than black or Hispanic students, but nonwhite students were disproportionately suspended compared to their representation in the student body. Boys were greatly overrepresented in the suspension numbers. Many suspended children were from single parent and stepparent families and/or were on free or reduced lunch.[4] Detrimental behavior accounted for 96 percent of suspensions and 38 percent of expulsions in the 1995–96 school year. Deadly weapons accounted for over 22 percent of the expulsions, and controlled substances for 17 percent of the remainder of the expulsions that year.[5]

Table 15

District 11 Selected Results of Suspension Referrals over Time

| | | | | | | | | 1995 | 1996 |
| Referrals | 1988 | 1989 | 1990 | 1991 | 1992 | 1993 | 1994 | –96 (to | –97 (to |
resulting in	–89	–90	–91	–92	–93	–94	–95	5/22)	11/6)
Expulsion	5	7	8	14	27	85	131	222	39
Administrative Placement	64	63	60	63	76	51	39	48	2
Tutoring	36	26	18	36	20	16	n/a	n/a	n/a
Homeschooling	82	78	70	65	66	46	60	122	9
Dropouts	11	18	14	6	1	2	0	0	0
Cancelation	7	12	8	20	20	16	8	17	3

Source: Office of Student Discipline Services, "Suspension Referral and Discipline Reports," Colorado Springs Public Schools, Colorado Springs, CO, 1988–1996.

Thus, the overall trends in school violence in Colorado Springs seem similar to those in Denver and the state as a whole. Like Denver, the Colorado Springs district has begun improvements in its incident reporting and security enforcement capabilities. It is likely experiencing and will likely experience in the future an appearance of increasing levels of school violence and incidents as the central district office gathers and reports more comprehensive and systematic data. The current and past suspension reports are fairly extensive. They offer some interesting breakdowns on socioeconomic factors that were not seen in Denver, allowing for some discussion of disparities and conditioning factors beyond basic racial and ethnic categories. As one school board member put it in pointing out and arguing for an alternative form of data collection than what the state mandates,

> What I'm saying is that the real issues have to do with this issue, the family situation and the economic status of the family, and it just happens that more of those are black and Hispanic than they are white . . . My feeling is that it is certainly a situation where you should consider, OK, what's the real cause? Because what happens when you put the race label on it is everybody wants to say that's the cause. That's more of an incidental result, except for the fact that, you know, if you can prove that they're poor because of discrimination, or . . . that they are that way because of factors beyond their control.

It is clear here that the ways in which data are categorized and reported reflect assumptions on the part of policy makers and school officials about values and factors that shape school violence.

Approach to School Violence: Problem Definition, Policies, and Programs

The Colorado Springs approach to school violence fits closely within the dominant state problem definition. It is generally similar to that in Denver. It combines a strict disciplinary policy with school-level and some district-level alternative programs and educational solutions. It allows the schools to operate within an overall district disciplinary structure. The district has increased its emphasis on safety and security programs and capabilities and its search for alternative educational settings for disruptive youth so that school-level administrators can enforce order and control in their schools. As one security administrator put it,

> I think that there's a lot of merit to *seeking order to seek safety*, and we do a pretty good job on that, in most of our schools. But, frankly, there are some where I think we could do a better job. And that was another thing that happened at this middle school across the way here was that the order in the building was restored, and when that order was restored, the discipline referrals and the calls for police service dropped by half, by about half, by 50 percent. And that takes not just the administrator or the staff, and it's not just the security staff. It's not just the teachers. It's everybody, parents and teachers and everybody working together.

District 11 Student Conduct and Discipline Policy

The district's discipline policy combines the legally prescribed requirements (see chapters three and four) with a ladder approach that divides disciplinary infractions and actions into four levels, with level four being the most serious and including expulsion as mandated by the state. The Colorado Springs policy is more accessible, however. It is printed in an easily readable booklet that is distributed to all first-time students in the district.[6] This booklet carefully explains district policies and alternatives. It was the product of a substantial, inclusive, committee-meeting process following the state law changes in 1993. Since then, the district has had information and training meetings for staff on the more recent discipline law changes. It has mailed out supplements to the handbook to parents.[7]

Dress Codes

A recent policy change in Colorado Springs is the institution of a district-wide student and staff dress code policy. The dress code's primary focus is on reducing gang influences in the schools. It was formulated through a series of meetings that solicited student input throughout the district. Additionally, the dress code aims to improve student discipline and the school climate overall. The district fit the new policy into its overall mission:

> We believe that every student has the ability to learn in an educational environment that is concerned, structured and responsive to the needs of students and the community. We also believe that the educational process must provide an environment in which all students are afforded the opportunity to obtain lifetime competencies and survive as productive members of society. Additionally, School District Eleven is committed to the establishment of practices and programs which will insure the intellectual, physical, and emotional well-being of all students. To that end, our goal is to enhance school pride, school safety, student morale, attitude, performance, reduce violence, and discourage gang activity, thereby providing a healthy environment conducive to academic achievement. Hair and dress codes have not been a topic of much concern for school principals or legal advisers since the 1970's, but recent concern with school violence and efforts to reduce gang visibility at school have caused school districts across America to revisit issues raised in the earlier cases. As you know, violence and other forms of learning distractions in the public schools are increasing. Membership in gangs has broadened to include both older and younger members as well as females. In some communities, fear of gangs

has become so pervasive that it threatens students' ability and opportunity to learn. In order to resolve the problem, school boards and administrators must take measures to reduce the power of gangs and to redirect focus on learning through well-written policies . . . Because as a school district we want learning environments that are safe and free from disruptions, the following student dress restrictions will be enforced.[8]

This letter also helps to reveal the district's definition of the problem, its acknowledgment that things have gotten worse; its connection of violence, disruption, and learning; and its connection of current concerns with attention given to the problem in the 1970s. One district administrator, commenting on the student representatives' reaction to the proposed dress code, noted the importance of student input and the short-terms results of an ongoing test project:

The suggested list that we had given them about the things not to wear were substantiated by them. They felt that they were a distraction and potentially a safety hazard in school. And some of the language that we've used has been changed to the student language that they would understand, which was helpful. Because now I know, when we put something there and the kid sees it, they'll say, "Oh, I know what that means." And they said we use a lot of jargon, which we do. But they put it in a format they thought they could understand . . . The board is really interested in expanding the input into this thing, because it's such a controversial issue. We have an elementary school now that's using a uniform, and they're weighing the results of that. And it's too early to tell yet, but it seems like it's already had an impact on leveling the field, in terms of students coming to school with the same kinds of uniforms and not whether or not they've got the Nikes and all that sort of stuff. The tendency is to . . . operate a little bit and then see what the test scores are for this quarter, and see whether that's going to make a difference or not.

The Helen Hunt Elementary School, where the uniform project was implemented, instituted uniforms as part of a broader plan that used federal Chapter I funds, donations, a federal Evenstart grant, and a federal Goals 2000 grant to begin a Student Achievement Initiative. Student discipline problems have reportedly decreased as a result of this school-level reform.[9] It will be difficult to discern the results of the uniforms themselves, due to their being part of a more comprehensive initiative. Additionally, the tendency to measure the effectiveness of these programs in terms of test scores, and not disciplinary incidents, for example, is clear in the above quote.

Security and Alternative Educational Approaches

Like Denver, Colorado Springs has a combination of security and educational approaches to violence prevention, intervention, and treatment, many of which are handled at the local school level. Surveillance cameras have been piloted in two high schools. The district awaits further funding before placing cameras in more settings.[10] The district has an Alternatives for Drop Outs Program that counsels dropouts on how to return to school. This program reported a 76 percent success rate in counseling students back into educational programs. The district also operates five alternative secondary programs, such as the Educational Opportunity Program, the Palmer Night School, and the Doherty Night School, which offer learning opportunities for students who are having trouble in the regular academic settings.[11]

Grant Programs and Decentralization: Guidance and Consistency

Safe and Drug-Free Schools and Communities (SDFSC) money was used in Colorado Springs to implement prevention programs, train members of the student assistance program, administer a Pikes Peak Youth Lifestyles Survey, and distribute a monthly newsletter.[12] As in Denver, the Colorado Springs schools were largely given the responsibility for implementing the additional, prevention-oriented programs that would supplement the district's discipline policy parameters and fill in the many gaps that the district left open. This was true even though District 11 is not a site-based district.

The Colorado Springs district shows a lesser degree of decentralization than does Denver. Schools in Colorado Springs seem to have a fair amount of input into district decisions, particularly through the Building Accountability Advisory Committee and District Accountability Advisory Committee. Parental choice is fairly strong. Nevertheless, the district is formally a centralized system. The district office is the primary actor in the district.[13]

While it appears that Colorado Springs is much less decentralized than Denver, in the area of school violence and discipline, the district-school dynamic is consistent across the two districts. Both districts face similar issues of consistency and fairness in disciplinary practices across schools, in addition to a strong desire for local control. This tension in both districts parallels that between the districts and the state in terms of a desire for strong disciplinary tools and avoidance of micromanagement, although this latter concern seemed stronger in Colorado Springs.

One board member described the issues associated with centralization and variation across the schools:

> [District 11] is a little bit more centralized probably than a lot of them. Now, there's a fair amount of variability in terms of individual programs and individual focuses at the various high schools and middle schools. The grade schools, I'd say, tailor it pretty much to their clientele. They all run the same basic programs, pretty much. Where they differ is more in the support programs . . . Overall, as a district, we haven't strongly encouraged a lot of site-based variability. But we have encouraged choice where we could . . . One of the issues that I've seen if I back away, *we have tried to, in the discipline piece, get fairly reasonable consistency* . . . Here's the interpretation of the board's policy; here's . . . recommended basic approaches, and [we have] . . . tried to . . . encourage more and more . . . centralized training from the standpoint of interpretation and approaches and things, because one of the things that happens is if you have a real lenient principal one place and down the road you got a real strict one, that gets out real quick. And pretty soon people are moving back and forth as a result. And you really don't want to set up that type of internal variability . . . The other piece, which is this obvious one here, is *we have to be very careful about trying to be fair and consistent with regard to race.* And that has been already brought up against us . . . because the papers just love to write that kind of story that says, "look here, you've got a 10 percent black population, and 30 percent of the infractions are with black kids." And then you always leave the innuendo there that it's all because of racism and not because of other factors. But we try real hard not to have that happen . . . .The standards-based program in Colorado is much more now oriented toward more what you're going to be able to do in a certain time . . . And, so, I think, that's tending to go toward one-size-fits-all a little bit more, and then the other piece of it is . . . *mobility is extremely high.* And in a lot of the southern schools, or lower-income schools, the stability rate is pretty low, so we have kids moving all around . . . It's very hard to adjust . . . But those issues are a little bit of a damper to variability . . . But at the grade schools it's more tailored to individual staff member emphasis and the parental support situations, and other things.

The Colorado Springs district "promulgates," to use the word of one administrator, the state law. It trains its administrators how to apply the policies. Yet the district attempts to allow discretion for site administrators on the selection of programs. Some administrators felt that this level of balance was sufficient, but at least one board member thought that schools were too constrained by the central administration, state and federal mandates, and judicial decisions that overly favored students' rights:

> I think I'm a little old-fashioned. I guess I think that the teachers and principals need to have discretion, more discretion than they have now . . . Discretion in terms of running their show, whatever it is. In case of the teacher, it's her classroom, or his classroom, and in the case of the principal, it's the school. And certain things shouldn't be tolerated . . . They do have that ability [to choose who is in their classroom], but it's layers of central administration and court cases and special education laws . . . I mean, they can exercise discretion, but they have to do it carefully and judiciously; and, of course, that comes from the fact that probably kids were jerked around, and then there were all these things that were done to compensate, and then the pendulum swung too far.

Safety and Security: Centralization

As in Denver, the district has centralized its safety and security functions, hiring a new director who brought in a new problem definition similar to that of his Denver counterparts, with whom he often is in contact. One district administrator also noted the care with which the lessening of the principals' authority over security staff had to be accomplished:

> They centralized [the security department] . . . that's a real trick in any school district is centralizing a function, and I think centralizing the function and putting the responsibility for the function in one office was a big policy decision on their part. The implementation of that policy decision is ongoing. We're not there yet, not where we want to be at, but [we] also know and knew at the time that there's no way that we were going to come in and rip out forty people from a building, and the principals are going to sit still for it, so we did it very carefully . . . We had to move real carefully on that, but it's been an instructive process for everybody, and I think that the principals are now comfortable with what we're trying to do.

Evaluation: Decentralization

Another key similarity to Denver is the increasing inability of the district to accomplish an effective evaluation function, primarily due to central resource constraints. The district has pushed this role down to the school level:

> We only have one person who is full-time assigned to evaluations. And the priority tends to go to district-wide programs . . . We do a lot of survey

research in lieu of being able to do a lot of observations. We have to go with self-reports on implementations. And then the principals have a role in evaluation, and there are other central staff who then come in as far as the content areas, so it's a complex process. It's very institutionalized, you know. It's done through committee structures, and the committees change somewhat over time. But when we're going to do a curriculum review, it's an all-out effort, and there's people from our department and people from the curriculum department and lots of teachers . . . A lot of this is like, it's almost like a business where you have different people on a project, or they are supervising a particular area, and they would bring in resources or training, and they might or might not do their own immediate kind of evaluation. We're really looking at numbers here, is the ultimate, our statistics, staying in line with what, you know, not getting worse, getting better . . . We have a strategic plan that's in place, and there is a section of it that speaks to safety, and I'm helping to coordinate an overall evaluation of the strategic plan so . . . that we're getting similar-type information from the managers in the different areas that are reflected in the strategic plan, which actually is very comprehensive . . . *We're tending to do more intensive, typical, or traditional evaluation, where we're looking at one program with a defined set of objectives and goals in areas that are related to curriculum directly.*

The district is trying to coordinate and connect an overall evaluation according to its strategic plan, but program evaluation in the sense of examining specific programs related to discipline and violence is very limited at the district level in Colorado Springs.

Comparisons to Denver: Selected Problem Definition and Learning Themes

There are a number of areas, related to problem definition and policy-learning, that emerged in Colorado Springs and reflected similar issues prominent in the Denver case. This section discusses these areas thematically. It integrates additional reflections on the themes of the book.

Program and Policy Evaluation

As mentioned above, Colorado Springs exhibits a similar lack of concerted effort to comprehensively evaluate violence prevention, intervention, and rehabilitation programs. Again, we see the beginnings of efforts to produce monitoring information and data that is comparable. A long-term, ongoing, risk factor–monitoring study being done at the University of Colorado at Colorado Springs was mentioned in the district but did not seem to have too much impact on policy or programs. Again, this is not focused analysis and dissemination of results to the schools. There was little evidence here for complex learning based on this kind of information or process.

One board member described the difficulties of even gathering consistent data in a large school district. He additionally expressed an interest in seeing how things were working but did not discuss any formal attempt to evaluate the consequences of programs or policies:

> The other thing that has been done has been trying, in each school, keeping statistics on the discipline aspects: the various different level-one, -two, -three, and -four infractions, the numbers, the suspensions, the expulsions. This is a district-wide approach, and trying to see where that's going. Now, . . . they've had a little bit of a problem in getting the data clean because we changed in '94, and then we changed again this last year, and it's difficult to get a district with thirty-three thousand kids to all be consistent in the way they report things. The other thing that we're looking at from that, and kind of always in the back of our mind, is, let's keep looking at these things in terms of how they're working.

Time and Resource Constraints

As mentioned, the lack of time and resources affected Colorado Springs' ability to evaluate, as it did Denver's. Additional issues similarly were reminiscent of Denver's problems with money and staff resources. Colorado Springs recently passed its first bond issue in some twenty-five years. Perhaps the financial constraints will ease up a bit in the future, but the district has been on a limited budget for quite some time. A lack of time, money, and available attention limited the board's ability to act with a great deal of foresight on additional education programs for expelled students, as one board member noted:

> We haven't been able to generate, other than from what John [Griego, the director of School Management] has been trying to do [on one of the two state grants for a residential care facility], a good program for expelled students, partly because it's just out this year. We've been so busy with the bond and other things that we couldn't. It's not something that we're against, or that we won't work on, but the other piece of it is that you get all of these things, but you don't get any more money. *There's always an issue of where does the money come from.* That's why my approach has been more try to be proactive, and try to be more proactive when they're young, and try to maybe work harder on improving their educational capabilities.

This lack of funds has limited the district's ability to provide alternative programs, as one administrator lamented:

> Prevention's not a new phenomenon in public education. In fact, we're caretakers, and we've been doing that pretty well . . . We've been taking care of kids. I mean, we've done everything in our power to try to demonstrate our commitment to educating kids by providing a variety of alternatives and trying to identify those behaviors on the front end, i.e., in the elementary level, and prevent those kinds of behaviors from advancing or getting worse and progressing to the middle school and high school areas. In years past, when we weren't so hung up on the *resources* and we had some resources where we could place toward those focuses, we were more apt to do that. Now that the *competition for the dollars* is in place, we have less and less ability to build those kinds of alternatives that we so desperately need for the students who are not being successful in the regular public school setting. And so we've enacted a pretty active and aggressive dropout retrieval system. We've got a couple of alternative high schools going on right now. A lot of your schools, through special grants and title programs, are placing alternative programs in their schools to hopefully keep the students in school. We've got three charter schools right now active in School District 11. That provides another alternative for those kids who need something different than the public school setting that we offer right now. We're considering a fourth alternative school starting in the fall . . . We're expanding the Edison Project into a middle school concept, so we're, as a district, we're trying to do everything we can to promote this idea of student success and performance and achievement issues at a variety of levels. And, but like I said, it's becoming more and more difficult to do that.

So, as in Denver, schools and the district in Colorado Springs have had to rely on grants for alternative programs. They have matched programs to available funds. Alternative educational and prevention programs have met with resistance both from the board and from the conservative community in which the district is situated, due to their increased per-pupil cost and the perception that they take money away from traditional education programs, as one board member related:

> There are some alternative settings . . . But, very frankly, the school board is kind of hesitant to put too much of that in because it's expensive. In a conservative community you don't do a whole lot of that, because any time . . . you really make a difference, or you lower the student-teacher ratio, that's bucks. So, how much money should you put into kids who are misbehaving? . . . Some kids think, "Well, misbehave, you get three disruptions . . . and you can go to school over there." And instead of being

in a class of thirty-five, you're in a class of twelve. What a great deal . . . I don't know if kids look at it that way, but even if they don't look at it that way, you really have to think about taking resources from the great whole . . . . I mean, the district has had a terrible time getting money for capital. There's no progress. We've been trying for twenty-five years to get a bond issue passed. So when you can't get bond issues passed, you end up siphoning off money for capital. And so to do alternative programs, you're *siphoning money* from English classes. So all of sudden instead of thirty kids you've got thirty-five kids in the English class. And that's pretty important. Or the algebra class.

Demographic and Political Cultural Influences

Several political, cultural, and demographic aspects of the Colorado Springs district and community have affected problem definition and learning in the district. The social, political, and religious conservatism of the area has constrained the district's ability to raise funds and to spend them on alternative approaches to violence prevention. Another administrator described the dilemma this way, illustrating the difference between his more comprehensive definition of the problem and the realm of the possible or acceptable in the community:

> Now, I also think that we need to do some intervention programs there as well. Prevention programs are good for the student body at large, but then there's a much smaller segment of the student population who educators and security administrators can identify as being severely at risk for alcohol and drug abuse and gang involvement and violence. And [for] those kids, I would like to see us develop some real comprehensive, school-based intervention strategies, but also in having developed those school-based intervention strategies also bring in all of those outside agencies to bear on that kid's life. *Now we tried to do this with communities and schools, but we have a hugely conservative community here and communities and schools got all bound up with parental rights and perceived Social Services Department abuses and those kinds of things*, and, I think, really ended up hurting the kids that needed the services the most. I mean, communities and schools is nothing more than bringing together cops and social workers and health care workers and job counselors and boy scout leaders and all of that into one place where these kids can have access to these services, and *it just never happened in this district.*

Thus, coordinated learning in the community and the schools is hindered by a set of social norms surrounding limited government and the rights of parents. Another administrator viewed it this way:

The problem is politicians are always afraid that somebody's going to take issue with them because they will be seen, especially in this state, as being, quote, too liberal. Liberal has almost become like the scarlet letter. God forbid that you be branded as a liberal, oh my god. To me, being liberal doesn't mean anything other than that you're being a little open-minded and a little caring, a little humanistic. That doesn't mean you throw all the conservatives' values out the window. That's not what I'm saying at all, but why can't there be a little common ground rather than opposite extremes. Particularly when it comes to working with the youth . . . I think Colorado is a rather conservative state. Certainly El Paso County is. El Paso County is not conservative; *El Paso County is ultra conservative* . . . The whole issue of reaching out, and then the helping hand, that's seen as liberal. Why should it be perceived as being liberal? Why can't it be perceived as being human? And that's another thing; you know, we have some very conservative religious elements in communities, and these people go to church every single Sunday. They are very actively involved, but they're the biggest segregationists there are because they do it within their own church. Granted it's good, but can you imagine the impact of all churches getting together, not feuding over which religion is better, and they all chip in to exert some efforts in terms of helping our youth? Tremendous, tremendous possible impact there.

Demographically, Colorado Springs is smaller and less urban than Denver, yet interviewees, some explicitly comparing the two districts, described District 11 as the inner-city district in El Paso County. A similar dynamic was identified whereby middle-class and white families were leaving the district for wealthier suburban metropolitan communities. Similar racial and ethnic conflicts were mentioned, including the issue of disparities in disciplinary actions and academic achievement. This inner-city self and public image has made District 11 the focal point for discussions of violence and discipline problems in the area. This has made the district somewhat self-conscious about how the public perceives the district acting against violence and discipline problems. As in Denver, the district's institutional interest has contributed to its tough stance on violence and disruption. The norms of limited action and parental control have perhaps even more strongly here led to the selection of certain approaches, such as security and alternative schools, and the avoidance of others, such as comprehensive prevention and education programs.

Contrasting Problem Definitions

As in Denver, in addition to a dominant order-expulsion and security-control problem definition, contrasting views of the problem existed among individuals in Colorado Springs, some of whom were cognizant of the assorted ways of approaching the problem. In one case, a clear contrast between a board member and an administrator seemed to illustrate the competing problem definitions of the community and the district. The board, as representative of the community, was identified as being more conservative, or at least acting that way in order to be elected. According to one board member, this was even more true after the change in the electoral system so that board members were chosen in November rather than May:

> For a long time [the administration] wasn't tough enough. Protested a lot when the state discipline law went into place. Said it would take years to set policy, it doesn't make sense, resisted, a lot . . . When I first got on the board ten years ago, there was so much concern about at-risk kids, and very legitimately so. And I think there was so much bending over backwards for at-risk kids, and when you couple that with court cases that give kids due-process rights, I think that you just create *a culture where there's too much tolerance*, there's been too much tolerance of disruption. *I don't know if I worry so much about violence as I do about disruption of the learning process.* I mean, I think violence happens, and it happens here and there, and it kind of bubbles, and I don't mean to make light of it, because I know that kids get hurt. But the system that I've been in with thirty-two thousand kids, I don't remember anybody being irreparably harmed from another student . . . [The administration] knows the innards of these problems . . . but there's *a philosophical difference between [the administration] and the board, which is representative of the community* . . . In general, the board is probably not as conservative as the community because of who votes in the school board races. But I . . . saw the board become more conservative, more no-nonsense, more reflective of the community, and I think a lot of that had to do with the fact that the school board elections changed from May to November . . . I think people are thinking of elections in November; it's a logical time, so there are more voters, and when you have *more voters* in a school board election, it's harder for special-interest groups to control the election. And pretty much the teachers unions have controlled the school board elections . . . Statewide change. It's a good thing for reform. I mean, I know that schools still aren't changing rapidly, but they have school boards where the more people who vote in school board elections, the more school board members feel compelled to *represent the community ethos*.

The board, representing the community, was prone to having, or expressing, a less tolerant, less student-oriented problem definition than the administration. The administration was more concerned about student services but was constrained by the lack of time, funds, and board and community support as to the ways in which it could approach the problem. In this case, conflict learning was hindered by these competing problem definitions that prevented adequate assessment of particular approaches, dissemination of information, and openness to innovation.

The contrast, a contrast that was seen in Denver as well, is evident in the use of the terms "proactive" and "positive." Some individuals talked about such proactive measures as increased security awareness and tough discipline, while others defined proactive in more educational terms. Even in the security department, "prevention" took on a more comprehensive, educational, research-informed definition, as one official illustrated:

> One of the things that I certainly am is a *preventionist*. I don't think we've done as good of a job as we need to do. And prevention programs at the middle school level and intervention programs at the middle school levelÑprevention being things like DARE, where we bring kids in and teach them avoidance skills and give them a level of knowledge that they need to have in order to avoid drugs and violence and gangs and that kind of thing. But in Colorado Springs how that kind of evolved is we do DARE in fifth grade and some of that filters down in to the elementary building . . . so that kids really from K through five get I think, a reasonable dose of prevention . . . We could do more there, but from the time they hit sixth grade until from then on *there is no comprehensive district-wide prevention effort.* Nor is there a comprehensive district-wide intervention effort. I talked a little bit about the prevention effort first, and I should say that one of the things that educators ask me as well, you know, *What the hell does the school have to do with providing prevention? And my response to that is that . . . if kids don't feel safe and they aren't safe, they're not going to do very much learning* . . . And for that matter, if they're stoned or if they're off of a binge from the previous night, they're not going to do much learning either. And I think that to the extent that we can mitigate all of those things in their lives, they're going to be better learners. So what I would like to see us do in this district is to take a real hard look at developing a comprehensive prevention program grade six though eight. Studies have shown that . . . is the time when children make the decision about whether they're going to engage in premarital sex, whether they're going to engage in abuse of alcohol and other substances, tobacco, whether they're going to become gang involved, all of those things. There may be precursors to that down there in the earlier grades, and certainly we've got some fifth graders that are hard-core gang members now, but for the most part I think that those decisions are made in the middle school year, and that's where we have really dropped the ball.

The security administration has a similar background to that in Denver and is sharing information with its larger counterpart. Similar approaches include the surveillance pilot project, professionalization of staff, more central control, and an avoidance of turning the security force into a district "police force." As they are in regular contact, it appears that in this area the two districts are drawing lessons about effective practices from one another. They are using research and personal training and experience to inform their approaches. Similar contact and lesson-drawing was mentioned in Denver in the area of special education, where Colorado Springs is learning how to deal with problems that Denver has been facing for a number of years. These examples illustrate interaction within similar pockets of learning.

One District 11 board member used "proactive" and "positive" both ways, never really settling on one definition. At one point, security and tough discipline were positive and proactive for him:

> We have television systems installed to monitor the halls and so forth . . . I think it's better to be *proactive* than to sit there and say, "Gee, we let this get out of hand; we shouldn't have let this happen." But that's why we have toughened up that discipline policy a little . . . I think it's being proactive to say we want our classrooms to be safe. And there are going to be some kids who are going to violate most policies, and when they do, they should expect consequences. And I don't want to see any kid thrown out of school, but at the same time, I want those who go to school to have the opportunity to learn as much as they can learn, and do it in a safe environment, because, I mean, I don't think I could learn if I were in a classroom today, as a student, if I knew there was a kid sitting back in the far corner with a thirty-eight . . . They've tried to carry violence into the schools, and I think we've responded with *very positive measures.* They may not think it's very positive, but *positive in terms of we're proactive with these problems, and it was old Berretta used to say, "You do the crime, you do the time."*

At another point, for this board member, early childhood education was proactive and positive, and the other measures were punitive:

> If you get them when they're three and four years old, you can create an attitude about learning, you know. And, of course, I'm a Catholic, and the Catholic Church used to say, "Give me a kid until he's six and I've got him for life." And there's more to it than that, but . . . *I think that would be a proactive and a positive measure, rather than the punitive measures that we have had to use.* And again, that is not to say that we don't have a percentage, even if we start them at three years of age, but I think we can cut it down significantly.

What is the meaning of these terms then? A possible interpretation is that all of these measures, surveillance as well as preschool education, are proactive and preventive measures against future and current violence, elements of a more comprehensive problem definition. Again, however, just an awareness of the benefits of and need for early intervention and alternative educational approaches is not enough to expand these elements in the districts and the state. Institutional interests and norms and a lack of extensive evaluation and information-sharing efforts hinder moving the learning process in this direction.

Others perceived that there needed to be a wholesale change from the punitive problem definition to what they perceived as a real proactive problem definition. A district administrator wondered whether

> Again using that term *paradigm shift,* in terms of communities and the citizenry, and how we begin to address the problems of youth and families, is are we always going to take a *negative and reactive impunitive [sic] view* of what has to be done, or are we going to begin to take *a swing there, a shift in the way that we think and the way that we begin to be more proactive* and begin to work in neighborhoods and families and create mentoring programs in communities, a large expansion of mentoring programs, for example, that is really supported by the top government officials in communities? It's the mayor, the chief of police, the county commissioners, and the civic organizations that say mentoring is important because if we have a . . . 60 percent divorce rate and we have all these kids floating around that need a mentor, and we're not doing everything possible within our communities to provide some assistance to those kids out there hurting for somebody to be their guiding light so to speak, to head them in the right direction because that single parent is barely making ends meet. What's so wrong about that? I mean, that alone, if you stop to think about it, everybody talks about doing some *positive things,* but I wonder, if you would ask in any given audience how many of you are mentoring a kid, how many would raise their hands?

Another contrast in problem definitions in Colorado Springs again reflects a Denver issue. Is violence getting worse, or not? How bad is the problem? And, if it is a serious problem, then where do funds go to handle it? As in Denver, some in Colorado Springs thought that the public, largely because of the media, perceived that the problem was much worse than it actually was, while others argued that the public needed to be informed of the extent of the problem so that they would support efforts, such as increased security monitoring and enforcement, to combat it. One district official said that

> I think you have to look at the problem regarding youth violence from a very analytical point of view. Are you basing it on empirical research, or are you basing it on conjecture, because the media creates such a paranoia regarding youth violence that they really are obviously out to sell newspapers and to bring in the audience . . . But if you began to look at the real statistical data, then you begin to see clearly that the problem isn't as pervasive as it appears. It's just that politically it becomes very profitable for politicians to make this huge monster out of something that's, granted, is a problem but not to the extent that it is presented to the public.

State-District Relationship

As mentioned, the relationship between the state and District 11 is similar to that between the state and DPS, although there was more of an emphasis on local control and unfunded mandates in Colorado Springs. The state was portrayed as driving policy change and problem definition in District 11, sometimes in advance of district action and sometimes codifying and standardizing district initiatives, as one administrator noted:

> Well, I guess [the violence problem] is two pronged, and one is getting a handle on the frequency of serious violence and kind of having a policy in place and procedures in place that make it kind of an *even playing field across the schools*. That all the schools are using more or less the same; they're *applying consistently the definitions* that we have interpreted out of the law and out of the *state directives* in a consistent manner across the school district. And some of that speaks to clarity around what constitutes the serious infractions. And we do have a policy in place that has gone to every parent, every student, and every staff member, explaining what all the different levels are and what kinds of behaviors would call for those sorts of consequences . . . This has been stimulated by the legislation, but we were already working on that problem anyway . . . The indicators, the counts of suspensions and expulsions, when we first started counting them about three years ago, and . . . the School Finance Act of '88 called for the collection of indicator data which was to include graduation rate, dropout rate, and I believe that the law specified suspensions and expulsions. But that's about when we started with some systems to collect several different statistics, including the suspensions, and of course, we found, like you do, commonly, when you first collect information on anything, across a school district . . . *there were different criteria being applied, different standards, different philosophies . . . and definitions*, of course, so we . . . had to work through a lot of those issues. And that seems to take about two to three

years to accomplish that, so now, I think, we've got pretty much everybody using the logistics, or the mechanics of using the [central data-tracking] computer program, and understanding about the different kinds of infractions. And, of course, *our policy became very strict . . . with the prescriptions of the new law*, that anything involving guns or certain kinds of behaviors would go right to a certain kind of reaction as far as a suspension, expulsion. And so schools that were using suspensions as a disciplinary measure for less severe kinds of infractions had to kind of *redefine where they were, to get everybody kind of calibrated* to . . . three suspensions and you're out, kind of thing. Well, that's not going to work real well . . . for schools that were heavier users, so to speak, as a disciplinary measure.

The state legal changes were identified by an administrator as driving the increase in district suspensions and expulsions:

A lot of [the rise in suspension referrals in the 1995–96 school year] is a *direct result of the Safe School legislation* that came about and the special legislative session in 1993 and then began to be enacted in '94 and really came to full fruition in the '95–96 school year where . . . we are mandated to make referrals after . . . six significant disruptions in the classroom or in the school. We were mandated to refer those kids down for expulsion or consideration for expulsion. My suspicion is it's going to be more next year, because the state legislature has changed that from six to three . . . We've expelled more kids; we've heard more cases and expelled more kids. That also goes for weapon offenses and . . . there's a big jump in the number of referrals for weapons, and that stems from a *policy decision made by the superintendent* to be very tough and have essentially a zero-tolerance attitude toward weapons possession of any kind or possessing a facsimile of a firearm. And so, well, I'm not sure that there were necessarily more firearms or more weapons in schools, it's just that, typically, a lot of those lower-level weapons offenses, say a kid bringing a knife to school, had been dealt with at the building and wouldn't get referred to down here [to the central office]. And now they're pretty much all referred down here, and again that's kind of an *outlook of that whole get-tough attitude on student discipline and safety.*

The state was portrayed as having a "schizophrenic" kind of approach after it added, and here again the language is revealing, a more "proactive" approach in 1996. The district was said by an official to have taken

A very, very hard stance about no drugs, no tolerance for drugs, no tolerance for weapons, and that's *legislated in the safe schools legislation of 1993*, all of the legislation that was enacted then, and then just this last legislative session there was some more legislation that *made it even tougher* . . . In District 11 they have gotten really tough on drugs. If a kid has a drug pipe or has I don't care what amount of marijuana, for example, we have to expel them. It doesn't say what length to expel them, but if they're selling it's expulsion for a year, mandatory . . . Our expulsions have increased probably about 700 percent over the last five or six years, and the question then is, are kids getting worse, or are we getting tougher on the policies? . . . Both. Kids are getting worse, but it's more an issue of *much tougher policies and state laws* . . . The new *state law now mandates all school districts to implement some proactive efforts* and is very specific about the first time that a kid gets suspended out of school for a material disruption of the school environment, that a remedial discipline plan be initiated . . . so that, hopefully, he or she is prevented from getting expelled from school . . . I think that it's going to generate a lot more expulsions. I've seen some of them already, but remember this is mid-November; we still have what, six months more. By the end of the school year all of those kids are rambunctious, you know. Well, how many times certain kids—how long will it take for them before they get the third one? I mean, we're going to be tossing kids out all over this state, left and right, *even though this state has been a little bit schizophrenic in saying, "We're getting tougher, but, oh, by the way, let's put in some proactive measures here."* And we're getting tougher and we're bumping kids out, but . . . the state legislature is saying, "OK, we want you to kick these kids out, but we're not going to provide any money for programs so that these kids aren't out there floating around." And what I was saying . . . is, with some exceptions, most of those kids that we're expelling out of the school system in the state are not the kids that are going to be at home watching *Mr. Rogers' Neighborhood*. Those are the kids that are going to be out robbing Mr. Rogers' neighborhood . . . Public schools draw from the entire community. Why should it be just the public school system's problem? It belongs—it's a societal problem.

There was resistance in the district by some individuals to state encroachments and mandates. And in Colorado Springs there appeared to be, in general, more resistance to state interference, particularly when an unfunded mandate was involved. But this resistance was selective. When a state dictum involved or was grounded in a different problem definition than that of the individual in the district, or represented what was perceived to be an incomplete problem definition from the individual's point of view, the individual clearly reacted against the state approach. Another example of this pattern is the sharing of information between the Denver and Colorado Springs school security departments, two similar pockets of learning.[14]

As in Denver, the conflict between law and policy, on the one hand, and procedures and implementation, on the other, illustrates the difficulty in top-down management, control by decree, and consistency across district and school sites. One board member, commenting on the length of time it took for the school administration to implement board policy and state law, identified this as an institutional problem:

> It's just an example of how *hard it is to change things in public schools.* And law makers can make these rules, and you have [an administrator] sitting there, and he doesn't think it's a good idea, and he finds some obscure court case somewhere and cuts out a little piece of it and thinks that he's doing the right thing . . . But, see, when I was talking to the superintendent, . . . I was talking about policies that were in place, but they weren't being followed, so it wasn't like we had to change the policies. *The policies were there. It was that they weren't following the policies* from the school district. So, there were policies put in place with the help of a very able law firm after the [state] law was passed . . . Well, it's just kind of an interesting case study, not only of discipline, but of *how institutions work.*

As districts muddled through with their implementation of state laws, so the state has muddled through with its legislative process. Interviews revealed that the state was responding to feedback from the school districts, feedback which was channeled primarily through the Colorado Department of Education, legislative committees, and professional organizations. Thus, there was a two-way, or circular, process and information network from the districts to the state, in the form of disciplinary complaints; from the state to the districts, in the form of tough laws; and again from the districts to the state, in terms of reactions to and problems with implementing the laws. In terms of learning, it will take more time to determine whether this incremental, trial-and-error approach will lead to a more comprehensive redefinition of the problem. As mentioned in chapter 3, evaluation components were built into the state laws in 1996, but it remains to be seen whether they will continue to promote the solving of the same problem, expulsion; whether they will provide enough resources and support to promote effective evaluations; and whether that evaluation information will be effectively shared with districts and schools.

Innovation

Just as the state perceived itself as an innovator in terms of disciplinary legislation, prevention, and education reform, and Denver perceived itself as an innovator in terms of special education,

Colorado Springs saw itself as an innovator in terms of discipline. One administrator described sending out District 11's student conduct and discipline handbook to other districts and states that wanted to follow its example. And, like Denver, Colorado Springs was piloting surveillance and city police officers in some schools, although it is unclear who got these ideas first. An interesting dynamic identified in both districts, however, might be called "re-innovation," or "rediscovering the wheel."

In Denver, this occurred with the district's crisis team and in returning to former programs from Denver and elsewhere, including uniforms, neighborhood schools, and a zero-tolerance approach. One administrator there described the cyclical changes, even after he had previously described how much networking he was involved in, in order to avoid "reinventing a lot of wheels":

> I've been here for thirty years. As a matter of fact, I've seen a complete cycle. And almost, of course, I'm another one of those that believes that *things do work in cycles,* and if you wait around long enough in one place, soon everything will come back to you. I have seen us go from . . . the seventies . . . the free expression era, . . . do what you want to do . . . kind of an ultraliberal approach, to today, where we've kind of turned around, more and more, to zero-tolerance-type levels, where we are saying, "no, we can't do this, and no, . . . you are not allowed to do it." And I think, right now, we are, I think *we're on the beam, so to speak,* to be falling either way. We could either become so restrictive that our schools do end up looking like penal institutions, or we could go to the exact opposite, where we don't take the action necessary to do the things that we have to do, such as environmental design of our schools . . . I think we're at a *crossroads.* I think we're at a real crossroads in this school district as to which way we go. I'm not, I don't believe much in burying your head in the sand and saying it can't happen here, because it can and, in fact, is happening here. On the same hand, I'm a very, very firm believer on individual rights. And . . . my job is to figure out how to balance pure safety with pure individual rights.

Some observers would argue that incremental learning and progress have occurred, despite the seemingly cyclical nature of school reforms.[15] And perhaps, as districts have adopted older programs and adapted them to current circumstances, they have learned over time, redefining the current problem in a better way and recognizing past successes and failures. But there are limits to this progress, and to state-district communication as a part of that, as one Colorado Springs administrator suggested:

So we've got to get everybody to the point of having that same kind of investment in our community, and to be able to look at ourselves and some of these programs, which may mean that you volunteer and don't get paid for it, and that's OK. *So we've got to reenact some old things that have kind of occurred in the past that I think will probably, maybe with a different twist, be just as successful in the future* . . . It's all relationship oriented. I mean, we've got to start building some better relationships and better communication and start doing some bonding with our community, the kids in our community, because right now they don't feel like they're appreciated enough. So those are some of the areas that I think we need to work on, and *help our legislators understand* what we really face, and get them down to the schools and communities to really experience the kinds of things that are happening. Sometimes they're detached from that and don't really understand that to the extent that I think that some of the decision-making that they make could be affected in a different manner. I would like to see them do a little bit more outreach to the schools and the communities, to have community sessions where the input could be given to a particular item before it's enacted; and instead of asking people to go to Denver, that they would send a committee to different parts of Colorado, western slope, those places. Announce it; say, "We're having a meeting here for this reason." Allow local people to come to those meetings, because right now they're very hands off, because you've got to go all the way to the state capital to be able to give any kind of input, and *it's not accessible*. Now, for me, I could, because I'm in a job where it allows me to do those kinds of things, but I think if you really want the grassroots opinion in those communities, and if the state really wants to hear the grassroots opinion on a variety of socioeconomic levels, they've got to get into the communities.

Conclusions

The examination of Colorado Springs in comparison to the Denver Public Schools was revealing, not so much for the differences it illustrated as for the confirmation of previously observed tendencies gained from it. While the contrasts in the demographic environment and the political culture of the district showed the importance of taking these factors into account when considering school violence, learning, and the policy process in different institutional contexts, the numerous similarities lend support for the conclusions reached in chapters 3 and 4.

In Colorado Springs District 11, personnel change was a key factor in bringing in new problem definitions and causing change, "awakening," as one administrator put it, the district to the safety and security problem. Crisis, public fear, and district responsiveness to its constituency stimulated tough action in Colorado Springs, as the "summer of violence" in Denver and some high-profile local cases led the district to label the problem as such. The importance of the state, the role of the individual in constructing problem definitions, the competition between problem definitions in different segments of the institution, and the role of the school in providing alternative prevention programs are themes that resonated in both districts.

The limitations on systematic evaluation of programs and policies in the area of school violence were clear as well. Constrained by both staff time and financial inadequacies, Colorado Springs exhibited little in the way of the analysis, reflection, and problem setting characterized by the propositions raised in this study. Complex learning within the whole district was on the level of that in Denver, mixed and fragmented, without a clear overall mission or attempt to focus on and define the school violence problem in a shared and comprehensive manner.

Chapter 6
Conclusion
Learning about Learning

> Well, there's family issues, but there's also societal issues. See, I think the biggest crime in society aside from violence and weapons is *indifference*, indifference as American citizens, as Colorado citizens. We're far too apathetic . . . We create our own monster through our indifference and then we complain about it. *We're either part of the problem or we're part of the solution.*
> —a Colorado Springs district administrator

This book has examined the state of Colorado and two of its larger school districts in order to assess policy-learning as a process of problem redefinition through the window of school violence policy-making. The study reveals a number of important aspects of problem definition and policy-learning in these institutional contexts regarding the school violence policy problem, some of which may offer insights into this problem and these processes in other states, institutions, and policy areas.

This chapter begins with an assessment of the guiding propositions of the book, integrating results from state, district, and school levels. Several main arguments connect the various elements of the study and they can be divided into two general areas: reflections on the school violence problem in school districts in particular and reflections on problem definition and policy-learning. The chapter discusses each of these areas in turn, presenting the main conclusions from the study, and suggesting lessons relevant for each one. It presents a list of recommendations to practitioners who wish to improve the complex learning curve in their organization. It then concludes with a discussion of some of the basic issues raised by the research.

Reflections on the Guiding Policy-Learning and Problem Definition Propositions

Reflecting on the guiding propositions posed by this study and looking at the state, district, and school levels in Colorado, it appears that available data tend to support many of them. However, not enough conclusive evidence was found in several areas to offer substantial support for or against some notions. In large part, this was due to the lack of time that had passed since recent legislative changes. These changes may or may not offer insight into several of the hypotheses over the long term.

> 1a. An institutional focus that emphasizes problem solving rather than problem setting leads to a lack of innovation and learning and produces or continues an insufficient or limited definition of the problem.

This proposition was generally confirmed through interviews and examination of archival data, inasmuch as the expulsion-oriented problem definition and debate have dominated the search for policy solutions. The tendency in many of the state institutions has been to look at prevention only as an afterthought. Where the state legislature and the governor have acted, they have focused on punishing and expelling disruptive students, with the main goal of securing safety for other students in school and promoting an orderly learning environment. One sees this in the 1993 safe-schools legislation, and even the governor's task force on expulsion. The crisis learning that occurred in the 1993 special legislative session produced only simple learning and not a departure from cultural and public opinion norms.

The 1996 legislative changes, with their encouragement of expulsion prevention programs, show movement toward a broader outlook. However, these laws continue to try to solve the problem of expulsion and suspension. Prevention in the laws was designed to limit expulsions and suspensions. The laws were still not necessarily confronting other factors associated with violence. The legislature took a problem-solving approach. It did not innovate in such directions as comprehensive peace education, conflict resolution, or curricular reform. The legislature may have set up a future basis for learning through its structuring of evaluation programs (see below).

Pockets of more complex learning did exist in the state, but usually not within state decision-making institutions. Competing approaches and definitions were shown by LARASA (Latin American Research and Service Agency), the Colorado Lawyers Committee (CLC), and the Conflict Center, for example. It appears that LARASA and the CLC set out with more of a problem-setting posture in their research, even as they started from the presumptive standpoint of solving the problem of racial and ethnic disparity in disciplinary practices. These two groups were more open to examining the expulsion problem in a broader sense. They began to add dimensions to the problem of school violence overall by focusing on student and family rights, basic underlying reasons for disruption and violence, and difficulties in the way laws were applied. A CLC task force member explained their study process, clearly indicating an attempt at learning:

> We had a number of task force meetings with the intention of finding all the information out about what actually was happening. What was working, what wasn't working. What attitudes were within the school districts. Where the numbers were. We saw some preliminary numbers out of the Colorado Department of Education about what kind of a population was being disciplined, and what wasn't. We worked fairly closely with CDE on that, and tried to understand those issues, and then we got into a number of programs from other places in the country for dealing with discipline problems.

Here we see the search for accuracy in terms of data and assumptions about the school violence problem. This is an examination of trends. The member continued,

> We got acquainted locally with a principal out in the Aurora system . . . who had managed to get through an entire year without an expulsion by the management of an in-school environment for his suspension program. We concluded that that was a worthwhile thing that desired further study, that perhaps some encouragement to other schools to experiment in that way would be worthwhile. And so we kind of built that into our thought processes. We concluded fairly early that there was no question that the legislation that required expulsion for certain weapons, and in certain violence kinds of circumstances, was not going to be changed in the legislature, that that was a fact of life that we had to recognize. *But we began to explore it from the point of view of a kid's right to an education, and what happened when you took a kid out of the schools on a full-year basis and said, "You can't come back to school for a year," because of this circumstance or that, and what do we do with that kid.* And we had just come through the summer when gang violence in Denver had been at its peak, and we began to perceive that if all we were doing was putting kids back into the community, which was where their problem probably originated in the first place, and put them back into the home, which we suspected was the real origination of their malfunction, that we were probably compounding the problem rather than solving the problem.

Now comes an understanding and reevaluation of goals, projections for the future, and policy alternatives, along with a recognition of the broader nature of the problem.

And so we conceived of an idea to build some schools on a pilot basis, to take kids out of the expulsion population and put them together in a much more rigid educational environment, something that required them to go to school longer hours, longer months, essentially a full-time school environment. And then we even conceived of the idea of making it a residential facility as opposed to a walk-in facility, so that we had truly removed the student from the influences that were causing the dysfunction in the first place. We did take a hard look at the Eagle Rock school in Estes Park, which is funded by the Honda people. *Met with a number of the students from up there, to learn about what it was that drove them and inspired them and motivated them. And then we sat down, and we drafted some legislation that we thought was comprehensive,* and we persuaded Jeanne Adkins to sponsor it. She persuaded the senate president to cosponsor it in the senate, and we launched about a full-press effort to see to its adoption. And it got adopted.

Finally, we see active lesson-drawing about values and alternatives, with an action element in a particular direction. In the end, both CLC and LARASA produced reports that emphasized the expulsion and suspension issue. It appears that the state's dominant problem definition, reified through multiple pieces of legislation, was continuing a limited definition of the problem even in pockets where learning was beginning to take place.[1]

At the district level, this proposition was convincingly confirmed. From the focus on discipline and removing "bad" students so others could learn, as handed down by the state and confirmed in the districts, to the lack of district engagement in promoting the creation and sharing of innovations, the districts have been content at an administrative level to accept the state's problem definition. Evidence of the problem-solving orientation and the general "satisficing" overall includes the fear of innovating, the lack of real sharing identified at principal meetings, and the lack of research focus in the district. In Denver, it must be emphasized that individuals in different pockets in the district are problem setting and redefining the problem, but the comprehensive joining of isolated problem definitions based in different departments has not occurred in the district. School violence and discipline are not considered priorities on the agenda, as several board members noted. One does not get the sense that the district as a whole has a broad mission to deal with school violence in a way which joins the safety and security, discipline, violence prevention education, psychological intervention, and community and parent involvement perspectives, to name a few.

The districts are doing a lot of seeking of minimally sufficient actions. The lack of a research focus illustrates this. In Denver, Student Services employees described the benefits of a staff retreat that led to group reflection on necessary protocols for the crisis team. This seemed to be more oriented toward problem setting. At the same time, they argued that the district did not place any value on research. Since they received no occupational reward and did not have the time, they avoided research work in favor of direct practice, as one Student Services administrator noted:

> So, for a lot of reasons, we need to identify what's effective and we need to find ways to demonstrate that, so that there is some continuity . . . I think the biggest barrier to that, in our practice, one that I've heard over and over in a lot of different contexts, not just this one, is time . . . just finding the time to do it. I mean, we've had some just absolutely wonderful programs that have been proposed and research projects that have been thought of. We have a tremendously talented staff of psychologists here, and not just saying that as a member of the staff. We've got . . . a lot of people that are working with outside agencies, that are teaching . . . We've got a lot of talent here, and a lot of experience. But with the best intentions, you end up just fulfilling the needs that the schools have, and you don't have time to do the things you'd like to do. Then it becomes a second priority to do . . . I think that's one of the biggest obstacles . . . [An information clearinghouse] would be good. Prepackaged information. That would be great. Somebody to do the legwork. There isn't much of a value, I don't think, in most districts for those kinds of activities that we can provide, like researching, like, you know, development and program evaluation. What we tend to hear is "direct service to students." That's the key phrase. If you're not involved in something that is a direct service to students, which they view as testing or counseling, . . . you're not doing what we want you to do. And we have been told that in a number of ways. There's not really a value for it, and I don't know where that comes from. I don't know how you put that in place.

> 1b. A critical awareness and discussion of problem definitions within an institution will lead to more complex learning.

The Conflict Center and the Colorado School Mediation Project, groups with a more alternative approach to school violence, also shared a more open, problem-setting perspective. While starting from a particular philosophical standpoint on conflict and violence, these groups nevertheless were extremely inclusive in terms of the groups, individuals, and research they were bringing together in their conferences and institutional programs. They were learning through a more academic and critical comparison of approaches to and definitions of school violence. However, at the overall state level, and in institutions that were responsible for making policy, this learning was again having limited effect.

In the Colorado Department of Education (CDE), some individuals were focusing on defining the problem of school violence. Among these individuals, and the agency to some extent, more complex learning had occurred. This was exemplified by problem definitions that took into account multiple goals, alternatives, and causal stories. A key question is, Why was this more comprehensive, problem-setting approach not impacting the state legislature to a greater degree? Funding limitations could be one explanation, but public sentiment and the political leanings in the Republican-dominated legislature is another. In the realm of the possible, the narrower, problem-solving approach was more practical and popular. The CDE was an agency in a more reactive, administrative role. It was not setting policy for the legislature.

In the districts and schools, this proposition leads to a particular conclusion. *Individuals* who were aware of and discussed contrasting problem definitions, referring to them as philosophies, perspectives, and viewpoints, seemed to have a more comprehensive definition of the school violence problem overall. They were able to compare perspectives and justify their own. They had learned about the problem over time. They either were trying to address many aspects themselves or were selecting one portion of the problem in their domain and acting on that, recognizing that others were responsible for handling other parts of the problem. In Denver's Department of Student Services, as one official there discussed, the district has institutionalized a set of services that, as discussed, are oriented towards a problem-setting perspective and a broad outlook on the school violence issue:

> So it's really a district-wide effort. We're using Safe and Drug-Free School money to do the training and to provide schools with some additional resources to deal with things like discipline problems and attendance problems and behavior problems and other kinds of issues, all related. And so we don't really view it as a pilot, we view it as a *systemic change,* that we're giving schools an opportunity to really orchestrate some resources and do something about this. That's, by the way, a few years ago, when we organized the Department of Student Services in Denver, . . . part of the *philosophy* was to be able to take a *broader systemic look* at issues like discipline, and to be able to organize and coordinate a greater number of

resources to address singular issues like discipline or attendance. And we're doing that in a far more coordinated way than we've done in the past.

Again, the next key step appears to be expanding the learning from a base such as this to the district board and administration, the policy level and the schools.

2a. Institutions that promote processes of reflection, diagnosis, and analysis based on evaluation of information and experiences will be more likely to experience complex learning.

In Colorado, the Department of Education role will be important in examining this proposition in the future. What kind of learning will result from 1996 mandates on program evaluation? Under the aegis of the state board, the CDE is responsible for administering the grant program and collecting the evaluations of funded programs and, if they are funded, pilot schools. Thus, the legislature has mandated program evaluations. Whether these evaluations will produce reflection, diagnosis, and analysis of the programs themselves remains to be seen. Similarly, whether the CDE will foster these processes is unknown. Resource constraints may limit these processes in both cases. Furthermore, if the CDE reflects on, diagnoses the problems associated with, and analyzes the newly available evaluations, it may or may not experience more complex learning. Based on my discussions with representatives of the CDE, I believe that it will. However, the key question at that point will be whether the state board and, even more problematical, the legislature will listen to the CDE and provide for policy changes that might be recommended.

To date we may not have seen enough of these processes to say whether they will produce complex learning. We may have to wait and see what happens after the 1996 laws are implemented and the evaluations come in. Contradictory evidence from both the governor's task force and the Violence Prevention Advisory Committee, however, does exist. Granted, the task force was charged with looking at expelled students, so it was no surprise that it began with the expulsion-oriented problem definition and that the solutions it offered to the problem were logically derived from that definition. So, while the task force story supports proposition 1a, it also seems not to support 2a. Given the amount of reflection, diagnosis, and analysis of experience and information that the task force conducted, it still produced relatively simple learning, as defined by this study. In other words, with the central problem definition taken for granted, and an initial problem-solving approach adopted, the procedures of analysis suggested in proposition 2a appear to have been overridden by the powers of the problem-solving approach presented in 1a.

The districts and schools are in the middle on this proposition. The districts, and in turn the schools, have begun to implement significant improvements in information gathering. They have increased their intelligence capabilities, an important first step that may lead to more complex learning. There is more monitoring, and the districts are learning about the state of the problem in many areas, such as literacy and disciplinary-incident reports. In Denver, these incident reports will now be standardized with the city's, thus allowing for improved comparison and tracking of offenders and offenses.

Discussions and data reports indicate that the districts and schools are not promoting extensive processes of reflection, diagnosis, and analysis based on this information as a whole. Yes, in the area of safety and security these processes have led to major changes there. But again, this has not occurred across the districts in a unified sense, linking multiple problem definitions and impacting policy. The sharing of good information and the drawing of lessons is inhibited, as one Denver special education administrator noted:

> Now, around the country, I know a lot's going on, but, you know . . . you get so busy just doing your day-to-day job. You don't have time to find out how Detroit is dealing with violent kids. You just don't, unless you happen to read it in the paper or it's in one of the journals that I get and I try and read. Fine, but do I go out and do research on it, no I don't. Nor does anybody else in the district that I know of.

This proposition is somewhat disproved by Denver's experience, for example, with the Ad Hoc Discipline Committee. The committee's intent was to systematically examine the discipline problem. It set out with a particular definition of that problem in mind, but given its multidisciplinary composition and its survey, it had the opportunity to experience complex learning. Yet it did not. It reaffirmed the district policy as it stood and took the definition of "discipline" for granted.

> 2b. Program evaluation alone may lead to solving or not solving the same problem, or the wrong problem, rather than a redefinition of the problem as a whole.

As mentioned above, we may have to wait and see what happens with Colorado's 1996 programs to fully address this proposition. Once again, a lack of adequate funding for such activities could impact their efficacy. Nevertheless, reading deeper into the legislative mandates and structures, one sees a continuing focus on suspension and expulsion. If schools and communities take the legislative cue, they may only focus on programs that directly address suspended and expelled students and students at risk of such. Evaluating these programs based on their ability to reduce suspensions, expulsions, and recidivism may lead to more simple learning about suspension and expulsion. The limited definition of the problem would remain. There is no guarantee that grantees will experiment and innovate more broadly, produce deeper reflection on what the problem is, and lead the state legislature to redefine the problem more comprehensively. In fact, given the Request for Proposals (RFP) issued by the Colorado Department of Education, an RFP based directly on the 1996 legislation, schools and communities must apply for programs that directly address the suspension and expulsion problem. Thus, there is an initial bias toward the dominant problem definition in program selection. While innovation and evaluation are now encouraged by the state, the deck is stacked against problem redefinition—complex learning—by the way the accepted problem definition structures the grant and evaluation process.

At the district and school levels, this proposition was supported by the particular focus of both districts' program evaluation efforts. In Denver, the Program Evaluation Office evaluates programs based on the requests of board members or the superintendent for information about and success rates of those particular programs. This evaluation process is another step in the right direction in terms of improved and more complex information gathering and assessment, this office suffers from its almost exclusive focus on academic achievement as an outcome measure and the fact that program cost seems to be the key impetus driving the choice of programs to evaluate. The programs that the office looks at tend to be those serving "special needs" populations, and thus costing more on a per-pupil basis than regular district programs. The office does not evaluate the curriculum as a whole, or general policies. Program evaluation in Colorado Springs presented a strikingly similar picture.

The cost effectiveness and academic achievement focus of these offices lead them to approach the same questions, How much is this program improving academic achievement and is it worth the money that the district is paying for it? seemingly regardless of the particular program's substance. For example, the one violence-oriented program that the Denver office has evaluated, the Alternative Middle School, was criticized for its lack of academic goals and the priority that it placed on retaining kids:

> They had one goal . . . I mean, it wasn't anything that was real easy to hold onto. It was real vague. And so, it was a real hard one to evaluate. So we had to ask lots of questions, and then you have to decide, with a program like that, what is the basic premise. Is it just to keep kids there, or is it to learn something. For all the other programs that we evaluate we were able to look at achievement and do some measure of it, before they got into the program, and now that they're in the program, and was there some measure of achievement. This program, obviously, didn't have that as one of its high priorities, and so the instruction and those kinds of things were scrutinized pretty carefully, and not, of course, in any kind of a measure that would compare to other kinds of programs that we have in the district. So, it was tough. You know, if you know alternative education, it's just a different kind of thing. It's a different kind of prioritizing, and our job is to get in with the real hard-core, draw the line, report the numbers, give us the data. And *they're not data people. They're not numbers people.* They're not; they're people that are very affective in their approach to everything, and so that makes it . . . real hard to report to the Board of Education the data that they want. *The board wants data. Alternative programs often avoid data at all costs. Everything is much more narrative. Much more affective . . .* You can't take portfolios to the Board of Education and say, "Hi, read all thirty-five of these." You can't do that. You can't; there's no way to quantify most of what you do. *And so when you try to quantify, they get very upset. They don't like you to . . .* Maybe if you had a whole lot of staff and a whole lot of people, but not if you just have two weeks to get in there, look at it really hard and spend a lot of time in a classroom, come back, pull all the data, throw it together, report to the board . . . If you had a committee and eight people that could go in over a long, eight-month period of time, yeah, but that's not realistic . . . Can't afford that. So then you have to say, "What are we in business here to do? Are we in business to keep kids off the street, or are we in business to educate kids? And if we're in business to educate kids, what is the quality of the education they're receiving? Or are we giving . . . *behavioral relief to the other middle schools* that wanted the kids out . . . ?" You know, at some point somebody has to establish priorities and decide why we do this kind of stuff . . . I don't remember anybody [on the board] that was just too terribly supportive [of this program report], actually. They were very concerned because *their focus is education . . . We couldn't find much evidence of learning.*

Given its mandate, this office has to look at certain areas of concern, such as academic achievement, in order to satisfy the interests of the board and the superintendent. For better or worse, that seems to have led to solving the same problem. The evaluation of the Alternative Middle School (AMS), in any event, did not lead to a redefinition of the problem.

The AMS experience illustrates the difficulties associated with many alternative programs, such as conflict resolution programs, violence prevention curricula, or anger management classes. They represent alternative problem definitions. They should not necessarily be evaluated using the same goals, criteria, and outcomes as standard educational programs. Affective and narrative approaches and data are difficult for evaluators to handle, particularly with limited time and resources. They are difficult for policy makers to digest because these people are used to short, quantifiable, comparable reports. This suggests the need for alternative research methods, joining qualitative and quantitative methods, to more effectively analyze these types of programs. Additionally, policy makers, such as board members, may need to be trained in how to assess such complex data.

> 3. Institutional interests and norms of behavior will constrain and bias the learning process.

This proposition was largely supported. Among all the institutions examined, stated and interpreted norms and interests clearly affected the school violence problem definition, and thus the learning process. The legislature and governor, for example, both needed to be seen to be acting. To appease the public and to gain reelection, they had to be tough, or at the least show "tough love."[2] Protecting the majority of good students had to be the first priority. It was in both the Democratic governor's interests, the Republican legislative majority's interests, and the Democratic legislative minority's interests to come together in a bipartisan way to pass tough legislation. While individual legislators disagreed with the actions taken, or perhaps saw the potential for resulting problems in 1993, the norm was decisive action in a way that reaffirmed individual responsibility, right and wrong, authority, and order.

The Colorado Department of Education (CDE) was more methodical, working from a research base and focusing on the learning needs of children and families. However, the CDE recognized its reliance on the state legislature for funding and the political reality of what it could accomplish. Thus, it followed a norm of compromise, of getting enough to get by and to do a little bit. This limited its ability to be comprehensive as it had to tinker around the margins instead of setting the problem in a comprehensive manner. Funding and direction from the federal government, however, in some ways bypassed the state legislature and gave the CDE the ability to carry out prevention-oriented programs at the local level. The Safe and Drug-Free Schools money was limited. The CDE could have used supplementary help from the state, but the money has provided for a number of prevention programs that would not have been in place otherwise. This is an example of a way in which federal intervention can lead states to take actions that they would not take otherwise, steps that could lead eventually to complex learning at the state and national level.

Related to this, the state has an interest in being successful in the national education goals. This has prompted action. While the Safe and Drug-Free Schools programs are generally carried out behind the scenes, the public does see the reports on how the state is doing on goal seven overall. Again, federal involvement makes a difference. Yet the language of goal seven fits with the state's problem definition of safe, secure schools with good learning environments. The state and the national government have been unable to venture too far from public opinion in a forthright manner. An essential role of government, the education of the public about problematic issues, and thus the promotion of learning, has not been taking place. This is in part due to the circular process whereby the state government has needed to appeal to public opinion by offering a limited problem definition in order to gain electoral favor. Yet it has been trapped by that problem definition, which has stifled the development of complex learning in the state government and among the public.

At the state level, there has been a willingness to admit that there is a problem, at least. This is something that is not necessarily true at the district or school level. This is in the state's interests, however, for, if the problem is defined as such, it then justifies state action. State action in the manner taken rewards legislators and the governor, while not placing blame on them for bad results. The state is only giving the right disciplinary tools to schools and districts and mandating tough action where it has not already occurred. At the district and school levels, however, admitting that there is a problem can cause multiple headaches for administrators, teachers, and principals. It may be in their interests to avoid recognizing problems at all.[3]

The clearest instance of this is the districts' quandary involving public information about violence levels. For a district, and in particular for a Department of Safety and Security, the public needs to comprehend the magnitude of the violence problem so that they will understand and support the district's request and allocation of funds for increased security personnel and technology in the schools. Simultaneously, the districts are worried about their public image and about appearing to be too violent and unsafe. Denver fears continuing to lose enrollment to the suburbs just when enrollment is rising, in part due to the end of the desegregation order. The dilemma for this district is plain. It has tried to walk a careful line between publicity and defensiveness. This institutional interest has made it difficult for the district and the schools to be completely open about the school violence problem and to engage the community in a more extensive, inclusive approach to defining and managing it.

One security person described the changes going on in this area and their causes:

> Nobody wants to be in the newspaper for having an incident at their school, so it's . . . swept quietly downtown maybe. But we're starting to do things like having incident reports that the security people . . . are now having to fill out, in hopes that we'll get a more *accurate* idea of what really is going on in the building. And now the school security force are not under the supervision of the principal, so that's helped. You know, they are now under the supervision of [central] security. The principal can't say, "Keep quiet about this issue," and it's now reported downtown . . . We've finally figured out that it takes more than educators to run a district . . . *Security really isn't an education issue, other than it keeps kids from getting an education. But it's not an issue that most educators thought was important.* So that we now have business people with backgrounds in something other than education who came to the district and looked at some of the things that we're doing and said, "You know, this isn't working." And who also believe you have to be honest with the public and say, "You know, we have a major problem with security. We have a major problem with violence in the schools, and before we kill somebody in the building, let's deal with it and try not to have that happen." So a lot of times, you have to hit the public upside the head with that kind of an issue before they say security is an important thing to fund . . . Come flat out and say this is a problem . . . and here are the reports, if you want to see them. This is what happened; this is the incident. Because the public will never believe unless you have proof, and they're never going to fund whatever we need funded unless you can prove that it needs money. And I don't know why we haven't figured that out

. . . It's hard on your *reputation*, and it probably could cost you students, because parents are going to say, "Oh my god, if they're in that much trouble, I'm going to put my kid in private school." Or send them to Cherry Creek, or whatever school district . . . I think you probably have that time when you start being honest, that you're going to have those downsides. But I think after a while it's going to bring it back up, because they're going to say, "Well, they're honest about this." And the more honest you are about everything, the more the public says, "Well, you know, I can trust the schools again. They're telling us everything." So I think it will probably be hard at first, but I think it would actually, if you would say, well, we have a problem and this is what we're doing to deal with it, rather than, we don't have a problem, and, but we're trying to deal with it. *Right now we're saying we don't have a problem, but we need more security, and they're going, you don't have a problem, then why do you need it.*

The district is also concerned about raising the awareness of school staff about violence issues. This would help it to explain and implement improved security measures, but as one security administrator indicated, the district is worried about scaring the staff too much:

Through the security and this school-oriented policing, we're trying to develop the cultural changes. And I've had good support, you know, from the staff on these things, but we have to move slow and easy . . . You just can't cram this stuff down people's throats. It's . . . like playing a chess game . . . [It's a shift in] *culture, and, as I say, security culture, or school culture. It is. It's a real shift in attitude.* Because at the same time, I don't want to scare people to death. I don't want to put everybody in a panic out there . . . I could go out and tell everybody how far at risk they are, and bring in pictures of bombs, of people blown up, and kids who've shot teachers and all this stuff, and do a wonderful dog and pony show that would just raise the level . . . and just, you know, they'd be scared to come to school, come to work. I won't do that. Can't do that. First of all, I don't believe in the effect on the education world. *If we scare the teachers and make them think all the kids they're dealing with are going to kill them, how are they going to teach them?* And every one they're going to look at is a possible, I mean, you really want to kill me, don't you? You don't want to learn. So we got to be very cautious, and that's one of the reasons also on the sharing of information, between the public and—I got a principal right now that's on my case to share with him all known gang members in our schools. He wants a list. And when I asked him, "Why do you want the list," he says, "So I can compare it against my student population and identify which ones are in gangs." And I said, "Identify is the problem. What are you going to do when you identify them as a gang member?" "Oh, well, keep my eye on them." That's the problem, because unless he's done something wrong, the mere fact that he's a gang member should have no bearing whatsoever on how you treat him as a student. And that's why I won't give you the gang listings.

The notion of a culture shift is related to the norms of the district and school institutions. Another such norm in the district is, or was, the segmentation of the district into offices with separate, and sometimes competing, foci and missions. As mentioned, the differing problem definitions in these offices are apparent. A district administrator described the changes that were being implemented in the norms of balkanization and autonomy in the various district and school areas since the arrival of new district leadership:

Well, I know there's a lot more communication and collaboration. A lot more. And the education folks would probably say there's a lot more sharing. I just call it flat out communication and coordination. Yeah, there's a lot more, and there's a lot more trust; the trust level has gone up . . . Based on what I've heard, you know, *there was a lot of parochialism, even departmental parochialism*, and [the superintendent] said we're not islands. We don't do island management here. We're all on the Titanic, and we're not going to hit an iceberg. He's at the helm, and we're steering clear of those suckers, and this thing's moving.

What we see here is the tension between specialization and integration. In both the Denver and Colorado Springs districts, learning and problem definition were clearly influenced by institutional interests and norms of behavior.

4a. A decentralized institution that allows its component parts to experiment with new policies, evaluates those policies, uses that assessment information to inform its policy decisions, and disseminates that information throughout the organization is more likely to experience complex learning.

There has been little evidence of this kind of systematic action at the state level in Colorado. While there were no positive examples of this occurring, examples that would support this proposition, the general lack of examples combined with the lack of complex learning would tend to support the proposition. The legislature attempted to put this kind of process into place with the 1996 law changes, yet it remains to be seen whether and how it will use resulting evaluation information in its future policy decisions.

The state has tried to be decentralized and to inform constituents of policy changes, but in some ways it has been a two-way street, with ground-up information sharing and then top-down dissemination. Some of the key nongovernmental and nonprofit groups mentioned, such as the Colorado Association of School Boards, the Colorado Association of School Executives, and the Conflict Center, have played important roles in both producing research and informing their constituents about policy changes. Local elected officials, particularly the mayor of Denver and his office, have also contributed to the information gathering and policy selection activities at the state level.

At the CDE, the complex learning occurring has not completely enveloped the organization or policy makers. One exchange with a CDE administrator illustrates this:

> Administrator: The evidence is overwhelmingly clear that supporting kids early on, families early on, you get a different kid. You clearly get a different kid. And that's our job in the department, I think, along with others that say where you need to be in the era of limited resources.

> Interviewer: It sounds like you've got kind of a consistent view about early childhood education, about early intervention and prevention, that regardless of the issue that comes up, you're relating it to that approach. Would that be correct?

> Administrator: I do. Our team doesn't, necessarily, but I do, because for me that's what prevention is. It's getting kids off to the right foot developmentally in the first place, giving parents skills to be parents.

> Interviewer: What are some of the hindrances that you face, obstacles that you face in talking to the legislature, to policy makers, about what's working, what's not working?

> Administrator: The biggest hindrance I face is that's not the real issue for them. The real issue for them is a political agenda. They're politicians. It was real popular in 1994 to say all these government programs don't work. We're just wasting the taxpayers' money.

In other words, the various offices in the agency continued to remain focused on particular segmented issues, with the department as a whole not clearly espousing a recognizable problem definition or attempted redefinition. Furthermore, communicating that problem definition to politicians was easier said than done.

At the district and school levels, similar patterns of experience can be seen. The converse of proposition 4a, that a decentralized institution that does not engage in these practices is less likely to experience complex learning, is strongly supported in Denver and Colorado Springs. As has been discussed, Denver and Colorado Springs both allow their schools a great deal of flexibility outside of the strictly defined discipline policy area. Yet the districts, at least in the area of school violence but less so in the area of literacy and academic achievement, have not evaluated those policies and programs and utilized the information to really examine the problem in a broad sense. In Denver, the district does disseminate program and policy information through meetings and in-service workshops. This was identified as helpful and fairly successful in providing school administrators with an understanding of discipline policy changes and requirements and model programs that they could adopt.

Part of the conclusion here is that decentralization does not always work to promote experimentation and learning as intended. Or, if that was not the intention and, for example, cost savings and local control were the goals, then decentralization can be a hindrance to effective learning about problems, policies, and programs throughout a district. For example, the crisis team adopted centrally by Denver Student Services and then devolved to the schools was recentralized in order to make it more effective and able to respond to incidents throughout the district. It was pointed out that sometimes outside intervention in a school was necessary when a crisis intimately involved in-school counselors, administrators, and so forth. Decentralization can also be about the diffusion of responsibility; this may lower accountability at the central level.

Another example is the recentralization of school security control and reporting in both districts. To get away from the situation where mixed incident reporting was occurring, in part due to a principal's interest in keeping problems quiet and within the confines of the school, control has been shifted to a stronger, more professional, central staff and office. This is an activity that seems to be essentially a central, district office role, as suggested by interviews with those in both the district offices and with some administrators in the schools who were pleased with the improvements being made in this area. However, as discussed, some administrators did not see the need for security staff in their school and refused to have the central office place them there:

> I would guess . . . that we have the fewest discipline problems of any of the middle schools. The fact that we don't need a security aide says that right there. That there's no need. And that's our decision, not the district's,

because they wanted to pawn one off last year, pawn another one off this year, and the CDM and the faculty and I said no. However, we would like the money, because I would like to have someone work in the library, you know, stuff like that, but we don't get the money either.

The conflicting problem definitions between the central security office and this particular school are evident.

A broader issue concerning decentralization is its potential to hinder the learning process throughout the district. It was argued by some that decentralization complicated the learning process because it reduced the central office staff and resources to such an extent that it was nearly impossible to do the kinds of research and information sharing necessary to accomplish effective district-wide learning. That is to say, if information gathering and sharing are necessary precursors to complex learning, then hindrances to these practices will stifle the learning process overall. State and federal money was one of the only supplements that made such practices possible at all. Denver's Department of Student Services, recently established, was seen as a positive source for learning. Overall, though, it was disconnected from the Program Evaluation office and learning was becoming more difficult:

Well, I think we're learning what's more effective than not, and what types of interventions, and how placed, and when we do them, with whom we work, and I think we're constantly learning along those lines. And we try to, whenever we find a piece of research that may give us some indication, we try to disseminate that among schools and among those Community and School Assistance Teams for students, and among our own staff. So, every time we learn something, we try and communicate it with people. I think we're learning . . . I would say *the structure of having a unified Department of Student Services greatly helps because it becomes kind of a clearinghouse and a feeding system for that kind of information.* Clearing it, and then feeding it back out to schools from a sole source, I think that helps a great deal. And also, we have the people on staff who have some responsibility for gathering that information now . . . The Evaluation Department so far has had more of an *academic orientation*, although it does evaluate different programs . . . I think [the district is] moderately decentralized. I think we have some very strong central departments that increasingly are taking kind of a service orientation towards schools and towards their decentralized needs and authority and responsibilities within the sites. But we still have departments that serve schools, such as Student Services, but we recognize that *our role is to really serve the school and the school sites. And they are our consumers, and in that respect the district is greatly decentralized in terms of its philosophy . . . With sort of reduced staff, on a central level, it makes it increasingly difficult* to do the kind of identification . . . of effective research and then the dissemination of that, and the monitoring of it, the support for it, the training. It's increasingly difficult with reduced staff. And I would say that it would be virtually impossible if we didn't have state and federal money, such as Safe and Drug-Free School money, with which to operate.

4b. Institutions that promote only the gradual accumulation of knowledge through trial-and-error study will produce simple learning.

This proposition was fairly convincingly supported by 1993 to 1996 state legislative changes, which represented reactive tinkering and "stabs in the dark." The delay in getting alternative schools for expelled students up and running represented a lack of vision about the overall problem of school violence. These schools are still not funded, even though they were authorized. Secondly, even the problem-correcting focus of the 1996 legislation was the result not of systematic evaluation and study but rather of loud messages from interest groups, constituents, and local school officials. The "satisficing" behavior of the Department of Education, as one example, additionally failed to confront political and financial constraints in order to significantly expand the prevailing problem definition.

Overall, the districts and schools were not engaged in much study in this area, either trial and error or otherwise. Some pilot programs, such as the surveillance systems or Denver's Alternative Middle School (AMS), were district-run endeavors. It remains to be seen what happens with the surveillance programs that have just begun. The AMS was seen to be insufficiently planned, given its lack of established goals and procedures. It seemed to be a rushed attempt to deal with the rising number of students who were not making it in the regular school setting. The overall impact of evaluation from the Program Evaluation office seemed to occur mainly in relation to funding levels, personnel decisions, program refining, and having the programs themselves define who they were. But this office does not have a broad planning or policy-defining role, although this is supposed to happen in the Department of Planning, Research, and Program Evaluation, from which the Program Evaluation office was recently separated. This office could be used to evaluate, or help schools to evaluate, various kinds of violence prevention, intervention, and alternative programs.

Schools themselves have mainly engaged in trial-and-error program experimentation, perhaps based on grant opportunities or serendipitous program discoveries through a research report or an organizational meeting. Evaluation of such programs is scarce. School administrators may have learned over time through their own experiences. In a chicken-and-egg dilemma, it is difficult to determine whether experiences with particular programs led individuals to change their problem definition over time and learn in a complex manner, or whether preexisting individual problem definitions led individuals to favor particular programs or approaches in the first place. None of those interviewed discussed strong cognitive-change reactions to various program experiences, although at least one mentioned that experiences with particular programs had led her to support or avoid them in the future:

> Some conflict resolution programs work. The kids you want to take conflict resolution, because all programs are voluntary, aren't the ones that need the conflict resolution programs. Motivational speakers? Do you think, in an afternoon of one hour of speaking, it might turn a kid's life around? And maybe one is better than none. That's few and far between that that happens, so the problems—now do we have programs for staff development that help teachers deal with more violent students? Don't confront them, don't, those kinds of things, yes, we have that. And we have conflict resolution programs for our kids, but I will tell you in general I don't think those work very effectively. I think the ones for staff development for teachers do. What are gang signs, what are things to be aware of, self-defense classes for teachers. We have that . . . I will tell you that I don't believe that the conflict resolution class that we had with our students [worked] . . . What we did was we took the repeat offenders and put them through the conflict resolution program, and then we had the student evaluate . . . Did that help them improve their behavior. And to be totally candid, they said "Hell no, why did we have to go through this? And we didn't learn anything more about . . . " They know that they're supposed to talk out their problems. They know they're supposed to walk away from it. They know . . . all the things that they have been taught all the way through school and through their childhood, but they don't care at that point, when they're angry enough. So, OK, maybe we need to have anger workshops . . . They do know better, they just choose not to use it.

> 4c. Incremental change will be less likely to produce complex learning (overall problem redefinition).

This related proposition requires more time to be fully assessed. Time will tell, but this does seem to hold true. Even with myriad causes and goals debated publicly, not that much actual systemic change has occurred. Institutions have generally gone along with the dominant problem definition. The incrementalism of the legislative approach, what Lindblom called "disjointed decision-making" and "decision-making through mutual adjustment," has not yet produced complex learning in Colorado in the area of school violence.[4] Gradually, the problem definition may shift as new elements are added to or alter portions of the current expulsion-oriented problem definition.

Yet this slow process and the multiple, sometimes marginal policy changes that occurred over the past four years have led many to feel that enough is enough and that they need to give these changes time to sink in. Thus, a bias toward the revised status quo has been reinforced. In fact, the 1993 changes were perceived to be massive and radical, setting up a huge obstacle to further policy shifts. It may be that future changes in the problem definition and associated policy reforms will have to occur quietly in the Department of Education and at the district and school levels, as large-scale legislative changes would appear unlikely. Such localized, incremental change will be complicated by tough state mandates.

As with the state, this was a difficult hypothesis to assess at the district and school levels due to the limited time period of this study. The most complex learning in the districts appears to have occurred as the result of major personnel changes and restructuring efforts, such as the division of the Denver district into educational and business and operations segments, the reorganization of the departments of Safety and Security and Student Services, and the institutionalization of the Community and School Assistance Teams. The success to date of such efforts in leading to changes in thinking and practice argue for the role of more systemic restructuring efforts in producing learning. On the other hand, incremental change is difficult to measure, particularly when it involves individual perception. It may be that over a much longer period of time than this study was able to evaluate, incremental shifts have occurred that have produced a more comprehensive overall problem redefinition than previously existed in the district. Yet the weight of the experiences assessed in this study seems to indicate that without a focus on problem setting, incrementalism has failed to promote more complex learning.

5. Complex learning may require changing the structure, direction, and mission of an institution itself to make it more open to a problem-setting approach.

In the two main state institutions under discussion, the legislature and the state Department of Education, this was confirmed. For the legislature, the compromise, bargaining, and checks of the legislative process, along with constituent responsiveness, prevented legislators and the governor from considering alternatives, such as those that would go against majority clamors for toughness or that were offered by those on the other side of the aisle. As one senator described in terms of an attempt to pass a related bill, "I've failed two years in a row. It's passed, but then it's failed in the house, for no other reason than I'm from the minority party. They just find another pretense to kill it." The sense of what was in the realm of the possible deterred policy makers from considering and, perhaps, proposing ideas that were projected to fail. And partisan politics and individual legislative personalities, as discussed above, were key elements in considering a bill.

Cooperation and coordination between such agencies as the Department of Education, the Youth Offender System, the Department of Corrections, and the Department of Social Services may be required to achieve significant progress in the area of school violence, but this type of action is not facilitated by the traditional segmentation of agencies and their related turf.[5] The 1996 legislation sought to improve information sharing between agencies. Multiple agency committees have been meeting to facilitate cooperation in the state. However, significant public and legislative barriers remain against sharing information about children, with bills proposed in 1997 that would limit psychological testing of students and public school inquiries about student or parent or guardian beliefs and practices.[6] Furthermore, many of those interviewed continued to perceive this problem as a family, school, criminal justice, or social services issue. Again, we see contrasting and distinctive problem definitions based in various institutional pockets. Integrating these pieces of the problem may require changing institutional structures and norms.

In terms of the Colorado Department of Education, if its structure and mission were to promote overall learning and achievement, then it would seem logical to get the troublemakers out of the schools. However, if the mission was to get every child an education, then perhaps a different policy outlook would prevail. The department was struggling to balance these potentially competing goals and alternatives in 1996. While evaluation processes were built into the department's structure and the notion of trying to pursue "best practices" was ingrained in the department, in terms of the school violence issue, the department had not reconciled the two missions. Nor had it produced a problem definition that encompassed a broader outlook on the school violence issue, one that integrated the notions of safe schools for all students and a positive education experience for every student.

Following on the above, this proposition gained further support through looking at the school districts and some of the Denver schools. District leadership in defining the mission and goals of the districts had great impact in particular areas, such as safety and security and literacy. The lack of such a strong guiding principle on school violence, or at least the lack of coordination on and dissemination of such a mission, hinders a district's learning process in this area overall. In Denver, an administrator defined the problem this way:

> In fact the superintendent has developed a command structure that is very integrated. Support services and the education component, two sides of the house, but I think we're very integrated in terms of collaboration and sharing information, much, much more than it was prior to his arrival . . . A major cultural change [has been] applied. Communicate, collaborate, graduate. But that doesn't mean we always agree.

In the schools, administrators played the role of influencing change in structure, direction, and mission. They were redefining this problem in their schools. There was a melding of the administrators' own previously accepted problem definitions that they brought with them to their new schools and the particular preexisting cultural and environmental context of those schools. As one Denver district administrator put it,

> [Security staff] are supposed to be part of the culture of the school. And every school culture's a little different. [We've] got to make sure that [we've] got people that are compatible and flexible to deal within that school culture. The principal commands the school.

A principal described the change in philosophy he brought to his school and his utilization of the new district Community and School Assistance Team approach:

> When I came in [to this school], I said [to the faculty], "Hey, when I leave home, it's not like I leave home and I go to work. I leave home and I'm coming home because I spend a lot of time here." I think that when people who work in schools can take that concept, then you're going to put more into it. I don't care what hours you put in, those hours that you put in, they're going to be valuable, valuable hours because, see, no matter what child you work with within the seven and a half hours, that child will benefit because once you show them that you really care, violence will curb, achievement will go up, and you will have a harmonious environment. Now, I'm not saying everything here is perfect. This school, if you remember the last couple of years, was in the newspaper front page for excess discipline referrals. Well, with the creation of our CSAT team, we cut referrals by 1,000. We cut the suspensions by what, 280? And that was just in one year . . . And it's mostly due to the CSAT and a *change in philosophy* and teacher buy-in as far as, hey, following the correct procedures and getting teachers to understand that I know that kids can be nerve-wracking at times, but some of the nerve-wracking things that they do is just acting out because they know no other way to get your attention than to act out. So it's a build-up of patience and tolerance and then trying to get the child to understand: this is why you're doing this and now *let's address the real problem.*

However, in both the districts and the schools, it was uncertain whether an institutional process for future complex learning had been established or whether an individual's presentation of a new and perhaps more comprehensive definition of the school violence problem constituted complex learning for the district or school as it then existed. In other words, was it learning just because the problem definition in that institution changed, even though the institutional learning process was not necessarily an ongoing experience and the new individual's problem definition may not have changed at all since that person brought it with him or her?

Reflections on the School Districts and School Violence Problem

Several main themes in this area deserve further discussion. First, funding, resources, and mandates for evaluation are key influences on whether policy and program appraisal takes place and how it contributes to learning. Second, clearinghouse-type activities seem essential for policy and program replication, although replication is difficult to accomplish. Third, implementation at the local level is a strong force in directing policy, programs, and learning. Fourth, higher education needs to be involved in addressing the school violence problem. Fifth, academic success and the violence problem are interrelated, but it is unclear how. Sixth, school violence policies and programs must balance individual rights and community concerns. Seventh, several study biases and limitations were identified that are particularly relevant in this policy area with this type of study. And finally, a suggestion for possible research in this area is proposed.

Evaluation: Funding, Resources, and Mandates

Evaluation is a key element of most of the study propositions, and that is due to its centrality in theories about policy-learning. The general notion is that individuals learn based on their understanding of new information, and that individuals translate that learning into institutional change. This study looked at evaluation as an impetus for problem redefinition. It examined institutional and other barriers to and facilitators of that learning process. A key problem that emerged in the school violence policy area was the lack of much systematic evaluation of relevant programs, regulations, and policies, and hence the lack of use of such information. A central conclusion is that if individuals and institutions are to have even the *opportunity* to learn from better information how to make better policies, then better evaluations need to be done. This study found evidence that individuals who, on their own initiative, read research and attended meetings tended to look at the school violence problem in a more comprehensive manner.

It seems apparent that more funding, staff, and institutional resources need to be devoted to evaluating more types of school violence programs and policies, from security approaches to education approaches to changes in discipline policies. Time needs to be allowed for such interventions to work and for such evaluations to be conducted. The information then needs to be utilized. Where evaluation was mandated, as in specific grant programs, it occurred. However, the resources provided in these cases were still insufficient to meet the criteria suggested above. Even when evaluations were requested, there was no guarantee that individuals would comply adequately with the request or utilize the resulting information. This was particularly true if they were convinced that personal experience was the most valuable source of learning or that every school was inherently unique and different. For example, Denver mandates evaluations through its School Improvement and Accountability (SIAC) process, but they continue not to be completed. State, district, and school people all agreed that there were not enough evaluation resources. They even questioned whether the newly mandated evaluations accompanying the state in-school suspension grants would take place.

Information Sharing

Study participants called for better and more accessible information about school violence. Individuals both explicitly requested the creation of an information clearinghouse for school violence–related programs and described their discovery of such knowledge largely through happenstance, state and national organizational meetings, district in-service trainings, and personal research. In this policy area, there is both too much information, in that it overwhelms the researcher and practitioner, and too little information, in that good studies are difficult to find. This helps to explain the overall lack of effect of information on policy-learning in this area. However, such information clearinghouses as Partnerships against Violence, a federal multiagency program run through the federal Department of Justice and the National School Safety Center in California, do exist.[7] The question is, Why isn't this information reaching practitioners more effectively?

Part of the problem may be time, since those at the district and school level were quick to point out that they had little time to reflect either on personal experience or potential programs. Another issue may be the preestablished problem definition at both the individual and the institutional level. Individuals noted their search for available programs that had resources attached and fit their previously constructed needs assessment for the problem at their school or in the district. They chose from a menu provided by the district, the state, or a granting organization. Money was thus a key influence again, but in the context of choosing a program that fit with a problem definition. Decision makers wanted clearly understandable, readable program materials that explained goals and activities and how the program would fit into their context. As one interviewee noted, program replication is difficult to accomplish.

Again, it is true that how the information is structured and presented to individuals and institutions can greatly affect its eventual impact. The problem definition process is important in simplifying the school violence problem so that it is manageable, while making the problem definition more comprehensive, more accurate, and more integrated. Individuals and institutions can and should strive to achieve this kind of self-aware process, even within the limits of what Simon called bounded rationality.[8]

Implementation

Local control and implementation issues were dominant themes that emerged in the research. The "street-level bureaucrats" in this study included not only district administrators looking at state and federal programs and mandates, but school level administrators and, importantly, teachers in individual classrooms. Local control was a key philosophy in both districts, even though, formally, Denver was more site-based. Yet in some ways, the informal notions of teacher control in the class and principal control in the school were just as strong in determining program adoption and success. One respondent argued that any program was effective so long as a motivated and committed individual adopted it, promoted it, and developed it over time. Without that individual, programs would be significantly less successful. While the institutionalization of a problem definition has powerful effects, as discussed further below, top-level administrators cannot forget the importance of program and policy implementation and the inability of higher policy levels to move too quickly against district- and school-level opinion.

Higher Education

For a more comprehensive problem definition in this area to evolve over time, it seems that teachers and administrators, as well as legislators and community members, will have to learn over time, through experience and training, about wider elements of the problem. For this to be accomplished, a piece that seems lacking in the established problem definition, and one that this research had not yet considered, needs to be joined to the debate and to reform efforts. That is the role that higher education plays in educating teachers and administrators.

A more obvious role for higher education is in its research capacity, and in its need to present more usable information to policy makers and practitioners. But the role of teacher-training institutions and administrative and management programs in educating teachers, future assistant principals and principals, district-level administrators, and board members—and some individuals in this study fit all or most of those categories at one time or another—is essential in presenting the most current and comprehensive information and approaches. More time needs to be devoted to training these individuals in classroom management techniques, behavioral interventions, conflict resolution, safety and security practices, discipline law, and violence prevention alternatives, as well as working with agencies outside the school, utilizing available research, and applying for grants. This should help to prepare educators to deal with the problem more comprehensively and to learn over time.

Academic Success and Violence

It is becoming increasingly difficult for educators at all levels to doubt the relevance of violence, discipline, disruption, and safety issues to the education process, and to societal problems writ large. The national education goals, state educational standards, and district mission statements all connect the school violence problem to learning. Violence inhibits the learning process for the majority of nonviolent kids. However, violence also destroys the learning process for those students who are violent themselves. And, more importantly, it may be the failure of the learning process itself that promotes student violence and disruptive behavior. In other words, this is yet another paradoxical, chicken-and-egg situation in this problem.

Many respondents discussed this issue in some detail. Some argued that students had to be removed from school if they prevented others from learning; others argued that students were disruptive because for various reasons they were unable to succeed academically; some supported both positions. Students were said to fail academically for any number of reasons, including family dysfunction, poverty, family mobility, learning disabilities, behavioral disorders, personality, and ethnic, racial, or cultural differences and conflicts. Academic failure and learning problems seemed then to compound on one another over time, getting progressively worse as a student moved through grades and eventually leading that student to act out in one way or another. This was largely due to the fact that the student had little interest in school or in class because she or he could not understand the lessons, perhaps could not read or write, and tended to act out to cover up her or his lack of academic ability.

Thus, academic achievement and school violence are related, but the connections between the two are complex and not easily untangled. Some of the same causes of learning failure contribute to violent behavior. It may be a downward spiral where the two pathologies reinforce one another. These connections were made explicitly by some of those interviewed and implicitly by others. They would seem to suggest that integrating school violence prevention, intervention, and rehabilitation approaches with more purely academic efforts would be a positive way to deal with issues that the same students may be facing in both areas.

Individual and Community

The treatment and removal of violent or disruptive children from school raises many issues of individual and community rights, including the right of the individual to an education and the right of the community to safety. Yet both the disruptive student and the well-behaved student have a right to be educated. And the community has a right to be free of undue government interference, as well as a right to be safe and secure. In talking with people in the districts, schools, and the state, these conflicts were continually apparent. Some minority respondents represented a civil rights–oriented perspective, advocating the use of consistent laws and rules to prevent ethnic and racial discrimination. Other individuals and district policies stressed the right of all students to a safe learning environment. The difficulty lay in determining what to do with those who violated the rules and were thus inconsistent with creating and maintaining such an environment. Decisions had to be made in light of the public's and policy makers' hesitancy to pour money into alternative educational environments for these students.

Additionally, many of the tough law-and-order and control mechanisms now being put into place across the states and schools raise concerns about the intrusiveness of the state into people's lives. Security cameras, locker searches, information databases and sharing of discipline-related personal information, strict disciplinary policies and mandatory consequences, gang membership lists, and community or school-oriented policing are all frightening in some ways, in the sense that they get into the lives of students and families before an event has occurred, creating strong norms of obedience to the control of authority. School uniforms, prohibited student apparel, expulsion for a calendar year, these all slowly chip away at the gains students and families have made, for better or worse, in securing their rights to privacy, equal access, and protection from abuse. Due process procedures appear to be entrenched and gaining strength for students and families, but mandatory penalties take away the discretion of administrators, and appeals are useless unless procedures are followed incorrectly.

This is a controversial area, and I raise these issues here because they were raised by members of the study. Balance and conflicts between individual and community rights represent a consistent thread that runs throughout many of the problem definitions portrayed in the interviews and in state, district, and school laws, policies, and codes. It is an issue that deserves attention when considering school violence policy approaches, problem definitions, and the directions in which individuals and institutions are learning over time.

Study Biases and Limitations

As with any study, this one has its biases and limitations. In addition to those that are generally associated with case study and comparative case study approaches and qualitative interview data, this particular policy area revealed some contextual issues that need to be considered. General questions associated with a *collective* and *instrumental* case study approach such as this one include the ability to generalize from results obtained from one or several cases and the importance of choosing appropriate cases for consideration.[9] A study such as this focuses on interpretation of large amounts of qualitative data, some gained through semistructured interviews, some through a scaled opinion survey, and some through examination of policy reports, news accounts, memos, laws, policy manuals, and public relations materials. This raises questions of interviewer subjectivity and bias, as well as such credibility issues as transparency, coherence of themes, consistency of individuals, consistency across cases, and communicability.[10]

These issues are the subject of debate among researchers. It is my opinion that the findings of this study are reliable and consistent and that they represent in large part the themes, processes, and problem definitions under study accurately and comprehensively. The deeper understanding gained through a study such as this in a few contexts compensates for the smaller overall scope of the research. The goal of this study was not generalization across all cases or times. As such, this study aims only to offer a source for reflection for other school districts, states, and scholars, so that they can determine according to other contexts and theoretical approaches whether the information contained here helps them approach this and other policy problems.

That said, there is at least one specific study bias related to this particular problem area that was raised by study participants and should be addressed. It was suggested that the time of the school year was important in determining how well students were behaving. There was disagreement on this, with some administrators arguing that the beginning of the year was worse because students had not gotten into their usual routine and others pointing out that the end of the year was worse because students wanted to get out of school by late spring. In either case, the fact that the interviews for this study were conducted between the summer vacation and the end of the fall semester could have biased the comments of interviewees who were reacting either to the previous spring's events or the past fall's relative quiet, or vice versa. Data were not examined that would confirm that violence rates rose or fell significantly during the course of the school year.

Finally, another more general research issue concerns the analysis and composition of the study once the data have been collected. I have found it difficult in writing up the findings to balance the desire for truth and comprehensiveness in reporting and interpretation with the goal of protecting confidentiality and not making people look bad. A summary of the original research study was sent to all participants, and a full copy was available on request, in order to inform respondents and perhaps lead to improved decision-making in the state, districts, and schools. This helps to keep the author on target, support honesty and attention to evidence, and promote balance in assessing the data as a whole, due to the fact that in the back of the researcher's mind, he or she knows that any one of the people interviewed could be reading anything that is being written. This factuality and the reflective process of feeding the study back to participants have their benefits, but the bottom line is that the researcher, once through with the study, moves on, while the participants must live with the legacy of the work once it is reintroduced into their environment. Thus, I attempted to strike a balance, attempting to say what I felt needed to be said, protecting confidentiality as much as possible, and keeping in mind a regard for the impact of the writing.

Future Research

There are many possible directions that future research on school violence can and should take. Particular policies and program interventions need to be evaluated using control groups over time in a systematic, comparative manner. States need to be compared in terms of the impact of state discipline legislation on school violence and youth violence overall. School violence problem definitions need to be compared to other research on state and local political culture to examine the role that values and beliefs play in policy formulation.

A more specific study of school violence policy could attempt to track the effects of laws and policies on school and youth violence and incident levels as well as on student attitudes toward violent behavior. One of the claims of those who are strongly against expulsion as a means of resolving the school violence problem is that expulsion only serves to shift the problem into communities and makes expelled students more likely to get involved in the justice and prison systems. There is little data that would be good enough for such a study today. It would be worthwhile to measure baseline levels of youth violence and incidents and where those incidents occurred in multiple school districts, cities, or states before or immediately upon the passage of a particular discipline law. Similar data could then be gathered over time. The places where incidents occurred could be examined in order to determine whether tough school discipline legislation, such as that in Colorado, was pushing violence out of the schools and into the community. Useful supplements to such a study would be the tracking over time of expelled students to see where they went; some of this is being done by such groups as the Colorado Foundation for Families and Children. Surveys with students would also help to measure the impact of such policies on their behavior and attitudes over time.

Reflections on Education Policy

My research raised some interesting broader education policy issues in addition to the specific school violence–related themes. These include the decline of the school district and the insufficiencies of decentralization. Both patterns have ramifications for thinking about education policy as a whole, as well as about some specific education reform approaches.

Decline of the School District

One of the most curious implications of the focus on school violence policy for educational institutions is the general atrophy of the school district. While still playing a central role in budgeting, operational issues such as transportation and buildings management, and setting out policy parameters, the districts appeared caught between apparently conflicting trends. On the one hand, through site-based management, school-based accountability and decision-making committees, intra-district school choice programs, and the flexibility allowed to school administrators to choose their own alternative programs, the districts were devolving power and responsibility to the local school level. On the other hand, through increasing state and federal mandates and grant programs, the districts were losing control of policy-making to the state and federal governments. In the middle, with decreasing funds available for programming, less leeway in the face of legal constraints, and increasing demands for site-level control, the districts were losing their centrality.

In some cases, the state was going directly to the schools with programs and funding. The federal government was doing this as well, sometimes through coordinated grant programs such as Safe and Drug-Free Schools and Communities. Site-level administrators described the district as interpreting state law and setting out overall parameters, but also talked about the lack of district influence on what they did in their schools.

An interesting argument that could be explored is that the lack of professionalization of school boards limits their effectiveness and influence over both schools and district administrators. Like many school boards, the two examined in these cases were volunteer. They consisted of both educators, parents, and businesspeople. Since most had regular full-time jobs, their sometimes forty hours or more each week of board service meant a great deal of extra work for them. This impacted their time and attention given to district issues. This lack of a professionalized school board had significant impact on the ability of the community's representatives to reflect deeply on district issues and learn over time. It would be useful to think about school board members in light of arguments concerning the professionalization of state legislatures to see if this body of work sheds light on school district policy-making institutions, and even local school governance structures. Similarly, it would be interesting to examine problem redefinition based on personnel change in relation to the election of new school board members or the hiring of new administrators.

This is not to argue that the districts were or are totally irrelevant or will disappear any time soon. It is to say that they might be becoming less important over time. A comprehensive study of education policy issues needs to take into account the school, district, state, and even federal levels and the dynamic relationships between them in order to fully capture the complexities of various policy issues as they play out in specific contexts. The district appears to be more and more a mediating structure or set of institutions which supports schools, by interpreting state law and standards and providing funding and information, but leaving many optional programs and additional efforts up to the sites.

Decentralization

An important argument throughout this study has been the inadequacy of decentralization as it has been implemented in these contexts for promoting learning and the effective use of resources. It should be noted that decentralization arguments also include such goals as community involvement through closer connections to empowered schools and parents. Apart from that general notion, which was the subject of some debate in the interviews, decentralization, as represented in a number of the study propositions, is argued to promote experimentation, more effective programming, and better learning. What emerged in the study was the realization that the decentralization argument is largely incomplete as it is represented by scholars, educational institutions, and the public.

Decentralization is not enough. To accomplish more complex learning, educational institutions need to make more of a concerted effort to gather, process, integrate, and disseminate information about programs, policies, and individual site practices. The process needs to include reflection on success and failure and sharing of that wisdom with other sites and districts. Study participants argued that decentralization led to poor evaluation and slower learning. Partly, this was due to resource constraints, but clearly it was also due to a general lack of concerted effort to bring decentralized components back together to finish the process of learning. Site experimentation can be fruitful, but it can also reinvent wheels. There is no way for schools, districts, and states to know which process is occurring unless they are closely involved with one another in openly reflecting on what is happening at each level.

Thus, this study provides further evidence that it may be necessary to rethink some of the arguments in favor of decentralization, in light of the issues raised by a focus on policy-learning and problem definition. As Dryzek puts it, "Governmental decentralization proves no more compelling than privatization as a means for promoting efficiency and accountability."[11] Additional processes and resources appear essential for effective integration of and learning from the lessons produced in a decentralized system.

Reflections on Problem Definition and Policy-learning

The theoretical arguments put forward in this study revolved around the idea that institutional learning about public policy issues really is a process of defining and redefining policy problems in a more comprehensive, accurate, and integrative way. More complex learning involves problem redefinition over time in understandings of goals, trends, causes, predictions, and policy alternatives related to a particular problem. It involves accurate information and assumptions and the integration of fragmented pieces of a problem into a more systematic whole. Conceptually, this was a very useful approach to examining a particular policy problem in varied contexts. It allowed for the structuring of information gathering and reflection in such a way as to help clarify and comprehend a large amount of data on a complex problem. Theoretically and in practice, a number of issues surfaced related to this theoretical approach. These include the difficulties involved in assessing the changes in problem definitions; the importance of the institutionalization of problem definitions; the conception of change as learning or just following mandates; the consideration of learning in terms of policies, programs, or practices; and the notion that complex learning may consist of joining multiple problem definitions in an institution.

Difficulties in Assessing Problem Definition Change

There were a number of difficulties that I encountered in attempting to assess changes in problem definitions over time, or learning. First, this change was hard to measure. Questions structured on Lasswell's five "problem orientation categories," as identified above, were effective in eliciting a more complete sense of an individual's problem definition, and somewhat less so an institution's approach to the problem.[12] Questions were asked about change but were less successful in assessing whether, how much, and in which areas a person's problem definition had shifted over time. Even more difficult was determining what caused changes for individuals, although a number of factors, such as crisis events and personnel change, were identified as important, particularly in the institutional context.

Secondly, individuals for the most part lacked personal awareness of their own problem definition and so had difficulty discussing it. Interpretation was essential here, as was looking at such words as "paradigm," "philosophy," "culture," and "tone," which people used to describe their own, other people's, and institutional problem definitions. But this longitudinal, retrospective approach was sometimes misleading or unclear. For example, one individual referred a great deal to approaches that were "in vogue twenty-five to thirty years ago." In actuality, it seemed that most of the things that he was referring to were in vogue about forty years ago.

Assessing problem definition changes and then integrating them across individuals and institutions was difficult, though not impossible. More work could be done using content analysis or other systematic qualitative data analysis approaches to see whether a more quantifiable result could be obtained in this area. The presence of policy-learning, in general and in particular instances, was determined by assessing the comments of interviewees and district policy and program changes in a broadly interpretive manner. Overall, the conceptual framework of problem definition change was useful in this way for understanding how approaches to this policy problem had evolved more generally over time.

Institutionalization of Problem Definition

One of the most salient elements of a problem definition was its institutionalization in law, policy, or regulations. Achieving that kind of formal institutionalization gave a problem definition increased weight and influence over subsequent decisions and lower-level procedures. It was difficult to change institutionalized problem definitions that in many ways took on what March and Olsen refer to as institutional characteristics, defining norms and rules of behavior, both formally and informally.[13]

For example, at the federal level, the Safe and Drug-Free Schools and Communities program formally connects substance abuse and violence. It did not do so in the past, even though many criminologists and practitioners held that belief. In Colorado, for example, CDE was using SDFSC money to fund violence prevention before the federal law changed. Nevertheless, when the language of the federal law was altered to include "safe," it formally connected safety and drug use and institutionalized that problem definition. Preventing one pathology would help prevent the other. Approaches in one area could learn something from approaches in the other. This problem definition trickled down to the states, and then to the districts, and then to the schools, in the form of informational seminars projecting that problem definition and grant requirements structured explicitly around it. A similar dynamic was at work with Colorado's safe-schools legislation, one that institutionalized the concept of mandatory expulsion for certain offenses to protect the safety of the majority. It was also there in the national education goal that connected violence and learning.

These kinds of institutionalized problem definitions were not immune to change. But they became entrenched in such a way that they promoted rules and practices that set into the structure of state, district, and school institutions a particular view of the problem, a view divorced from any particular individual. Thus, it became an institutional problem definition that was more than just the sum of individual problem definitions at any one time. And learning became changing that institutional problem definition, which was not easy, given the bias of institutions to the status quo and the exhaustion of people after the passage of new pieces of legislation and the policy and regulatory changes that accompanied them.

Learning versus Following

This concept leads to another critical view of the learning concept. If an individual or an institution follows a mandate from a higher authoritative or institutional level, is that learning, or is it just obedience? For example, when school districts in 1993 and 1996 wrote policies and regulations to conform with state legal mandates on school discipline, were they learning, or was their adherence to, conformity with, and alignment with these laws, as many people put it, just following orders? In other words, the change shown in the district may have represented changes in several problem orientation categories, or more complex learning. But it was not necessarily cognitive change based on an agreement with what would be the correct approach to the problem. The problem definition changed institutionally, and individuals and schools would now have to comply with those changes, but they were not necessarily learning per se. Were they reassessing their goals? Their understanding of the causes of school violence? The merits and drawbacks of policy solutions? In most cases, I would say that they were not. Yet change was occurring. This is a difficulty with the learning concept. Dominant problem definitions can be forced on people and institutions, leading to change but no real reflection on the problem.

Policy-learning versus Programs and Practices

Another conceptual difficulty is the differentiation between policy-learning and learning about effective programs and practices. The problem definition construct identifies policy alternatives as one of its five elements, and within policy alternatives are policies, programs, regulations, procedures, and so forth. Policy-learning in this study was viewed as change in most of the five categories, including alternatives, which would include policies and programs. Yet most evaluation and discussion of effectiveness and information took place on a programmatic rather than a policy level. In other words, policies, such as "three strikes and you're out" discipline legislation codified in the district's student conduct and discipline policy, were written. Within that, various programs were designed to deal with alternatives to expulsion, or violence prevention. Procedures and regulations were written by the administration to govern how discipline was to be administered.

The difficulty is that policy-learning encompasses all of these elements, and they are ill-defined and not well differentiated in the literature. They are really different levels of action and orientation with a problem area. A study of learning could focus on all or only one of them. From the problem definition perspective, even focusing on all of these policy and programmatic levels is simple learning if one focuses only on each level as an alternative solution rather than taking into account goals, trends, conditions, and projections involved in each. Thus, it is important in studies of policy-learning to clarify the levels on which one is concentrating in order to clarify the policy process more fully.

Complex Learning Joining Multiple Problem Definitions

Assessing institutional learning and changes in institutional problem definitions involved a complex understanding of large and fragmented institutions. The relationships between individual and institutional problem definitions were difficult to determine. Multiple problem definitions existed among individuals and parts of institutions, with individual problem definitions often influenced by personal experiences and roles in the institution. These problem definitions were sometimes competing and conflicting but more often were complementary and not mutually exclusive.

Institutions are themselves aggregations of individual problem definitions in terms of both current occupants of offices and roles and the historical legacy of formal and informal policies, rules, and procedures that have been established by previous tenants. Pockets of learning and pockets of stasis, represented by both individuals and groups, can be identified within institutions. I would argue that one way in which institutions learn is through the active and explicit joining of pockets of learning.

The decentralized institution must take advantage of the creativity, innovation, and local support that are encouraged by the devolution of responsibility and control. This institution must complete the learning cycle by joining lower-level problem definitions and learning experiences. Furthermore, it must reflect overall learning back down to these levels to share lessons throughout the organization. The segmented institution must take advantage of the specialized approaches and attention to particular parts of a policy problem, parts which are fostered by the identification of particular needs and areas of expertise. This institution must complete the learning cycle by integrating the pieces of a policy problem with an overall set of goals in mind, all of which are subject to revision.

Thus, one way to resolve the quandary of determining an overall institutional problem definition, say in a school district, and to assess learning and change in that problem definition would be to join these multiple problem definitions to form one larger, comprehensive problem definition. This definition would be more than the sum of its parts. It would be a more abstract or intangible concept, the institutional problem definition.

The district, for example, could be imagined to be like an octopus whose tentacles are various departments, programs, rules, policies, and individuals, each with its own problem definition. Separately, these definitions often appear incomplete, capturing one part of the problem from one particular perspective. Joined together, they may represent a more comprehensive definition of the problem evolving over time and perhaps more complex learning. What this book has argued is that there needs to be more of a concerted effort on the part of the institutional leadership to define a mission in this problem area which joins these various parts explicitly and improves communication and coordination among them. In some areas in the districts and the state this was happening, but it was not occurring to much of an extent in the area of school violence. What is required is a problem-setting perspective in a broader sense in order to improve the ability of those individuals and parts of the district to see that their problem definitions can be complementary in a way that sets a more comprehensive definition of the problem overall. Thus, the most valued problem definition, one that results from complex learning, is comprehensive, based on accurate information from a variety of sources, and integrative across institutional boundaries.

Recommendations for Improving Complex Institutional Learning

This study has touched on numerous stories of learning failures, learning successes, and partial successes. Table 16 illustrates a set of recommendations for education practitioners, including administrators, teachers, principals, board members, and parents, who wish to maximize learning in their school, school system, or organization.

Conclusions: Pockets of Learning in Fragmented Institutions

This study has argued that pockets of learning exist in institutions that are fragmented, both vertically and horizontally, to such an extent that they do not facilitate the joining of these pockets into a larger, more comprehensive problem definition. This fragmentation is symbolized and perpetuated by the distinguishing of elements of the school violence problem, itself an element of such larger social problems as poverty, youth violence, the prevalence of guns, dysfunctional families, and so forth, into particular pieces. These pieces are labeled and assigned to particular missions, such as safety and security, student services, special education, crisis team, discipline policy, hearing officer, gang task force, and alternative education. As Edelman argues,

> We establish separate departments of government to deal with these supposedly distinct problems . . . and staff them with people trained to focus upon a particular set of symptoms and to believe in a distinctive set of causes for each of them. Such a classification evokes beliefs and perceptions that we normally accept uncritically, precisely because they are generated subtly by the terms used to designate them. The classification scheme implies, first, that these various problems are distinct from one another, with different causes, just as they have separate symptoms . . . When we name and classify a problem, we unconsciously establish the status and the roles of those involved with it, including their self-conceptions . . . How the problem is named involves alternative scenarios, each with its own facts, value judgments, and emotions.[14]

While not fully agreeing with Edelman's argument that the real underlying causes of all these related social problems are economic, I would suggest that the school violence problem within institutions such as school districts suffers from this institutional specialization problem, whereby the pockets of learning that exist are prevented from being joined in a more holistic, systems-oriented problem definition that defies the institutionalized fragmentation. Our experience with institutions may suggest that they are only capable of simple, incremental learning, that this is what the American legislative and administrative process is all about. Yet we can and should expect more from our institutions. While Lindblom argues that through the incrementalist process, "the problem confronting the decision maker is continually redefined," incrementalism has been criticized for being tied to the status quo and for lacking conceptual guidelines for making decisions.[15] Problem definitions are devices through which the integration of various pieces of complex social problems helps institutions to overcome limits on their rationality. A problem definition perspective as discussed here helps institutions overcome their reliance on past programs and procedures. It provides them with conceptual tools that they can use to more successfully address complex policy problems.

Table 16

Recommendations for Improving Institutional Learning

---

1. *Adopt a problem-setting perspective.* Focus on defining problems in a comprehensive manner, integrating multiple pieces of the problem, linking pockets of learning, and maintaining a broad view of the issues at hand.

2. *Improve inter-institutional and intra-institutional cooperation and coordination.* Include multiple agencies and departments in both formal and informal processes of definition of and action on recognized and shared problems.

3. *Find, fund, produce, and deliver accurate and useful information.* Resources and mandates for evaluation and information sharing over an extended period of time are essential for learning lessons from the past and from other people and places.

4. *Train people to read available research, reflect on their and others' experiences, and act according to their knowledge.* Institutionalize these processes through higher education programs, membership in national and state organizations, grant opportunities, and organizational retreats.

5. *Take the lead in defining the problem and sustain your involvement.* As a superintendent, principal, teacher, parent, or board member, you can prove indispensable in leading and promoting changes in problem definition and successes in programs over time. The problem definitions of institutional leaders matter. You can change your school or school system.

Perhaps one of the impediments to such an integration of the various components of the school violence problem is the resistance shown by both individuals and institutions to change and to information sharing. Problem definitions were enshrined in law and institutional policy or cognitively based on personal experience and training. Individuals and organizations resisted new ideas that did not fit within their conceptualization of the problem. Institutional compartmentalization, devolution, and standardization made information sharing and learning difficult.

This study has illustrated the complexity of the problem definition and policy-learning processes in actual institutional contexts. It has raised questions as to the ability of these institutions to engage in complex learning over time. It has taken the problem definition focus as part of the definition of the problem itself, thus directing its course of study at understanding how views of the school violence problem are constructed. My own value bias is toward a more comprehensive definition of the school violence problem in order to improve decision-making and thus reduce violence and improve the willingness and ability of children to act nonviolently.

Thus, this study approached complex learning as comprehensive change in the problem definition. It did not specify in what direction that change should take place, but only that it should occur across the problem orientation categories. But it must be acknowledged that I proceeded with a particular direction in mind, that being a fuller assessment of educational violence prevention solutions and a joining of multiple strategies for violence prevention with discipline policy, safety and security, and family and community involvement approaches. There is an assumption that a more comprehensive problem redefinition will go in this direction, which is not punitive or preventive, but both, and more. This assumption is based on an assessment and integration of the existing literature on school violence. I believe that schools should be more than just holding places for kids to keep them out of trouble in the community, whether in regular or alternative schools. Schools should proactively teach kids how to live without violence. Improving the ways in which educational institutions approach problems will help them to accomplish this goal.

Afterword
Life after Columbine

Sometimes events occur that are so tragic, so shocking that they become symbols, ensconced in our collective and individual memories as permament representations of our own perception of a particular issue. Such is Columbine. I have been saddened and amazed in the months since April 1999 when two Colorado students entered Columbine High School, a school of some eighteen hundred students in a middle-class suburb of Denver, and proceeded to kill their classmates and themselves. I have been saddened that such awful multiple murders and suicides occured and amazed at the extent to which the events of that day have galvanized the nation and the world and have taken on the mantel of "the violence that can happen anywhere."

I will not go into the details of the Columbine events here since they were summarized by the media in minute focus elsewhere.[1] Already observers have written of the lives of the two boys who turned into killers, of their victims, their legacy. They have looked for answers to the "why" of Columbine and have concentrated largely on the "how." They have portrayed Columbine as a symbol of our times, of what is wrong with America's youth and culture, and, as with most crises, called for action. What is most astounding in all of this is the level to which "Columbine," as a symbol, has been so dissociated from the details of its origin. Much like "Watergate" came over time to represent abuse of government, scandal, and the dangers of the cover-up, the word itself losing connections to the "Watergate Hotel break-in" from whence it came, "the violence at Columbine High School in Littleton, Colorado," has quite simply and quickly become "Columbine."[2] Enough said.

That such a word already has such power attests to the speed with which dramatic news travels in this age and the preexisting susceptibility of people to interest in the issues of crime and violence. The reactions to Columbine in Colorado, nationally, and around the globe are reminiscent of Colorado's earlier reactions to violence in the state, as discussed in chapter 3. Now, more than ever, this has become a national and international phenomenon whereby we see the crystallization of this horrified sentiment and the process of media sensationalization of live tragedy. Columbine. We have all, already, become familiar with the pictures of students, hands on their heads, rushing out of the building, so symbolic of Anytown High School, or falling out of a window, bloody, over and over again. And the CNN theme song and graphic were composed and recorded before parents were even notified.

In Colorado, a call for a state-wide meeting turns into a fight between the governor and his lieutenant governor because the assembly is scheduled during the week of the traditional African American celebration of Juneteenth. Nationally, we see an immediate push for gun control legislation, which, for the most part, fizzles. And later in Washington, the Million Mom March continues to insist on legislative action. Locally, and in every state, there is introspection. Can it happen here? How did it happen there? It must have been the parents, zero tolerance, expulsion.

I hope that readers of this book will have learned to take a more critical perspective on Columbine, and on the school violence problem as a whole. And I hope that they will see the path toward deconstructing some of the competing problem definitions that are being offered up as explanations, for each definition carries its own preferred solutions: gun control; parental-responsibility laws; tougher sentencing for first-time juvenile offenders; tolerance-building programs; money for counselors in schools; money for police in schools. The list goes on.

Track the progress of analysis, and one will see the construction of the problem. As Karr-Morse would predict, the media have begun to look for answers in the very earliest experiences of the perpetrators and in their upbringing. Look to their roots, and in the biological, social-developmental perspective, we can see "why they did it." But these were good kids from good homes, were they not? So we do not seem to find any meaningful answers there. There are strong arguments being made in general about the need for early childhood and parental education, but those policies would not have made a difference with these boys.[3]

We do see that the boys who perpetrated the crime, Harris in particular, sent some signals that could have been picked up and treated more successfully. But they were, right? They went through a juvenile diversion program with very positive reviews and seemed to be making a fresh start. They were not failing classes. Dylan Klebold went to the prom. Yes, when one gets into the details, over time, we will perhaps pull out specific decisions and contacts, or lack thereof, which, with hindsight, will lead professionals to say, "We could have worked better with all of the parents concerned." Or, "We, the juvenile justice community, and the police community could have worked better with the school and the school counseling staff to make sure that we were following these kids more closely once they had completed their community service." Or, "We, the parents, and we, the school, could have read those websites, searched those rooms and that garage, listened to concerned friends and their parents, and found that Dyan and Eric were two very angry, alienated, and potentially violent kids."

But now, families of Columbine victims and victims of other serious incidents of school violence and their communities are looking for someone to blame, some explanation of *why*, and some means to cause someone or some agency to take action so that this will not happen again to other families, to other students. Who or what is to blame? Other parents, gun manufacturers, the media, the schools, the police, someone.[4] In the case of Columbine, this trend has already split the victims' families, with some actively pursuing suits against the parents of the shooters, themselves suffering the suicides of their sons. Devastated by the shooting of her child, the mother of one Columbine victim recently took her own life. The president of the American Federation of Teachers advises parents to "SNOOP!" in addition to advocating for gun control, school counseling, and deemphasizing violent products in the media.[5]

Yet we are informed that in a survey of some one thousand children in grades three through twelve, 61 percent of Dads and 66 percent of Moms were graded an "A" or a "B" for "Knowing what goes on with me," while 22.5 percent of Dads and 19 percent of Moms received a "D" or an "F" on this factor. Overall, this survey shows the large majority of parents being there for their kids and doing the right thing. Only 10 percent of kids wished their mothers would spend more time with them, and 15.5 percent said the same about their fathers. Quality time is as important to kids as ever, but the author of the survey asks us to improve both "focused" and "hang-around" times with our children.[6] So most parents are doing a good job, but it is clear that there is an ever-present disconnection between kids and their parents.

We can blame other parents only to the point at which "their" children become "our" children, at which time we see that almost any child or adolescent is capable of keeping secrets, acting out, fighting, carrying a weapon, being suspended or expelled, or worse. A recent survey of two thousand young men and women, the GenY2K Report, found that of those aged sixteen to nineteen, 41 percent "say there are people they want to get even with," and 43 percent "say they sometimes are pushed too far and feel they will explode." The authors of this study argue that "controlling parents may be to blame for kids' volatility. 'Most people assume that teens who exhibit . . . violent tendencies are the result of hands-off parenting,' Nickles says. 'In the population we studied the opposite is the case.' Says Ashcraft, 'Overscheduled, pressured children are an emotional powder keg.'"[7]

And we know that much violence originates and is modeled in the home. Coming from a social-developmental perspective, Rhodes, for example, argues that violence incubates in the family domain, a sector until recently off-limits to public examination. Children reared with violence are at significantly more risk of initiating violence themselves.[8] So much for snooping.

And we as a society are starting to recognize the connections between homicide and suicide, or interpersonal and intrapersonal violence. We must see that many of the recent violent school events were instances of both. In Colorado, Klebold and Harris made it clear in a videotaped confession filmed just prior to their attack, that they did not intend to come out alive. They also argued that they acted without anyone else's assistance or knowledge, particularly that of the young man who provided them with one of their most powerful firearms and who was sentenced to six years in prison. Many victims' families used the occasion of his sentencing hearing to lay blame on him for facilitating the violence and to ask for a stiff sentence to act as a future deterrent to such abetting of juvenile crimes.[9] Blame. Catharsis. Few answers.

Looking back at the suicide and homicide statistics in Colorado in chapter 3, we see that suicide has been a consistently significant problem there for many years and that it rivals homicide in terms of magnitude and impact. Colorado has one of the highest suicide rates in the country. U.S. surgeon general David Satcher recently announced that he will focus on suicide prevention as a major public health issue, pointing to connections between suicide and gun prevalence and other significant trends. In 1997, for example, guns were used in 17,566 suicides, compared with 13,522 homicides, according to the National Vital Statistics Report. There were 30,232 suicides overall in America in 1989, 31,284 in 1995, and 29,264 in

1998. The suicide rate for black youths aged ten to nineteen, traditionally lower than that for white youths, more than doubled since 1980 to 4.5 per 100,000 in 1995 from 2.1 per 100,000 in 1980.[10] In a recent comparative study, we find that the U.S. suicide rate of 13 per 100,000 is higher than that of the European Union's average of 11.9 per 100,000 but lower than that of some northern european nations, such as Switzerland (20.1), Sweden (14.2), and Finland (26.3).[11]

I think that every American community can attest to the impact and prevalence of suicides in their midst, whether connected to aggressive homicidal behavior or carried out in horrific public and private ways. In wealthy Fairfield County, Connecticut, at least two youths recently chose to make powerful statements by killing themselves in ways that ensured that people noticed. One high-achieving, well-regarded athlete and student drank gasoline and set himself on fire at home in the middle of the night. He gave no reason. Another young man hung himself at Darien High School from a climbing rope in the wrestling room. It is a fine line indeed that distinguishes these acts from those in Colorado, Oregon, Arkansas, or Mississippi. Guns provide some of the answer, in their role as enablers of mass violence. But all these acts have largely taken place in caring school communities under the watchful eyes of averagely involved parents. Thus is the power of Columbine: the seeming normality of Littleton's middle class, largely white community. Herein lies the feeling that "if it could happen there . . . ."

At Columbine in the fall after the violence there were new wariness, new security measures, including bomb-sniffing dogs, and traumatic memories.[12] There are still disagreements over what to do with the library, scene of so much terror, and what lessons to learn. At other schools around the country there have been bomb threats, violence scares, expulsions, and copycat incidents (in Cleveland, in Atlanta, in Newark).[13] And everywhere are references in the media and in the minds and statements of educators, police, journalists, all of us, to Columbine and what it symbolizes. It seems that security measures, as expected, given the conclusions of this book, have taken first place, with physical, environmental, and order-control-expulsion problem definitions taking hold. A recent summary of the fall's back-to-school measures included surveillance cameras, computerized I.D. cards, caller I.D. devices, metal detectors, uniformed officers, disaster drills, and backpack bans.[14]

One might call this last measure "backpack reform," where book bags are banned, ordered to be see-through to avoid concealment of weapons, or deemed unnecessary when schools dismantle lockers and provide or require two sets of books—one for home and one for school—so as to avoid the need for students to have a means to carry books to and fro. Combined with the surge in popularity of school uniforms, to avoid cliques, trenchcoats, gang paraphernalia, and so forth, the removal of lockers and backpacks further minimizes students' private space at school and emphasizes the importance of community safety over individual rights.

A recent cartoon captured the changed atmosphere succinctly. Two young children return to the school hallway to find a "Welcome Back, Kids" banner, underneath which are four doors, each with a name plate on it: Teachers' lounge, SWAT lounge, Grief Counselors' lounge, Media lounge.[15] As never before, Columbine has kept the issue of school violence just under the surface of the American consciousness. On the CBS *Sixty Minutes* news program (March 5, 2000), a lead story entitled "The Columbine Effect" focused not on Columbine, but on the efforts of Alabama to ban a habitually disruptive, emotionally disabled boy from the state's public schools. The conflict was evident between the rights of the majority to a safe school environment and the right of the individual to a free public education. The symbol and lessons of Columbine were lurking beneath the surface: remove the deviant, potentially harmful students from school before they really hurt somebody.

With national attention being focused on school shootings and, by them, on youth violence in general, President Clinton announced $100 million in grants for programs that work to prevent violence as part of the federal "Safe Schools/Healthy Schools Initiative."[16] And, "spurred by the deadly rampage at Columbine High School, the Federal Bureau of Alcohol, Tobacco and Firearms is working with a threat-evaluation company to develop a computer information program to help administrators spot troubled students who might be near the brink of violence."[17] The so-called Mosaic-2000 program will attempt to prevent violence by profiling potentially dangerous students in order to predict their chances of causing harm. While based on developmental knowledge, this is still mainly a security-oriented approach.

As James Q. Wilson summarized just after Columbine (it is interesting to note that he referred then to "Littleton, Colo.," and not to Columbine, the symbol not being quite determined or established yet), the incident led all of us to "repeat our favorite remedies for eliminating violence," among them reducing violence in the media, controlling guns, putting armed guards and metal detectors in the schools, and reducing cliques in the schools. Columbine also led him to repeat his own, less "fashionable" remedies, including promoting parental accountability and principles of good citizenship in the schools (molding character, providing good counseling, and identifying those "social loners" and others displaying symptoms that could hint at violence). Wilson argues for money to experiment with solutions and then closes with two of his personal, immediate favorite solutions: establishing dress codes to avoid cliques around dress and ceasing to tell schools "that they cannot teach about religious alternatives to modish culture."[18]

We each have our own problem definitions and preferred strategies, and Wilson has his, particularly his emphasis on these last two policies. But overall, Wilson tried immediately after Columbine to place the incident in context and to argue for an expanded, more comprehensive view of the school violence problem and for experimentation to find some right solutions. As James Garbarino, among others, has argued, there is no one right solution to a problem with multiple causes, and working on risk factors and sustaining resilience is the best strategy we have available. He has argued that the alienated Klebold and Harris developed a secret life, relying on each other and on violence to gain acceptance and identity.[19]

I think that those are the lessons I would emphasize from my perspective on Columbine. Violence can happen anywhere, and we cannot accurately predict precisely where or when. And violence will happen somewhere, despite our best efforts to prevent it. But we must go beyond the easy solutions, the reactionary and politically oriented stances. As more of the public demands more comprehensive, accurate, and integrated definitions of this and other complex social policy problems, our politicians and policy makers will have to respond with more effective solutions. As we locally search for better information and evaluate what is and is not working for us in our schools, districts, and states, we can share our lessons with one another and with policy makers and funding agencies. We need to acknowledge that school violence is all of our problem. Victims' families, as is so often the case, are leading us with an excellent example. We see it with counselors and family members from

Springfield, West Paducah, and Jonesboro assisting families in Colorado and demanding action. In Britain, after the Dunblane school massacre, handguns were banned throughout the country. Brazil, reacting to high rates of firearm violence, banned the sale of firearms, and the Brazilian President is hoping to completely ban the possession of arms across the country.[20] The public health approach to violence prevention is catching on in America. Anything is possible.

Appendix A
Interview Questionnaire

I. Interviewer Introduction

I am interested in understanding how individuals within school districts, and these districts as a whole, perceive the school violence problem, and how they have dealt with this issue. I am interested in your recollection of how the district has defined the school violence problem, what the school district has done in the area of school violence policy-making, if these policies have changed over time, and, if so, why? I must advise you that you have the right to withdraw your consent or discontinue participating at any time, and all the information that you provide will be kept confidential.

II. Overall Individual Problem Definition

I'd like to start by asking you about your personal views on school violence, discipline, and safety:

1. How do you see the school violence problem?

2. Has your perception of the school violence problem changed over time? How and why?

3. In your view, has violence gotten worse in the district in the past decade? If so, how?
a. What gives you that impression?
b. How do you find out about violence in the district?

4. What do you think are the causes of school violence in the district?
a. What led you to identify these factors as causing the problem?

5. How do you think the nature of the school violence problem will change in the future in the district?
a. How have your expectations about the future nature of school violence changed over time (since you first joined the school board; since you began working in the district; since you became a principal; etc.)?

6. What do you think should be the goals of a school violence policy?
a. Have these goals changed for you?

7. What do you think should be done about school violence? What would be some effective policy solutions to the school violence problem? Why?

III. Overall District Problem Definition

Shifting the focus away from your personal views, now I would like to ask you about the *school district's* policies on school violence, discipline, and safety:

1. Overall, how does the district approach the issue of school violence?
a. Are there particular school violence, safety, or discipline policies in place or under discussion?
b. To summarize, could you list the three most prominent school violence policies now under discussion in the district?

2. What are the goals of the district's school violence policies?

3. What is the district's understanding about the extent and nature of school violence in the district?
a. How does the district keep track of how much violence there is? Are there particular sources or indicators of which you are aware?

4. What does the district see as the causes of school violence?

5. Does the district expect the problem to get worse or get better in the future? Why?

IV. Learning

Now I'd like to focus on changes in the school district's school violence, safety, and disciplinary policies over time:

1. Have there been changes in school violence, safety, and disciplinary policies in the district over the past decade or so? How, when, and why have they changed?
a. What would cause the current policies to change in the next few years?
b. How would you characterize the evolution or development of school violence policies in the district?
c. To summarize, could you briefly list the three most important changes in district school violence policy in the past decade?
d. Could you list the three most important causes of change in these district policies?

2. How have the district's experiences with school violence affected your thinking about the issue?

3. Are you aware of ways in which the district was able to use its own past experiences and programs as a guide for future policy-making in the area of school violence?
a. Are there evaluations or monitoring arrangements that you know of for school violence policies in place?
b. How effective are they?

4. Are you aware of the district utilizing pilot programs at selected schools to test out new policy strategies?
a. Do you know if pilot programs have been used in the area of school violence?
b. How are these programs evaluated?
c. What happens to the evaluation information?

5. Does the district use information about school violence policies from other districts, this state, other states, or the federal government to make policy decisions?
b. What kind of information?
a. How does the district get this information?

6. Are you aware of any specific policy reports about school violence, reports that have played a role in changing district school violence policies?
a. If so, where did these reports come from?
b. How did the district obtain them?
c. What did they say?

7. How does the district know when a school violence policy is not working?
a. What has the district done, or what would the district do when confronted with such a situation?

8. Do you think that the district has learned over time to make more effective school violence policies? How and why?

V. Decentralization and Governance

We talked about the district's changes (or lack thereof) in school violence policy-making over time. Now I'd like to talk about the institutional structure of the district as it affects the policy process:

1. Who makes school violence policies in the district?
a. How did they come by that power or responsibility?
b. To summarize, could you list the three most important players involved in changes in district school violence policies?

2. Is there anything about how the district is organized that you think may have helped or hindered the learning process in relation to school violence policy-making?

3. Are there particular individuals or groups who have brought about changes in district policy-making in the school violence area?
a. Would you characterize these groups or individuals as insiders or outsiders in terms of their role in the district decision-making process?
b. Could you characterize the general approaches to school violence, discipline, and safety policies of some of these individuals or groups?

4. How centralized or decentralized is the school district?

a. Are there some areas in which the district actually moves decision-making control and authority to local schools? How so?

5. Do you think that this decentralization in the district, or lack thereof, has affected the ability to make effective school violence policies? How and why or why not?
a. Can you give me an example that comes to mind?

6. If you could do one thing to change how the district handles school violence, what would you do? Why isn't the district doing that?

VI. Conclusion

As we wrap up our discussion, I want to make sure that you have had an opportunity to mention everything that you feel is relevant, that I might have missed.

1. Is there anything that I've left out? Any questions that I should have asked to better understand the problem?

2. Are there other people with whom I should talk?

3. If you don't mind, I'd like to get some demographic information from you and also make sure that I have your position in or relationship to the district correct.

Appendix B
School Violence Survey

Please respond to the following statements of opinion by circling a number from –5 ("I disagree strongly") to +5 ("I agree strongly"), with 0 indicating that you are neutral or have no opinion about the statement:

1. Principals should expel any student who is caught with a weapon.

2. Expelling a student who is caught with a gun will not change that student's behavior.

3. Mandatory student expulsion will act as a deterrent toward future student gun possession in school.

4. The school system needs alternatives to suspending and expelling teens who get caught with guns and knives.

5. Conflict resolution programs that teach students how to solve problems amicably should be implemented at all school levels.

6. Violence prevention curricula are not helpful in reducing aggressive behavior by high school students.

7. The lack of a strong school disciplinary structure contributes to student violence.

8. Disruptive students should be sent to separate education programs within the district.

9. Students should be trained as "peer mediators" to help their classmates solve problems.

10. Public authorities are unable to control violence in our society or our schools.

Notes

Chapter 1

1. Note: Parts of the research and writing of this chapter were supported by the Education Commission of the States under a grant from the Metropolitan Life Foundation.

2. O'Neill, "An Overview of Promising Violence Reduction Strategies."

3. Department of Education, *America 2000 Communities.*

4. National Education Goals Panel, *The National Education Goals Report,* xvii. It is noteworthy that violence- and drug-free schools has made the short list of national education goals since its inception, revealing the level of concern about this issue in the country.

5. I. M. Harris, "From World Peace to Peace in the 'Hood."

6. L. Harris, *Metropolitan Life Survey of the American Teacher, 1993,* 113.

7. McCart, ed., *Kids and Violence.*

8. R. D. Stephens, *Congressional Testimony.*

9. Kadel and Follman, *Reducing School Violence,* 61–62.

10. "Saving Youth from Violence," 3.

11. Bastian and Taylor, *School Crime,* 1.

12. National School Boards Association, *Violence in the Schools,* 5.

13. The Harris poll found that 14 percent of all teachers felt that violence was a factor in teachers' decisions to leave their school. This number increased to 29 percent for teachers in schools with all or many minority students, and to 25 percent for teachers in schools with all or many lower income students. L. Harris, *Metropolitan Life Survey of the American Teacher, 1993.*

14. Kadel and Follman, *Reducing School Violence,* 19.

15. R. D. Stephens, *Congressional Testimony.*

16. L. Harris, *Metropolitan Life Survey of the American Teacher, 1993,* 8.

17. The preceding narrative section closely follows news articles as reported

in the *New York Times Index* from the year 1954, January through December. It remains true to the language of the time as closely as possible.

18.   In prior years, articles dealing with similar subjects may have been indexed under other headings, such as "Crime—Teenage Gangs" or "Education and Schools—Handicapped and Problem Students." This is illustrated by the 1954 narrative. The large number of articles in 1992 and 1993 could show the rise of a particular problem label, or even definition, i.e., that of "school violence," as well as an increase in actual violent incidents.

19.   "New York's Schools," *Economist*, Nov. 30, 1996, 26.

20.   See Fischhoff et al., *Acceptable Risk*, on the subjective construction of risk.

21.   "Crime Puzzle," *Denver Post*, May 15, 1994, 21A, 24A.

22.   Brownstein, "The Media."

23.   Furlong and Morrison, "Introduction to Miniseries," 141.

24.   Additionally, from 1992 to 1993, crime news reported on the three major television networks doubled and the coverage of murders tripled, according to a survey conducted by the Center for Media and Public Affairs in Washington, D.C. "Crime Puzzle," *Denver Post*, May 15, 1994, 21A, 24A.

25.   Thomas, "Our 'Subculture of Violence,'" 37.

26.   See Innes, *Knowledge and Public Policy*, on faulty crime indicators; Cochran, *Grandma Moses*, on the distortion of data; Greenberg, *The Cost-Benefit Analysis of Imprisonment*, on measuring the results of incarceration; *Economist*, Oct. 15, 1994, on similar problems in other countries; Reiss and Roth, eds., *Understanding and Preventing Violence*, for an overview of crime and violence reporting issues.

27.   Reiss and Roth, eds., *Understanding and Preventing Violence*, 3–5. Aggravated assaults are "those with weapons or causing serious nonfatal injury," 3. Aggravated assaults constituted 61 percent of all reported violent crimes in 1995 (FBI, *Uniform Crime Report*).

28.   Bender, "Crime Rate Dips," 2A; FBI, *Uniform Crime Report*.

29.   Elliott, "Youth Violence."

30. Butterfield, "Violent Crime Falls," 3A.

31. Furlong and Morrison, "Introduction to Miniseries," 141 (italics in original).

32. Reese, "*Reefer Madness* and *A Clockwork Orange*," 355.

33. Ibid., 356.

34. Ibid., 355–361.

35. National School Boards Association (NSBA), *Violence in the Schools*, 3–5. It is unclear to what extent school board opinions/responses were based on actual district data.

36. Reiss and Roth, *Understanding and Preventing Violence*, 57.

37. NSBA, *Violence in the Schools*, 3.

38. Center to Prevent Handgun Violence, *Caught in the Crossfire*, 1; Furlong and Morrison, "Introduction to Miniseries," 145.

39. Cole, "Guns and Violence," 103–107.

40. Mickish and Hinish, "Family Violence: An Overview," 71–77.

41. Gilbert, "Child Deaths."

42. National Education Goals Panel, *The National Education Goals Report*, 56–59.

43. L. Harris, *Metropolitan Life Survey of the American Teacher, 1993*; L. Harris, *Metropolitan Life Survey of the American Teacher, 1994*; Furlong and Morrison, "Introduction to Miniseries"; National School Boards Association (NSBA), *Violence in the Schools*; National Education Goals Panel, *The National Education Goals Report*; National School Safety Center, *School Crime and Violence*.

44. See Jenkins-Smith, "Analytical Debates and Policy Learning."

45. National School Safety Center, *School Crime and Violence*. The problem of improvements in reporting measures leading to higher incidence levels remains relevant here, however.

46. See Rochefort and Cobb, *The Politics of Problem Definition*.

47. Toby, "The Schools."

48. Schools have blamed parents for a lack of supervision that contributes to violent behavior, and the parents have called for strict punishment for student aggressors in order to protect the majority of nonviolent youth in the school. About half of all students with poor grades in the Harris poll felt that their parents spent hardly any or no time talking to them about schoolwork or taking part in school activities. This is consistent with other findings concerning the relationship between parental involvement in learning and academic achievement. Thirty-six percent of students with poor grades (as opposed to 13 percent of all students) reported that they had carried a weapon to school (see table 2). L. Harris, *Metropolitan Life Survey of the American Teacher, 1993,* 6, 91. Thus the parents who should be the most concerned about their child's safety and actions may be the least concerned of all, while those parents who spend the most time with their children may be the most involved in the school violence dialogue with the schools. This may negatively affect the policies adopted to counteract violence by overbalancing the interests of the majority of nonviolent students against those aggressive students who need the most help. There may be a causal relationship between parental involvement in their child's education and both academic achievement and dangerous behavior on the part of that student. Additionally, there may be a causal relationship between academic achievement and dangerous behavior, with academic failure or difficulties in learning promoting disruptive or violent behavior.

49. L. Harris, *Metropolitan Life Survey of the American Teacher, 1993,* 8.

50. See Reese, "*Reefer Madness* and *A Clockwork Orange*"; Sedlak et al., *Selling Students Short*; Johnson and Johnson, *Reducing School Violence*; Wilson, "*The Truly Disadvantaged* Revisited"; Myrdal, *An American Dilemma*.

51. Reiss and Roth, *Understanding and Preventing Violence.*

52. Ibid., 102.

53. Ibid., 20.

54. Hawkins and Catalano, Jr., *Communities That Care*; Hawkins et al., "Effects of a Skills Training Intervention;" Hawkins et al., "Childhood Predictors."

55. Morrison, Furlong, and Morrison, "School Violence to School Safety," 242–243. For more on risk factors, protective factors, and fostering resiliency in children, see Benson, *The Troubled Journey*; Bernard, *Fostering Resiliency in Kids.*

56. Reiss and Roth, *Understanding and Preventing Violence,* 103–115.

57.   Ibid., 115–129.

58.   Karr-Morse and Wiley, *Ghosts from the Nursery.*

59.   Reiss and Roth, *Understanding and Preventing Violence*, 129–147.

60.   Ibid., 133–138.

61.   Ibid., 147–149.

62.   Ibid., 370.

63.   As with most school violence studies, the National Institute of Education report studied "disruptive behavior," from talking to vandalism and violence. Reiss and Roth, *Understanding and Preventing Violence*, 155; National Institute of Education, *Violent Schools—Safe Schools*; National Institute of Education, *School Crime and Disruption.*

64.   Toby, "The Schools," 150.

65.   Guggenheim Foundation, *1993 Report*, 21.

66.   Morrison, Furlong, and Morrison, "School Violence to School Safety," 243.

67.   Reiss and Roth, *Understanding and Preventing Violence*, 156.

68.   Ibid., 156.

69.   Elliott et al., *Violence in American Schools.*

70.   Elliott, *Youth Violence*, 1.

71.   *Chronicle of Higher Education Almanac,* Aug. 29, 1997, 5.

72.   Bureau of the Census, *Current Population Reports*, 17–18.

73.   Bennett et al., *Body Count*, 1996.

74.   Reese, "*Reefer Madness* and *A Clockwork Orange*," 361–369.

75.   Prothrow-Stith, *Deadly Consequences*; Prothrow-Stith et al., "The Violence Prevention Project."

76.   Reiss and Roth, *Understanding and Preventing Violence*, 107–109, 125–127.

77.   Kadel and Follman, *Reducing School Violence*, 14.

78.   Reiss and Roth, *Understanding and Preventing Violence*, 148–149.

79.   Ibid., 150–151.

80.   See Quarles, "School Violence"; Toby, *Violence in School*; Wallis and Ford, *Crime Prevention*.

81.   Toby, "The Schools."

82.   On a deeper level, one could argue that these policies and the individuals who promote them attempt to further certain worldviews and notions of what is right. These include views on proper student conduct, punishment for deviant behavior, and the immorality of violence. From a more cynical standpoint, one could suggest that politicians and administrators seek power and money through certain policies. The "tough on crime" approach, applied to the schools, harvests votes and legislative support. Those who provide "safe schools" fill them with the children of concerned parents, while those who maintain dangerous schools lose pupils and the revenue that follows them from the state. Principals and district administrators who oversee violent schools could also lose their jobs and, in order to be seen as doing something, may be quick to act in an authoritative fashion. School institutions themselves may seek to protect their interests from challenges by students and community groups. Thus, they may choose to pursue policies that serve the institution rather than the students.

83.   Hess, "Massive 20-Year Crime Crackdown"; Baker and Dexter, "Crisis in Crime"; Methvin, "The Dirty Little Secret."

84.   Reiss and Roth, *Understanding and Preventing Violence*, 6.

85.   Elliott, *Youth Violence*.

86.   Tolan and Guerra, *What Works*.

87.   Ibid., 92–93.

88.   Ibid., 92–93.

89.   Reiss and Roth, *Understanding and Preventing Violence*, 108–109.

90.   Ibid., 148–149.

91.   Toby, "The Schools."

92. Kadel and Follman, *Reducing School Violence*, 14.

93. Elliott et al., *Violence in American Schools*, 379–386.

94. Colorado School Mediation Project, *Conflict Resolution in the Schools*; Metis Associates, Inc., *The Resolving Conflict Creatively Program*; Prothrow-Stith, *Deadly Consequences*, 191; I. M. Harris, "Teachers' Response to Conflict."

95. National Association for Mediation in Education, *The Fourth R.*

96. Ibid.; Lam, J., "Evaluating the Program." Research report. Amherst, MA, National Association for Mediation in Education, 1992.

97. Ibid.

98. Ibid.

99. See Leeuw et al., *Can Governments Learn?*

100. Education Commission of the States, *Clearinghouse Notes: Violence.*

101. Posner, "Research Raises Troubling Questions," 3.

102. Ibid., 38.

103. Florida Department of Education et al., *Final Report on Guiding Principles.*

104. Education Commission of the States, *Youth Violence: A Policymakers' Guide*, 6.

105. *The Washington Post,* Sept. 2, 1990.

106. *The New York Times,* Dec. 26, 1990, Education section.

107. Greene, "Viewpoints on School Violence"; Greene, "Redefining School Violence." See also Toby, "The Schools"; Prothrow-Stith, *Deadly Consequences*; R. D. Stephens, *Congressional Testimony*; Quarles, *School Violence.*

108. Woodson similarly notes the competing definitions of youth crime in terms of deterrence versus addressing root causes, and the relationship of these foci to the discussion of policy solutions (Woodson, *A Summons to Life*, 1–2).

109. Rose, *Lesson Drawing in Public Policy.*

Chapter 2

1. Weiss, "The Powers of Problem Definition"; Rochefort and Cobb, *The Politics of Problem Definition.*

2. Lasswell, *A Pre-view of Policy Sciences,* 56.

3. Thus, problem definition in this sense is explicitly empirical, contextual, and oriented toward resolving discrepancies between goal values and reality. The various elements of the Lasswellian framework, including the social process, decision process, and, particularly, the problem-orientation tasks, impact problem definition by expanding the analyst's perspective. The analyst can continually refer to the value categories and policy tasks that Lasswell identifies in order to revisit and modify the problem definition: "A contextual map . . . is an indispensable preliminary to the examination of any particular problem. The map does not, however, supply the answers. It provides a guide to the explorations that are necessary if specific issues are to be creatively dealt with." Lasswell, *A Pre-view of Policy Sciences,* 39.

4. Lasswell, *A Pre-view of Policy Sciences,* 40. Decision makers discover and define their own problems as well. They also play the role of symbol manipulators, using symbols, in this case in a problem-defining role, for both public solidarity-building and exploitation (Brunner, "Review of Murray Edelman"; cf. Lippmann, "The World Outside").

5. Simon, *Models of Man,* argues that the analyst and the practitioner are boundedly rational; and, in simplifying problems and being affected by social and psychological factors, the analyst misconstrues reality or is not capable of capturing it all. Brunner, "Global Climate Change," calls this the "common problem" of policy analysis.

6. Dery, *Problem Definition,* 4.

7. Dery's approach is again explicitly empirical and oriented toward innovation in terms of intervention to solve a problem. As a process, "[P]roblem definition here is viewed as stage setting which creates or defines certain activities as solutions; it may thus be likened to the perspective of a legislator, rather than a judge, with regard to the system of laws." Dery, *Problem Definition,* 6.

8. Dery argues against a simplistic notion of problem definition that looks to identify goals first and then discrepancies between a fixed "ought" and what currently "is." "This leads one to believe that a problem is defined by merely presenting the discrepancy." Dery, *Problem Definition,* 7. It is clear that although Lasswell begins with a discrepancy premise, his framework points to goal clarification, inclusion of missing values, and

an overall process of reconciliation among definitions. Goals are not "fixed." As he says, "Values change more by the unconscious redefinition of meaning than by rational analysis." Lasswell, *Psychopathology and Politics*, 201. Schön, "Generative Metaphor," argues that frame, or problem definition, conflicts center not on facts, but on values and beliefs. Wildavsky, "Choosing Preferences," argues that definitions of risk are subjective, and are the product of cultural influences on individuals.

9.   Dery, *Problem Definition*, 9.

10.   See Brunner, "Case-Wise Policy," on "case-wise" policy information versus data based on individual variables. He shows how the use of the less contextually based, less comprehensive variable-wise data results in the perpetuation of policy problems in the area of poverty. This argument shows that the *type* of data used may influence problem definition and thus policy action and outcomes.

11.   See Milburn, *Persuasion and Politics*, on schemas; Edner, "Intergovernmental Policy Development," on policy substance; Edelman, *Political Language*, on categorization; Schön, "Generative Metaphor," on generative metaphors; and Baumgartner and Jones, *Agendas and Instability*, on policy images.

12.   See Saussois and Laroche, "The Politics of Labeling"; Weiss, "The Powers of Problem Definition"; Dunn, *Public Policy Analysis*; Heclo, "Ideas, Interests, and Institutions."

13.   See March, "Theories of Choice;" Evans et al., *Bringing the State Back In*, Saussois and Laroche, "The Politics of Labeling"; Fischhoff et al., *Acceptable Risk*.

14.   Saussois and Laroche, "The Politics of Labeling," 105.

15.   Weiss, "The Powers of Problem Definition," 98. Advocates for competing problem definitions use symbols that have different weights depending on the political context but that serve as useful devices to generate public opinion and change problem definitions. Symbols remain latent in our culture when not in use, but the "complexity and cyclicity" of social and political dynamics "present frequent openings for defining and redefining problems." Weiss, "The Powers of Problem Definition," 110. These "openings" sound much like Kingdon's "windows of opportunity" (Kingdon, *Agendas*) for policy change.

16.   Weiss, "The Powers of Problem Definition," 98.

17.   Weiss explicitly relates problem definition to, but differentiates it from,

Kingdon's *Agendas*, agenda setting, as problem definition is concerned with how people think about issues while Kingdon focuses primarily on how problems come to public attention. However, Weiss notes that problem definition may play a part in getting an issue on the agenda. Weiss, "The Powers of Problem Definition," 118. This is what Lasswell, *A Pre-view of Policy Sciences*, would refer to as the promotion function in the policy process. Additionally, Weiss integrates the notion of policy entrepreneurs as actors in problem definition, just as they are agenda-setters for Kingdon. Further examples of advocacy definition include Mackinnon, "Pornography," in the realm of pornography; Moe, "The 'Reinventing Government' Exercise," in the realm of institutional reform; Oberman, "Sex," who looks at the problems of pregnant women who use drugs; Edelman, *Political Language*, on the poverty debate; Pickel, "Authoritarianism," on economic transformation to market economies in Eastern Europe; and Fineman, "Images," on single motherhood.

18.   See Dery, *Problem Definition*; March, "Theories of Choice."

19.   Roe, *Narrative Policy Analysis*, 2.

20.   See Rochefort and Cobb, *The Politics of Problem Definition*.

21.   Lasswell et al., *The Comparative Study of Symbols*, 11.

22.   Baumgartner and Jones, *Agendas and Instability*, 16.

23.   McCoy identifies the "most prevalent definition of learning" as "a cognitive change involving changes in beliefs and perceptions." McCoy, "Political Learning," 3.

24.   Learning processes are discussed in a number of distinct yet associated bodies of literature. These include social or policy learning; political learning; institutional or organizational learning; and innovation and diffusion. These literatures focus on policy change and improvement; how political values and perspectives change; organizational development and adaptation; and the creation, spread, and adoption of new technological, political, and policy ideas, respectively. There are numerous commonalities among these various branches of research, as well as several variables that distinguish the focus of the analysis and the emphasis on a particular aspect of learning. On social or policy learning, see Etheredge, *Can Governments Learn?*; Jenkins-Smith and Sabatier, "The Study of Public Policy Processes." On political learning, see McCoy, "Political Learning"; Adler and Haas, "Conclusion: Epistemic Communities." On institutional or organizational learning, see March and Olsen, *Rediscovering Institutions*. On innovation and diffusion, see Rogers, *Diffusion of Innovations*; Rose, *Lesson Drawing*.

25. McCoy, "Political Learning," 5.

26. See P. M. Haas, "Introduction: Epistemic Communities," on the former, and March and Olsen, *Rediscovering Institutions*, on the latter.

27. See McCoy, "Political Learning"; and Nye, "Nuclear Learning," on the former; and Levitt and March, "Organizational Learning"; and Leeuw, Rist, and Sonnichsen, *Can Governments Learn?* on the latter.

28. McCoy, "Political Learning," 3.

29. See March and Olsen, *Rediscovering Institutions*, 170.

30. Ibid., 59. March and Olsen identify six basic perspectives on institutional change, two of which fit this type of learning. What they call "variation and selection" is an evolutionary model wherein actors carrying out regular "[d]uties, obligations, and roles match a set of rules to a situation by criteria of appropriateness." Evolution over time produces rule-based learning. Secondly, "problem solving" involves actors applying a decision rule and comparing alternative choices in terms of expected outcomes based on prior established goals. This model involves intendedly rational choice. It is also representative of the incrementalist theory of decision making, "muddling through," or "satisficing." Ibid., 59. See Lindblom, *The Intelligence of Democracy*; and Simon, *Reason in Human Affairs*. Satisficing can be defined as "a decision-making process in which individuals or organizations reach a decision that is satisfactory and that provides benefits that meet the decisionmaker's situational needs . . . [This process] requires the decisionmaker to settle for less than the total outcome of a decision but to also be satisfied with the less-than-total product." Simon, *Models of Man*, in Kruschke and Jackson, *The Public Policy Dictionary*, 66. As Simon argues, "Reconciling points of view becomes somewhat easier if we adopt a *satisficing* point of view: if we look for *good enough* solutions, rather than insisting that only the best solutions will do." Simon, *Reason in Human Affairs*, 85. As Kruschke and Jackson point out, "[a]s a model of decision making, satisfycing [*sic*] allows the decisionmaker to achieve his or her main goals without involving comprehensive problem analysis or perfect information." Kruschke and Jackson, *The Public Policy Dictionary*, 66.

31. March and Olsen, *Rediscovering Institutions*, 59. March and Olsen's four additional perspectives on institutional change identify some of these sources of learning. In terms of experience, there is disagreement among scholars as to the role that success and failure play in learning. Success can lead to a "competency trap," where inferior procedures are improved and furthered due to initial performance success rather than replaced by better procedures overall. McCoy, "Political Learning," 8. See Levitt and March, "Organizational Learning"; March, "Theories of Choice"; and March and

Olsen, *Rediscovering Institutions*, 63. However, success can also lead to experimentation from a position of secure confidence. The stresses produced by failure may produce continued attachment to current policies rather than change. March and Olsen, *Rediscovering Institutions*, 60.

32. March and Olsen, *Rediscovering Institutions*, 59. Familiar here are pluralist theories of group competition and advocacy coalition and entrepreneurial roles in policy making. See Dahl, *Who Governs?*; Sabatier and Jenkins-Smith, *Policy Change and Learning*; and Kingdon, *Agendas*.

33. Rose, *Lesson Drawing*, 122, 25. "Contagion" learning borrows from an epidemiological model. It involves policy changes spreading from one institution to another. Here, ". . . variations in contact and in the attractiveness of the behaviors or beliefs being imitated affect the rate and pattern of spread." March and Olsen, *Rediscovering Institutions*, 59. This type of learning involves innovation in one context, and diffusion of that innovation to other institutions. See Rogers, *Diffusion of Innovations*; Walker, "The Diffusion of Innovations"; and E. B. Haas, *When Knowledge Is Power*. March and Olsen's sixth basic perspective on institutional change is "turnover" learning. This is a "regeneration" model, which can occur passively through general change in institutional personnel over time or intentionally through an institutional search for new leadership and ideas. March and Olsen, *Rediscovering Institutions*, 59. Here, new actors within institutions bring fresh perspectives on rules, norms, roles, and problems and thus may provoke learning in their new context.

34. For example, P. M. Haas, "Introduction: Epistemic Communities," and Adler and P. M. Haas, "Conclusion: Epistemic Communities," argue that in a situation of uncertainty, actors look for solutions and rely on "epistemic communities," groups of experts sharing consensual knowledge about a certain issue, what Kuhn, *The Structure of Scientific Revolutions*, might call paradigms, for guidance and solutions.

35. Roe, *Narrative Policy Analysis*, 2–3, italics in original. Roe presents narrative policy analysis, examining the stories that actors use to define a particular policy problem as a means of making sense of uncertain policy issues from an analytic standpoint. However, he argues that policy uncertainty is a *hindrance* to learning: "The preconditions for successful policymaking—low environmental uncertainty, stability in goals and objectives, institutional memory, and redundant resources—are also the preconditions for 'learning better from experience.'" Ibid., 35. Roe characterizes in simple terms a "learning process approach" as "trial and error" and advises practitioners and analysts not to focus on improving the learning process as such, but to make the best use of available policy narratives to construct policy "blueprints." Ibid., 34–35.

36. Lasswell, *The Decision Process*. This information can be utilized for

political or program justification purposes. Cochran, "Grandma Moses." But there are many forms of evaluation, some of which involve direct personal involvement in learning about a program. Variance in the way evaluations are structured affects the utilization of that information by decision makers. Mayne, "Utilizing Evaluation." Personal experience with programs and people and the accumulation of knowledge over the course of years in a field are powerful sources of direct learning experience and may impact learning from indirect experiences. Indirect experience encompasses contagion learning and what Rose refers to as lesson-drawing across space. Lesson-drawing across time could comprise either direct or indirect learning, depending on personal involvement, in the case of individual learning.

37. Hall, "Policy Paradigms," 278. Hall tries to avoid a narrow focus on state institutional actors as the locus for policy change by emphasizing the nexus between state and society. Hall confronts a "prevailing model of social learning as utilized by contemporary theorists of the state," a model that has three central features: policies are principally influenced by previous policies, "policy legacies," or "meaningful reactions to previous policies"; the key agents of policy change are experts within the state or working with the state from inside or elite positions; and the state generally acts autonomously from outside societal pressures. Ibid., 277–278. These parts correspond to third-, second-, and first-order policy changes, where third-order change is more "radical" and "wholesale" learning. Ibid., 279. See Nye, "Nuclear Learning," for distinctions between simple and complex learning, where as learning becomes more complex, it involves changes not only in means, but in underlying goals and priorities. Jenkins-Smith and Sabatier, "The Study of Public Policy Processes," 5–6, make the distinction between "core" and "secondary" beliefs, arguing that "policy-oriented learning" usually involves changes in secondary beliefs only, while changes among core public policy beliefs tend to happen only when one dominant coalition is replaced by another, which is hypothesized to occur as a result of exogenous changes to a system. McCoy suggests that learning can be simple—associated with changing means—or complex—associated with changing values and priorities, McCoy, "Political Learning," 3. Rist uses different terminology to express a similar distinction: "Single-loop learning . . . addresses ways of improving the present state of affairs, while double-loop learning brings about a fundamental reexamination of the condition and the current strategies to address it." Rist, "The Preconditions for Learning," 190. Much of the gray area in the literature involves linking the three dimensions outlined above.

38. See Bemelmans-Videc, Eriksen, and Goldenberg, "Facilitating Organizational Learning"; Vickers, *The Art of Judgment*"; McCoy, "Political Learning"; Nye, "Nuclear Learning"; and Rose, *Lesson Drawing*.

39.   Some authors have taken a step in this direction. Rose offers seven
        hypotheses about the ease of transfer of programs between various policy
        systems, such as local, state, or national governments. Rose's seventh
        hypothesis is most relevant here. He suggests that programs are more
        likely to be transferred to new locations when the values of the program
        and the values of those seeking to adopt a new program are generally
        consistent. Rose, *Lesson Drawing*, 119. Importantly, Rose points out that
        obstacles to program transfer are not static. "Many propositions that are
        true across space are not true across time. . . . In time, programs can
        become easier to transfer without any alteration in their intrinsic
        characteristics, as changes in policy environments remove obstacles."
        Ibid., 143. Over time, programs once deemed unacceptable can become
        valuable lessons as the policy environment within which decision makers
        exist evolves. For example, as national income rises in more countries,
        poor countries may begin to consider adopting European-style social
        programs that now seem prohibitively expensive. Ibid., 144.

40.   Following Rose, when the problem definitions in two locations are more
        compatible, it would be logical that a solution, or lesson, associated with
        a definition in location A would be a likely lesson to be drawn in location
        B. Additionally, as problem definitions evolve over time, solutions that
        are logically associated with those changing definitions could become
        more or less acceptable and viable. Hall's concept of policy paradigms,
        and their evolution over time, also offers connections between policy
        learning and problem definitions. Hall offers an argument that corresponds
        to Kuhn's theory of scientific paradigm shifts. Modeling policy change
        along the paradigm shift model, Hall argues that policy paradigms actually
        consist of ideas, or discourses, embedded in the actual language of politics
        and policy, which govern "not only the goals of policy and the kind of
        instruments that can be used to attain them, but also the very nature of the
        problems they are meant to be addressing." Hall, "Policy Paradigms," 279.
        Although he does not use the exact term, Hall is talking about problem
        definitions, which for him are paradigms governing social learning and
        policy selection. Hall's argument centers on the connection between
        policy paradigms and large-scale, or third-order, policy change. While
        first- and second-order changes can occur within the state and may be
        incremental, "satisficing," or routinized, or even directed toward concerted
        action, third-order change for him arises out of societal and political
        demands, mediated and expanded through the media. Ibid., 280.

41.   Note that Kuhn himself has questioned the transference of the "paradigm"
        concept from the natural sciences to other fields. See Kuhn, *The Structure
        of Scientific Revolutions*, 174ff. However, if not taken too literally, the
        concept seems useful here as a means of thinking about the role of problem
        definitions in structuring understanding about policy problems. Thus, Hall
        focuses on the importance of both political "powering" within society and
        institutions and expert "puzzling" within the state, where ideas, in the

form of policy paradigms, link the two spheres of state and society. Ibid., 289.

42.   McCoy, "Political Learning," 7, italics added. However, it seems that these authors have not directly made the link between policy learning and problem definition. They present in essence an argument that problem definitions impact the learning process in some fashion. Etheredge, *Can Governments Learn?*, offers another link between problem definition and policy-learning processes. In characterizing American foreign policy decision making as "dual-track," including both rational analysis and "imagination-derived thinking about power relationships," he shows how the latter channel strongly influences individual perceptions and definitions of foreign policy issues. This is an individual, subjective component in issue analysis and produces competing problem assessments and an overall decision environment that creates institutional "blockages" to learning. One can extend Etheredge's argument to view his second, subjective channel as the individual and group problem definition process. Etheredge's suggestions for honesty, integrity, and a critical posture toward the imagined world in order to improve decision making may then be transferred to the problem definition process overall, a process that Etheredge is limited in defining and explicating.

43.   See Hall, "Policy Paradigms," on policy paradigms. This view is not a radical departure from current directions in the literature on problem definition or policy learning. Jenkins-Smith and Sabatier, for example, emphasize "that policy evolution often involves multiple cycles. These are initiated by actors at different levels of government as various formulations of problems and solutions are conceived, partially tested, and reformulated." Jenkins-Smith and Sabatier argue that "policy elites" push these "formulations" in an institutionally complex and changing broader policy environment. Jenkins-Smith and Sabatier, "The Study of Public Policy Processes," 3. One can say that these actors are learning over time and that their conceptions of problems and their solutions involve problem definition processes. Rochefort and Cobb, *The Politics of Problem Definition*, from the problem definition perspective, identify myriad factors that impact problem definition over time. According to them, such elements as causal understandings, the level of severity attached to a problem, the novelty of an issue, and the complexity of an issue as defined affect the willingness and ability of actors to resolve problems. One could say, then, that these elements of the problem definition process impact the ability of actors and systems as a whole to learn over time how to better handle these problems, and how to redefine them so that they are more manageable. In another example of similar concepts that are used in both sets of literatures, Rochefort and Cobb discuss "problem ownership" as presented by Gusfield, *The Culture of Public Problems*. They argue that a "community of operatives" may own a problem if "the paradigm of explanation shaping policy development

goes without serious challenge, or when the challengers are effectively kept on the sidelines in the decisionmaking process." Hilgartner and Bosk, "The Rise and Fall of Social Problems," 14. The parallels to "epistemic communities," "issue networks," "advocacy coalitions," and so forth are clear.

44. Lasswell, *A Pre-view of Policy Sciences*.

45. The ability of actors and the institutions they occupy to engage in complex learning should not be confused with their ability to achieve "synoptic rationality." See, for example, Lindblom, *The Intelligence of Democracy*.

46. Simon's concept of "bounded rationality" is a more appropriate and applicable notion of individual and institutional ability. Simon, *Models of Man*, and *Reason in Human Affairs*.

47. This view goes beyond Lindblom's conception of incremental learning in a situation of uncertainty as a gradual trial-and-error process of testing alternative solutions. Complex learning does not require universal knowledge, but it does require assessing goals and future projections, for example, in addition to minor policy changes. Some might describe this problem definition approach as "integrative decision making" typical of "comprehensive rationalists" who assume that "goals are discoverable in advance and that 'perfect information is available.'" C. O. Jones, *An Introduction*, 240–241; Frohock, *Public Policy*, in C. O. Jones, *An Introduction*, 30–31. Thus, this approach would be dismissed as unrealistic or impossible in the realm of actual policy-making institutions. However, through integrating Simon's concept of bounded rationality, it is possible to advocate an approach to defining policy problems, one that is comprehensive, accurate, and integrative and evolves over time in real institutional contexts.

48. This is possible even when stipulating that people and institutions are capable of only bounded, not synoptic, rationality.

49. This is adapted from Rose, *Lesson Drawing*, 123.

50. See notes 8 and 9, this chapter.

51. See Geertz, "Thick Description"; Lijphart, "The Comparable-Cases Strategy"; and Stake, *The Art of Case Study Research*.

52. See Eckstein, "Case Study"; A. L. George, "Case Studies"; Lasswell, *A Pre-view of Policy Sciences*; O'Kane, "The Ladder of Abstraction"; Rubin and Rubin, *Qualitative Interviewing*; Schwartz, "Participation"; Skocpol and Somers, "The Uses of Comparative History"; Tilly, *Big Structures*; and

Weber, *The Theory of Social and Economic Organization.*

53. See Education Commission of the States, "A Framework," and Wirt and Kirst, *The Politics of Education.*

54. See Clarke and Hero, "Civic Capacity." Denver is included in a recent study of civic capacity and urban education reform (C. Stone, "School Reform") as well as in a recently started, four-city, two-year peer-mediation evaluation study funded by the Hewlett Foundation, a study that explores one perspective on the school violence issue. T. Jones, "Comprehensive Peer Mediation."

55. It is, according to Elazar's framework of state political cultures, more moralistic than traditionalistic, a characterization that Fitzpatrick and Hero found to correlate strongly with policy innovation. Elazar, *American Federalism*; Fitzpatrick and Hero, "Political Culture."

56. Greene, "Viewpoints on School Violence"; "Redefining School Violence."

57. These include decentralization, standardization, interagency cooperation, accountability, governance, reform, and restructuring. See Sarason, *Barometers of Change*, and *Revisiting "The Culture of the School"*; Fiske, *Smart Schools.*

58. Interviewing began in the Denver school district in June 1996. Thirty-five persons were interviewed in Denver through December 1996. Seven persons were interviewed in Colorado Springs from November through December, and twelve persons at the state level were interviewed from September through December 1996.

59. Lasswell, *A Pre-view of Policy Sciences*, see appendices.

60. Q.S.R.'s NUD*IST (Nonnumerical Unstructured Data Indexing, Searching, and Theory-building) program supports qualitative analysis of unstructured data, such as that from interview text. Text can be searched, indexed, coded, categorized, and edited, allowing for systematic, hierarchical organizing of the text. See Richards and Richards, "Using Computers in Qualitative Analysis"; "The NUD*IST Qualitative Data Analysis System."

61. Medler, "Reconciling the Two Directions of Reform," 9–11; Fiske, *Smart Schools*, 37. Colorado has passed a charter schools law.

62. Medler, "Reconciling the Two Directions of Reform," 11.

Chapter 3

1. Observers of state politics have argued that many factors impact state

policy actions and, particularly, decisions about education. These factors include state political culture; interest group organization and activity and the ethnic and/or racial diversity of the state's population; institutional factors, such as regulatory resources, ideology, and legislative party control; the inherently political nature of the education system; and the "policy environment" of state agencies, including the governor, the legislature, clientele groups, and professional organizations, to name just a few. See Marshal et al., *Culture and Education Policy*; Clarke and Hero, "Civic Capacity"; Fitzpatrick and Hero, "Political Culture;" Teske, "Interests and Institutions"; Kirst, *State, School, and Politics*; and Brudney and Hebert, "State Agencies," respectively.

2. Violence Prevention Advisory Committee et al., *Violence in Colorado*, 178, 175.

3. Ibid., 109.

4. Ibid., 110–111, 179.

5. Colorado Department of Public Safety, *Crime in Colorado*. The criminal homicide rate excludes negligent manslaughter. The assault rate excludes simple assaults. The violent crime rate includes murder, forcible rape, robbery, and aggravated assault.

6. Scanlon, "Juvenile Crime."

7. Johnston, "Youth Jail Proposed."

8. Colorado Department of Education, *Colorado: Results*, 7.

9. Ibid., 11–12, 45.

10. Telephone interview, Dec. 10, 1996.

11. King and Gomez, *Student Discipline and Expulsions*, 6–7.

12. Colorado Department of Education, "State Summary of Pupils Suspended and Expelled"; Colorado Foundation for Families and Children, *Facts Regarding School Expulsion & Suspension*.

13. Trujillo and Aaronson, "A Better Way."

14. Colorado Foundation for Families and Children, *Update on Costs*; Colorado Lawyers Committee, *Fact Sheet—H.B. 1203*; Colorado Lawyers Committee, *Memorandum: Discipline Task Force*.

15. Colorado Foundation for Families and Children, *Facts Regarding School*

Expulsion and Suspension.

16. Colorado Department of Education, "State Summary of Pupils Suspended and Expelled."

17. Bingham, "Policies on Ousting Students Vary."

18. Meier et al., "Black Representation"; Meier and Stewart, "Hispanic Representation."

19. Bingham, "State Sees Links"; Bingham, "State Graduation Rate Plummets."

20. Bingham, "State Sees Links."

21. See, for example, Pappas et al., *Voices from the Heart*; Woodson, *Youth Crime and Urban Policy.*

22. Frank, "State Coffers Brim."

23. Frank, "State Coffers Brim." The Colorado Department of Corrections projects steep growth in the prison population, has not been able to keep up with prison construction to meet demand, and is attempting to contract with private corporations to run some prison facilities (Booth, "State Faces Test"). The state passed a "three-strikes" law, the Super Habitual Criminal Law, in 1994. However, as of September 1996, there were reportedly no convictions under the law (Cannon, "3-Strikes Laws").

24. For a discussion of problems facing urban education, see Rothstein, *Handbook of Schooling.*

25. E. Anderson, "Denver Ranks 7th."

26. Brennan, "Gang Boom on Horizon."

27. Yoder, "Obsession with Crime."

28. Berke, "Crime Propels Rhetoric." See Quinney, *The Problem of Crime*, and Reiman, *The Rich Get Richer*, for critical discussions of the "crime problem" in America.

29. "Crime Fear/Crime Risk Paradox," *Los Angeles Times*, June 26, 1992, 1A; Booth, "Year of Violence."

30. Robinson and Kirksey, "Reported Crime Dives," quote from Professor Walt Copley, Metropolitan State University.

31.   Katz, "Rally against Violence."

32.   Booth, "Year of Violence."

33.   Lipsher, "Violence Fires Legislative Debate."

34.   McCart, ed., *Kids and Violence*, 38.

35.   U.S. Department of Education, *Safe and Drug-Free Schools and Communities Act*, 4–5.

36.   Terrill, "An Executive Summary," 1.

37.   Education Commission of the States, *Clearinghouse Notes: Discipline: Zero Tolerance/Gun Control—Detailed Version*, 1. By August 1996, all states had laws in compliance with the GFSA, with most having met the October 1995 deadline. The Gun-Free School Zones Act of 1990 enacted a federal ban on gun possession within 1,000 feet of schools. The U.S. Supreme Court, in a major decision, held in 1995 that the federal law was unconstitutional since it did not have enough to do with the regulation of interstate commerce to justify federal intervention in the area (Purdum, "Clinton Plans to Get around Ruling"). The Clinton administration proposed the Gun Free School Zones Amendments Act of 1995 in an attempt to circumvent this problem by stipulating that the government had to prove that the gun "moved in or the possession of such firearm otherwise affects interstate or foreign commerce." The White House, "Gun-Free School Zones."

38.   King and Gomez, *Student Discipline and Expulsions*, 1–2.

39.   Education Commission of the States, *Clearinghouse Notes: Discipline: Zero Tolerance/Gun Control—Detailed Version*, 2.

40.   King and Gomez, *Student Discipline and Expulsions*, 2.

41.   Breeskin, *Suspension and Expulsion*.

42.   George, "Armed Kids"; Sebastian, "Boulder High Principal."

43.   See Bingham, "State Graduation Rate Plummets," "Growing Pains," "State Sees Links." By 1996, these approaches included student meetings with instructional specialists as well as a district expulsion officer to obtain conditional return to the district in St. Vrain Valley; Expel School in Durango; an expulsion intervention program focusing on "corrective emotional experiences" in Mesa County; and a homebound computer-based program in Mapleton School District. Colorado Foundation for Families and Children, *What's Being Tried*.

44.   Education Commission of the States, *Youth Violence.*

45.   State of Colorado, "Governor's Expelled Student Task Force Report," 5.

46.   State of Colorado, "Governor's Expelled Student Task Force Report."

47.   Colorado Lawyers Committee, *Colorado Lawyers Committee: 1996 Report.*

48.   Colorado Lawyers Committee, *School Discipline Issues.*

49.   Colorado Lawyers Committee, *Colorado Lawyers Committee: 1996 Report*;
        Colorado Lawyers Committee, *Fact Sheet—H.B. 1203*; Colorado Lawyers
        Committee, *Summary of H.B. 1203.*

50.   Pappas et al., *Voices from the Heart*, 2.

51.   Ibid., 4.

52.   Ibid., 7–8.

53.   Colorado Foundation for Families and Children, *The Financial Costs of
        Failure*; Colorado Foundation for Families and Children, *School
        Expulsions.*

54.   Colorado School Mediation Project, "Violence in the Schools"; Colorado
        Foundation for Families and Children, *What's Being Tried.*

55.   Colorado Foundation for Families and Children, *Working with Suspended
        and Expelled Students.*

56.   Colorado School Mediation Project, "Violence in the Schools"; T. Jones,
        "Comprehensive Peer Mediation Evaluation Project."

57.   Colorado School Mediation Project, "Violence in the Schools."

58.   Carter, *Background.*

59.   Project PAVE, Inc., "1995 Project PAVE Fact Sheet."

60.   Center for the Study and Prevention of Violence, *CSPV Overview and
        Report of Progress*; Center for the Study and Prevention of Violence,
        "Schools and Adolescent Violence Project." See Elliott et al., *Violence in
        American Schools.*

61.   King and Gomez, *Student Discipline and Expulsions*. In addition to King's
        study, this author did a detailed study of school violence in the Boulder

Valley School District in 1993. See Greene, "Viewpoints on School Violence," *School Violence*, "Redefining School Violence."

62. King and Gomez, *Student Discipline and Expulsions*, 4, executive summary; and telephone interview with author, Jan. 23, 1997.

63. Additionally in 1996, a proposed "Parental Rights Amendment" to the Colorado Constitution failed to pass in November. This amendment, sponsored by a number of state and national conservative groups, would have stipulated that parents have an inalienable right "to direct and control the upbringing, education, values and discipline of their children." Heavily opposed by "liberals" and most in the "education and government establishment," the amendment signified the strength of the conservative movement in Colorado and the rebellion of some parents against educators' attempts to teach values, apply alternative forms of discipline in the schools, and question parental forms of discipline at home. Edsall, "Fighting over the Children."

64. Kingsbery and Hunt, "Changes to Student Discipline Laws."

65. Colorado Education Association, "From Schoolhouse to Statehouse."

66. Kingsbery and Hunt, "Changes to Student Discipline Laws," 4.

67. Aaronson, "Due Process Changes."

68. Ibid., 3.

69. Colorado Lawyers Committee, "In-School Suspension Act."

70. Colorado Lawyers Committee, "Colorado Pilot Schools Act."

71. See Smith, "Memorandum to Potential Grant Recipients"; Smith, "Memorandum to Superintendents"; and Colorado Department of Education, "Request for Proposal Packet."

72. Colorado Lawyers Committee, "Colorado Pilot Schools Act."

73. Brown and Frank, "Romer Sets '97 Agenda."

74. See Kingdon, *Agendas*.

75. See Lasswell, *A Pre-view of Policy Sciences*.

76. See Baca et al., "Bedrock of Youth Violence"; Knight, "Violence Spawns Theories"; Lipsher, "Juvenile Agencies Baffled"; Lipsher, "Violence Fires Legislative Debate"; Shilling, "Boot-Camp Jails."

77.   Lipsher, "Juvenile Agencies Baffled."

78.   *ABC News Primetime Live,* "Deadly Lessons."

79.   See Elazar, *American Federalism.*

80.   See Hero and Tolbert, "A Racial/Ethnic Diversity Interpretation"; Fitzpatrick and Hero, "Political Culture"; Hero, *Latinos.*

81.   Colorado Lawyers Committee, *Colorado Lawyers Committee: 1996 Report,* 7.

82.   See Hall, "Policy Paradigms"; Heclo, "Issue Networks"; Sabatier and Jenkins-Smith, *Policy Change and Learning.*

83.   Colorado Education Association, "Inclusion."

84.   Pappas et al., *Voices from the Heart,* 7–8.

85.   This example support's Hall's argument that routine, incremental, or "satisficing" policy changes can occur within "the state," but paradigmatic change arises out of societal and political demands. This more radical change in the goals and instruments of policy requires a change in the locus of authority to a source outside of "the state," into civil society. Hall, "Policy Paradigms," 280.

86.   P. M. Haas, "Introduction: Epistemic Communities"; Hall, "Policy Paradigms."

87.   Yoder, "Obsession with Crime."

Chapter 4

1.   See Button, "City Schools"; Rothstein, ed., *Handbook of Schooling,* 70–71; Hallett, ed., *Reinventing Central Office*; Kirst, *Who Controls Our Schools?*; Rapp, "A State Policy Maker's Guide."

2.   See Sarason, *Revisiting "The Culture of the School and the Problem of Change."*

3.   Colorado Department of Public Safety, *Crime in Colorado.*

4.   Ibid.

5.   Butterfield, "Violent Crimes."

6.   Violence Prevention Advisory Committee et al., *Violence in Colorado*, 210.

7.   Denver Public Schools, "Second Straight Year."

8.   Gottlieb, "DPS Seeks More Guards."

9.   Denver Public Schools, *Report to the Board*. See more detailed discussion of this process below. A CDM is intended to be an inclusive committee that will assist in making school-based decisions that reflect local priorities, within the framework of state laws and regulations and district policies and procedures. CDMs include the school principal, four teachers chosen by faculty vote, four parents or community representatives nominated by the PTSA or another community organization but elected by the majority of voting parents with children in the school, one classified employee chosen by classified employee vote, one business and/or employer representative nominated by the principal and approved by other CDM members, and, in the middle and high schools, two student representatives selected by the student council. Denver Classroom Teachers Association, "Agreement," 4–5.

10.   Denver Public Schools, *Report to the Board*, attachment 2.

11.   Amalgamated Transit Union, *School Bus Safety Survey*.

12.   Robey, "After-School Tutoring."

13.   National School Safety Center, *School Safety Assessment*, 4, 6.

14.   See Denver Public Schools, *Policy Manual*, section JK, "Student Conduct and Discipline," IV. C. As a grounds for suspension, "defiance" or "willful disobedience" is one of those gray areas in which teachers or administrators are allowed much room for interpretation of the policy.

15.   Department of Planning, Research, and Program Evaluation, *Report of Suspensions and Expulsions*. A recent report by the district's Black Education Advisory Council recommended that the district "[i]nvestigate expulsion and suspension of African American students." It noted that "African American students are succeeding at a disproportionate rate as Anglo students at all grade levels in reading at grade level, suspensions/expulsions and special education placements." Black Education Advisory Council, *A Call for Action*, 1, 16.

16.   Denver Public Schools, *Policy Manual*, section JK. "The mission of the Denver Public Schools, the center of learning for the community, is to guarantee that our children and youth acquire knowledge, skills, and values to become self-sufficient citizens and lifelong learners. We can achieve

this by providing personalized learning experiences for all students in collaborative partnerships with all segments of the community." See chapter 1 for a discussion of the National Education Goal.

17. Denver Public Schools, *Policy Manual*, section JK.

18. Ibid.

19. Denver Classroom Teachers Association, "Agreement," 9, article 5–8.

20. Ibid., 10, article 5–8–1–7.

21. Ibid., 37, articles 17, 18.

22. An ordinal ranking level using these factors was developed to rate the overall and comparative levels of decentralization in Denver and in Colorado Springs. A simple checklist and overall decentralization index score was developed. The presence and extent of a particular element of decentralization was indicated with a score from 0 (nonexistent) to 5 (formally established and initially implemented) to 10 (dominant and well-established characteristic), based on interpretation of formal district policies and discussions with interviewees. The maximum score would be a 60. DPS was given a score of 41.

23. Denver Public Schools, *Policy Manual*, sections IHBF, IHBG; Office of Program Evaluation, "The Alternative Middle School."

24. Office of Program Evaluation, "The Alternative Middle School," 1, 8.

25. Denver Public Schools, *Policy Manual*, section EB.

26. Ibid., section IHAMA.

27. Ibid., sections IHAMB, IHAMC.

28. Safe and Drug Free Schools and Communities, "Resiliency Flyer." The resiliency approach seeks to confront risk factors that impact children, enhance protective factors, and foster each child's resiliency, or ability to handle problems in their lives.

29. Department of Social Services, *Resource Guide*.

30. Denver Public Schools, "At-Risk Funds."

31. Denver Public Schools, "BEAC Presents Action Plan," and "Data Show Resurgence."

32.   See Witcher, "Forward to the Past."

33.   Denver Public Schools, *Report to the Board*, 1.

34.   Ibid., 3.

35.   Ibid., attachment 2.

36.   Ibid.

37.   Boigon, *Progress Report*.

38.   Ibid. See also Wheeler, "Six Clubs."

39.   Safe City Office, *Building a Safe City*; Stephens, "Memorandum to Supervisors."

40.   Mayor's Office, *Mayor Wellington E. Webb's Report*; Boigon, *Progress Report*.

41.   Michaud and Haney, "Letter to Ronald D. Stephens."

42.   Denver Public Schools and Denver Police Department Joint Task Force, *Denver Public Schools and Denver Police Department Joint Task Force*.

43.   Denver Public Schools, "Truancy Reduction Success."

44.   National School Safety Center, *School Safety Assessment*, 39–44.

45.   Denver Public Schools, *Policy Manual*, sections JK-R, 1-4-B.

46.   Denver Public Schools, "Changes in Discipline Policy Accepted."

47.   National School Safety Center, *School Safety Assessment*, 3.

48.   Bingham, "Growing Pains."

49.   Gottlieb, "Dance Ends in Beating."

50.   Nicholson, "City Will Drop Charges."

51.   Arthur Andersen and Co., S. C., Operational Consulting, *Denver Public Schools*.

52.   "Making Education Work for Chicano/Latino Students: An Action Plan for Our Students," submitted to Denver Public Schools, Board of Education, 1994, 7.

53.   Ibid., 4.

54.   Gottlieb, "Schools to Get Ultimatum; Gottlieb, "DPS' Get-Tough Policy"; Moskowitz, "Open Letter."

55.   Gottlieb, "DPS Seeks More Guards."

56.   Given more time and resources, it would have been useful to focus on several elementary schools as well. Interviews at the district level did provide information about and understanding of the school violence problem at the elementary level in Denver. Also, see research discussion in chapters 2 and 3.

Chapter 5

1.   Colorado Department of Public Safety, *Crime in Colorado.* Colorado Springs is the largest city in El Paso County, and reports from the Colorado Springs Police Department and the El Paso County Sheriff constitute almost all of the offenses reported for El Paso County. Other reporting agencies for the county are Fountain PD, Manitou Springs PD, Palmer Lake Marshall, Monument PD, and Green Mountain Falls PD.

2.   Office of School/Community Relations, *Colorado Springs Public Schools.*

3.   The DAAC and BAAC committee structure is similar to the SIAC structure in the Denver Public Schools. Both were created in line with a state mandate to improve accountability and reporting, but Denver Public Schools' School Improvement Advisory Committees (SIAC) coexist with the building Collaborative Decision Making (CDM) structures, making it difficult, according to one Denver respondent, to determine which committee was responsible for what, since they have overlapping responsibilities and membership.

4.   Office of Student Discipline Services, "Suspension Referral and Discipline Reports."

5.   Department of Planning Evaluation and Measurement, *Colorado Springs Public Schools.*

6.   Colorado Springs Public Schools, *Colorado Springs Public Schools.*

7.   Colorado Springs Public Schools, "Student Discipline;" Student Discipline Services, "House Bill 96-1203"; Student Discipline Services, "Senate Bill 96-63."

8.   Burnley, "Letter to Parent(s)/Guardian(s)."

9.   Colorado Springs Public School District Eleven, "Hunt Uniforms."

10.   Colorado Springs Public School District Eleven, "Security Cameras."

11.   Office of School/Community Relations, *Colorado Springs Public Schools*.

12.   Ibid.

13.   See chapter 4, especially footnote number 22, for a discussion of the decentralization scale developed to rate the districts. Colorado Springs was given a score of 28 out of 60 (as opposed to 41 for Denver).

14.   This is similar to Rose's notion that lesson-drawing is easier if the values in both the place of origin and the place of later adoption are comparable. Rose, *Lesson Drawing*.

15.   Tyack and Cuban, *Tinkering toward Utopia*.

Chapter 6

1.   For a related discussion of "metanarratives" see Roe, *Narrative Policy Analysis*.

2.   See, for example, Mayhew, *Congress*; Meier and McFarlane, "The Politics of Funding Abortion."

3.   See Weaver, "The Politics of Blame Avoidance."

4.   Lindblom, *The Intelligence of Democracy*, 178. For an application of this type of theory to education reform, see Tyack and Cuban, *Tinkering toward Utopia*.

5.   Edelman, *Political Language*.

6.   "Legislature '97," *Denver Post*, Jan. 9, 1997, 11A; Johnston, "School Tests Pass."

7.   U.S. Departments of Agriculture, Education, Health and Human Services, Housing and Urban Development, Justice, and Labor, *Partnerships Against Violence: Promising Programs*, and *Partnerships Against Violence: Information Sources*; National School Safety Center, *School Crime and Violence Statistical Review*.

8.   Simon, *Reason in Human Affairs*.

9.   Stake, *The Art of Case Study Research*, 4–9.

10.   Rubin and Rubin, *Qualitative Interviewing*, 85–91.

11.   Dryzek, *Discursive Democracy*, 138.

12.   Lasswell, *A Pre-view of Policy Sciences*.

13.   March and Olsen, *Rediscovering Institutions*.

14.   Edelman, *Political Language*, 26, 29.

15.   J. E. Anderson, *Public Policymaking*, 133–114.

Afterword

1.   Front page news in the *New York Times* ("2 Youths in Colorado School Said to Gun Down as Many as 23 and Kill Themselves in a Siege: A Suicide Mission," April 21, 1999, "15 Bodies Are Removed from School in Colorado: Portrait of Outcasts Seeking to Stand Out," April 22, 1999, "A Portrait of Two Killers at War with Themselves: Accounts of Behavior Do Little to Explain School Massacre," April 26, 1999). Special cover stories in *Newsweek*, for example, "Massacre in Colorado: Why? Portraits of the Killers. The Science of Teen Violence," May 3, 1999, "Beyond Littleton: How Well Do You Know Your Kid? Heading off Trouble. The Secret Life of Teens," May 10, 1999. And a more considered and thorough later discussion in a local paper, the *Denver Rocky Mountain News*, "Fatal Friendship: How Two Suburban Boys Traded Baseball and Bowling for Murder and Madness," Aug. 22, 1999. There have been continuing articles and headline stories through and past the one-year anniversary of the Columbine shootings.

2.   See Brunner, "Key Political Symbols."

3.   Karr-Morse, *Ghosts from the Nursery*; Elliott et al., *Violence in American Schools*.

4.   Belkin, "Parents Blaming Parents."

5.   Feldman, advertisement.

6.   Galinsky, "Do Working Parents Make the Grade?"

7.   Doyle, "Killers Among Us."

8.   Rhodes, "What Causes Brutality?"

9.   Janofsky, "Columbine Killers."

10. Butterfield, "Guns Used More for Suicide." See also Jamison, *Night Falls Fast.*

11. "What a lot of sterEUtypes," *Economist*, Oct. 23, 1999, 60.

12. Janofsky, "A Fresh Coat of Paint."

13. Fireston, "Boy Took Parent's Guns"; Associated Press, "White Students Accused"; Smothers, "Rumors of Violence."

14. Steinberg, "Barricading the School Door."

15. Handelsman, Walt. (*New York Times.* 8/29/99): 4.

16. Associated Press, "$100 Million to Reduce Violence."

17. Clines, "Computer Project."

18. J. Q. Wilson, "A Gap in the Curriculum."

19. Bartlett, "Breaking Silence"; See Garbarino, *Lost Boys.*

20. Rohter, "Brazil, High in Shootings."

Bibliography

Aaronson, N. "Due Process Changes Resulting from Passage of H.B. 1203." August 6, 1996.

ABC News Primetime Live. "Deadly Lessons (Transcript #272)." Nov. 19, 1992.

Adler, E., and P. M. Haas. "Conclusion: Epistemic Communities, World Order, and the Creation of a Reflective Research Program." *International Organization* 46, no. 1 (Winter 1992).

Almond, G. A. *A Discipline Divided: Schools and Sects in Political Science.* Newbury Park: Sage Publications, 1990.

Amalgamated Transit Union. *School Bus Safety Survey.* Denver: Amalgamated Transit Union, 1994.

American Psychological Association. *Violence and Youth: Psychology's Response.* Vol. 1, *Summary Report of the APA Commission on Violence and Youth.* Washington, DC: American Psychological Association, 1993.

Anderson, E. "Denver Ranks 7th in Area Crime: Glendale Tops among 25 Cities." *Denver Post,* March 6, 1994, 1A, 19A.

Anderson, J. E. *Public Policymaking: An Introduction.* Boston: Houghton Mifflin Co., 1990.

Arthur Andersen and Co., S. C., Operational Consulting. *Denver Public Schools: Management and Efficiency Project Read Outs 1, 2, 3, and Final Presentation.* Denver: Arthur Andersen and Co., 1994.

Associated Press. "$100 Million to Reduce Violence in Schools." *New York Times,* Sept. 12, 1999, A33.

———. "White Students Accused of Plot against Blacks." *New York Times,* Oct. 30, 1999, A16.

Baca, S., et al. "Bedrock of Youth Violence: Damaged Children." Special section on juvenile crime. *Denver Post,* Sept. 6, 1994, 9A–16A.

Baker, R., and P. Dexter. "Crisis in Crime: Can Prisons Make America Safe?" *Denver Post,* Feb. 2, 1994.

Barke, R. "Policy-learning and the Evolution of Federal Hazardous Waste Policy." *Policy Studies Journal* 14, no. 1 (September 1985): 123–131.

Bartlett, G. "Breaking Silence Can Save 'Lost Boys.'" *Wilton Bulletin*, Nov. 11, 1999, A1, 17.

Bastian, L., and B. M. Taylor. *School Crime: A National Crime Victimization Report*. No. NCJ-131645. Washington, DC: Department of Justice, 1991.

Baumgartner, F. R. *Conflict and Rhetoric in French Policymaking*. Pittsburgh, PA: University of Pittsburgh Press, 1989.

Baumgartner, F. R., and B. D. Jones. *Agendas and Instability in American Politics*. Chicago: University of Chicago Press, 1993.

Belkin, L. "Parents Blaming Parents: In the Wake of School Shootings, Victims' Families Are Turning to the Law for Retribution. And the Target Is Often a Murderer's Grieving Mom and Dad," *New York Times Magazine*, Oct. 31, 1999, 60–100.

Bemelmans-Videc, M. L., B. Eriksen, and E. N. Goldenberg. "Facilitating Organizational Learning: Human Resource Management and Program Evaluation." In *Can Governments Learn? Comparative Perspectives on Evaluation and Organizational Learning*, ed. F. L. Leeuw, R. C. Rist, and R. C. Sonnichsen. New Brunswick, NJ: Transaction Publishers, 1994.

Bender, P. "Crime Rate Dips for 5th Year in Row." *Denver Post*, Oct. 13, 1996, 2A.

Bennett, W. J., J. J. DiIulio, Jr., and J. P. Walters. *Body Count: Moral Poverty . . . and How to Win America's War against Crime and Drugs*. New York: Simon and Schuster, 1996.

Benson, P. L. *The Troubled Journey: A Profile of American Youth*. Minneapolis, MN: Respecteen, 1992.

Berke, R. L. "Crime Propels Rhetoric: Governors Brandish Theme in Speeches." *Denver Post*, Jan. 24, 1994, 1A, 8A.

Bernard, B. *Fostering Resiliency in Kids: Protective Factors in the Family, School, and Community*. Portland, OR: Western Regional Center for Drug-Free Schools and Communities, 1991.

Bingham, J. "Policies on Ousting Students Vary." *Denver Post*, Mar. 6, 1994.

———. "State Graduation Rate Plummets: Drop Coincides with Tough Expulsion Laws." *Denver Post*. Jan. 6, 1996, 1A, 12A.

———. "Growing Pains: Charter Expanding too Fast, Perez Says." *Denver Post*, Sept. 10, 1996, 1A, 15A.

———. "State Sees Links in Dropouts, Expulsions." *Denver Post*, Dec. 7, 1996, 1A, 18A.

———. "Denver's First Charter School to Close Down: Clayton Giving Way before Joint DPS-DU Facility Opens Nearby." *Denver Post*, Mar. 1, 1997, 1B.

———. "Charting a New Course." *Denver Post*, Mar. 2, 1997, 1A, 10–11A.

———. "Charting a New Course: Core Learning Gains Popularity." *Denver Post*, Mar. 3, 1997, 1A, 12A.

Black, T. M. *Straight Talk about American Education*. New York: Harcourt Brace, 1982.

Black Education Advisory Council. *A Call for Action: Presented to the Superintendent, Board of Education, Educators and the Community at Large Regarding Academic Achievement for African American Students in Denver Public Schools*. Denver: Denver Public Schools, 1995.

Bloom, A. *The Closing of the American Mind*. New York: Simon and Schuster, 1987.

Boigon, C. *Progress Report: Mayor's Office of Education and Advocacy, December 1995–September 1996*. Denver: Mayor's Office, City and County of Denver, 1996.

Booth, M. "Year of Violence: A Review of Denver's 130 Homicide Cases in 1993 Separates the Facts from the Fears." *Denver Post*, Jan. 23, 1994, 1A, 14–15A.

———. "State Faces Test on Private Prisons." *Denver Post*, Dec. 23, 1996, 1A, 9A.

Breeskin, M. W. *Suspension and Expulsion of Children with Disabilities*. Denver: Legal Center for People with Disabilities and Older People, 1996.

Brennan, C. "Gang Boom on Horizon, Expert Says: State Crime Fighters Map Strategy with Officials Reno Sent to Town." *Rocky Mountain News*, Oct. 29, 1993, 4A.

Breslauer, G. W., and P. E. Tetlock, eds. *Learning in U.S. and Soviet Foreign Policy*. Boulder, CO: Westview Press, 1991.

Brown, F., and T. Frank. "Romer Sets '97 Agenda: Priorities Lie with Children, Welfare, Roads." *Denver Post*, Jan. 10, 1997, 1A, 11A.

Brown, S. R. *Political Subjectivity: Applications of Q Methodology in Political Science*. New Haven: Yale University Press, 1980.

Brownstein, H. H. "The Media and the Construction of Random Drug Violence." *Social Justice* 18, no. 4 (1991): 85–99.

Brudney, J. L. and F. T. Hebert. "State Agencies and Their Environments: Examining the Influence of Important External Actors." *Journal of Politics* 49 (1987): 188–205.

Brunner, R. D. "Decentralized Energy Policies." *Public Policy* 28 (Winter 1980): 71–91.

———. "Case-Wise Policy Information Systems: Redefining Poverty." *Policy Sciences* 19 (1986): 201–223.

———. "Key Political Symbols: The Dissociation Process." *Policy Sciences* 20 (1987): 53–76.

———. "Review of Murray Edelman, *Constructing the Political Spectacle.*" *Policy Sciences* 22 (1989): 83–89.

———. "Global Climate Change: Defining the Policy Problem." *Policy Sciences* 24 (1991): 291–311.

Brunner, R. D., and W. Ascher. "Science and Social Responsibility." *Policy Sciences* 25 (1992): 295–331.

Brunner, R. D., J. S. Fitch, J. Grassia, L. Kathlene, and K. R. Hammond. "Improving Data Utilization: the Case-Wise Alternative." *Policy Sciences* 20 (1987): 365–394.

Budge, I., and D. McKay, eds. *Developing Democracy: Comparative Research in Honour of J. F. P. Blondel.* London: Sage Publications, 1994.

Burnley, K. S. *Letter to Parent(s)/Guardian(s).* Colorado Springs: Colorado Springs Public Schools, 1996.

Butterfield, F. "Violent Crime Falls 9 Percent, U.S. Reports." *Denver Post*, Sept. 18, 1996, 3A.

———. "Violent Crimes Continue Decline." *Denver Post*, Jan. 5, 1997, 2A.

———. "Guns Used More for Suicide Than Homicide: As Rate of Violent Crime Drops, New Attention to an Old Taboo," *New York Times*, Oct. 17, 1999, A18.

Button, H. W. "City Schools and School Systems: Sources of Centralization and Bureaucratization." In *Handbook of Schooling in Urban America*, ed. S. W. Rothstein, 43–65. Westport, CT: Greenwood Press, 1993.

Callison, W. L., and N. Richards-Colocino. "Crime, Violence, Gangs, and Drug Abuse: What Urban Schools Can Do about Them." In *Handbook of Schooling in Urban America*, ed. S. W. Rothstein, 339–364. Westport, CT: Greenwood Press, 1993.

Cannon, A. "3-Strikes Laws Swing and Miss, Survey Indicates." *Denver Post*, Sept. 10, 1996, 1A, 15A.

Carter, S. W. *Background on the Colorado Consortium for Community Policing.* Denver: Colorado Consortium for Community Policing, 1996.

Caughey, P. "Growing up Violent: Changing Social Conditions Have Raised the Stakes in Youth Crime." *Summit* (1995): 8–11.

Center for the Study and Prevention of Violence. *CSPV Overview and Report of Progress.* Boulder, CO: Center for the Study and Prevention of Violence, 1994.

————. "Schools and Adolescent Violence Project." Memorandum. Center for the Study and Prevention of Violence, Boulder, CO, 1996.

Center to Prevent Handgun Violence. "Caught in the Crossfire: A Report on Gun Violence in Our Nation's Schools." Washington, DC, September 1990.

Chronicle of Higher Education Almanac, Aug. 29, 1997, 5.

Clarke, S. E., and R. Hero. "Civic Capacity, Social Diversity, and Reform Politics: Denver." A paper presented at the Urban Affairs Annual Meeting in Portland, OR, 1995.

Clarke, S. E., R. Hero, and M. Sidney. "Ideas, Interests, and Institutions: Education Reform in Denver." A paper presented at the Annual Meeting of the Western Political Science Association in San Francisco, CA, 1996.

Clines, F. X. "Computer Project Seeks to Avert Youth Violence: Columbine Spurs Pilot Program at Schools." *New York Times*, Oct. 24, 1999, A20.

Cochran, N. "Grandma Moses and the 'Corruption' of Data." *Evaluation Quarterly* 2 (August 1978): 233–261.

————. "Society as Emergent and More Than Rational: An Essay on the Inappropriateness of Program Evaluation." *Policy Sciences* 12 (1980): 113–129.

Cole, S. "Guns and Violence." In *Violence in Colorado: Trends and Resources*, 103–107. Denver, CO: Colorado Department of Public Health and Environment, 1994.

Colorado Department of Education. "Colorado: Results of the 1995 Colorado Youth Risk Behavior Survey." Denver, CO, Colorado Department of Education, Oct. 6, 1995.

————. "Request for Proposal Packet." Denver, CO, Colorado Department of Education, 1996.

———. "State Summary of Pupils Suspended and Expelled by Gender and Ethnic/Racial Group and Counts of Suspensions and Expulsions by Reason." Denver, CO, Colorado Department of Education, Nov. 1996.

Colorado Department of Public Safety, Colorado Bureau of Investigation Crime Information Center. *Crime in Colorado: Annual Reports.* Denver, CO: Colorado Department of Public Safety, 1980–1995.

Colorado Education Association. "From Schoolhouse to Statehouse: Senate Bill 63." Memorandum to "Members of the Senate." Denver, CO, Colorado Education Association, 1996.

———. "Inclusion." Denver, CO, Colorado Education Association, n.d.

Colorado Foundation for Families and Children. *The Financial Costs of Failure: A Study of the Costs Incurred by 21 Youth Committed to the Colorado Office of Youth Services.* Denver, CO: Colorado Foundation for Families and Children, 1995.

———. *School Expulsions: A Cross-Systems Problem, Project Summary of the Year One Report.* Denver, CO: Colorado Foundation for Families and Children, 1995.

———. *Facts Regarding School Expulsion and Suspension in Colorado.* Denver, CO: Colorado Foundation for Families and Children, 1996.

———. *Update on Costs Associated with School Expulsion.* Denver, CO: Colorado Foundation for Families and Children, 1996.

———. *What's Being Tried in Colorado?* Denver, CO: Colorado Foundation for Families and Children, 1996.

———. *Working with Suspended and Expelled Students.* Denver, CO: Colorado Foundation for Families and Children, 1996.

Colorado Lawyers Committee. *School Discipline Issues: Rights and Responsibilities.* Denver, CO: Colorado Lawyers Committee, 1994.

———. *Colorado Lawyers Committee: 1996 Report.* Denver, CO: Colorado Lawyers Committee, 1996.

———. "Colorado Pilot Schools Act: C.R.S. 22-38-101 et seq." Memorandum. Colorado Lawyers Committee, Denver, CO, 1996.

———. *Fact Sheet—H.B. 1203.* Denver, CO: Colorado Lawyers Committee, 1996.

———. "In-School Suspension Act: C.R.S. 22-37-101 et seq." Memorandum. Colorado Lawyers Committee, Denver, CO, 1996.

———. "Memorandum: Discipline Task Force." Colorado Lawyers Committee, Denver, CO, 1996.

———. "Summary of H.B. 1203." Colorado Lawyers Committee, Denver, CO, 1996.

Colorado School Mediation Project. *Conflict Resolution in the Schools: Final Evaluation Report*. Boulder, CO: Colorado School Mediation Project, n.d.

———. "Violence in the Schools: Strengthening Skills for Resilient Youth." Proceedings. Annual Conference, Denver, CO, June 13–14, 1996.

Colorado Springs Public School District Eleven. "Hunt Uniforms One Aspect of Student Achievement Initiative." *D-11 Connection* 1, no. 1 (Fall 1996): 26.

———. "Security Cameras Promote Safe Learning Environment," *D-11 Connection* 1, no. 1 (Fall 1996): 27.

Colorado Springs Public Schools. *Colorado Springs Public Schools, School District No. 11, Colorado Springs, Colorado: Student Conduct and Discipline Code*. Colorado Springs, CO: Colorado Springs Public Schools, 1995.

———. "Student Discipline and Code of Conduct Training Sessions." Flyer. Colorado Springs, Colorado Springs Public Schools, 1996.

Corning, J. "Heading off Violence in Schools: Parents Involved in Different Approaches." *USAA Magazine* (Aug./Sept. 1996): 22–26.

Council of the Great City Schools. *Safety Initiatives in Urban Public Schools*. Washington, DC: Council of the Great City Schools, 1991.

Craig, A. "Environmental Monitoring: A Case of Learning through Evaluation?" *Policy Studies Review* 6, no. 2 (Nov. 1986): 366–373.

"Crime Fear/Crime Risk Paradox." *Los Angeles Times*, June 26, 1992, 1A.

"Crime Puzzle: Lower Statistics Belie Rising Fear." *Denver Post*, May 15, 1994, 21A, 24A.

Dahl, R. A. *Who Governs? Democracy and Power in an American City*. New Haven: Yale University Press, 1961.

Daneke, G. A. "Organizational Learning and Energy Policy." *Policy Studies Journal* 13, no. 2 (Dec. 1984): 309–318.

DeLeon, R. E. *Left Coast City: Progressive Politics in San Francisco, 1975–1991*. Lawrence: University Press of Kansas, 1992.

Denver Classroom Teachers Association and Denver Public Schools. "Agreement between Denver Classroom Teachers Association and School District No. 1 in the City and County of Denver and State of Colorado." Labor contract. Denver, CO, Denver Classroom Teachers Association and Denver Public Schools, 1994.

Denver Public Schools (DPS). "At-Risk Funds Help Elementary Schools Meet Critical Needs." *Board News* 2, no. 7 (Nov. 22, 1996).

———. "BEAC Presents Action Plan; Calls for 'New Day in DPS, Community, Parent Participation'" and "Data Show Resurgence among African American Students." *Board News* 2, no. 8 (Dec. 13, 1996).

———. "Changes in Discipline Policy Accepted." *Board News* 2, no. 2 (Sept. 20, 1996).

———. *Policy Manual*. Denver, CO: DPS, 1996.

———. "Second Straight Year of Strong Enrollment Growth Hints at Bright Prospects." *Board News* 2, no. 5 (Nov. 8, 1996).

———. "Truancy Reduction Success Relies on City-School Cooperation." *Board News* 2, no. 3 (Oct. 4, 1996).

Denver Public Schools, Ad Hoc Discipline Committee. *Report to the Board of Education: School Discipline Committee Recommendations*. Denver, CO: DPS, 1995.

Denver Public Schools and Denver Police Department Joint Task Force. "Denver Public Schools and Denver Police Department Joint Task Force." Denver, CO, DPS, 1995.

Department of Planning, Evaluation, and Measurement. *Colorado Springs Schools District Eleven: School Profiles 1995–96*. Colorado Springs: Colorado Springs Public Schools, 1996.

Department of Planning, Research and Program Evaluation. *Summary Reports of Pupil Membership*. Denver, CO: DPS, 1986–1995.

———. *Pupil Suspension Report*. Denver, CO: DPS, 1995.

———. *Report of 1996-1997 Student Membership by School, Grade, Gender, and Ethnicity*. Denver, CO: DPS, 1996.

———. *Report of Suspensions and Expulsions*. Denver, CO: DPS, 1996.

———. Unpublished data. DPS, Denver, CO, 1996.

Department of Social Services. *Resource Guide to Schools: City Prevention and Intervention Programs Addressing Social Challenges.* Denver: Denver Public Schools, 1994.

Dery, D. *Problem Definition in Policy Analysis.* Lawrence: University Press of Kansas, 1984.

Domhoff, G. W. *Who Really Rules? New Haven and Community Power Reexamined.* New Brunswick, NJ: Transaction Books, 1978.

Doyle, L. "Killers among Us: What Kind of Person Would Open Fire on Innocent Kids? An Animal—Just Like Any of Us," *New York Times Magazine,* Aug. 22, 1999, 13.

Dryzek, John. *Discursive Democracy.* Cambridge: Cambridge University Press, 1990.

Dunn, W. N. *Public Policy Analysis: An Introduction.* 2nd ed. Englewood Cliffs, NJ: Prentice Hall, 1994.

Eckstein, H. "Case Study and Theory in Political Science." In *Handbook of Political Science, Volume VII, Strategies of Inquiry,* ed. F. I. Greenstein and N. W. Polsby, 79–135. Reading, MA: Addison-Wesley, 1975.

Edelman, M. *Political Language: Words That Succeed and Policies That Fail.* New York: Academic Press, 1977.

Edner, S. "Intergovernmental Policy Development: The Importance of Problem Definition." 1973.

Edsall, T. B. "Fighting over the Children in Colorado: A Proposed Parental-Rights Amendment Pits the State's Conservatives against the Liberals." *Washington Post National Weekly Edition,* Oct. 28–Nov. 29, 1996, 29.

Education Commission of the States. *Clearinghouse Notes: Violence.* Denver, CO: Education Commission of the States, 1994.

———. *A Framework for Urban Hope: The New American Urban School District.* Denver: Education Commission of the States, 1995.

———. *Clearinghouse Notes: Discipline: Zero Tolerance/Gun Control—Detailed Version.* Denver: Education Commission of the States, 1996.

———. *Youth Violence: A Policymakers' Guide.* Denver, CO: Education Commission of the States, 1996.

Elazar, D. J. *American Federalism: A View from the States, 3rd ed.* New York: Harper and Row, 1984.

Elliott, D. S. *Youth Violence: An Overview*. No. F-693. Boulder, CO: Center for the Study and Prevention of Violence, 1994.

Elliott, D. S., B. A. Hamburg, and K. R. Williams, eds. *Violence in American Schools: A New Perspective*. New York: Cambridge University Press, 1998.

Etheredge, L. S. *Can Governments Learn? American Foreign Policy and Central American Revolutions*. New York: Pergamon, 1985.

Evans, P. B., D. Rueschemeyer, and T. Skocpol, eds. *Bringing the State Back In*. New York: Cambridge University Press, 1985.

Fearon, J. D. "Counterfactuals and Hypothesis Testing in Political Science." *World Politics* 43 (January 1991): 169–195.

Federal Bureau of Investigation (FBI). *Uniform Crime Report*. Washington, DC: Department of Justice, 1990–1996.

Feldman, S. Advertisement, *New York Times*, July 4, 1999, A7.

Fineman, M. "Images of Mothers in Poverty Discourses." *Duke Law Journal* (1991): 274–295.

Fireston, D. "Boy Took Parent's Guns for Attack, Sheriff Says." *New York Times*, May 22, 1999, A8.

Fischer, F. "Response: Reconstructing Policy Analysis: A Postpositivist Perspective." *Policy Sciences* 25 (1993): 333–339.

Fischhoff, B., S. Lichtenstein, P. Slovic, S. L. Derby, and R. L. Keeney. *Acceptable Risk*. Cambridge: Cambridge University Press, 1981.

Fischhoff, B., S. R. Watson, and C. Hope. "Defining Risk." *Policy Sciences* 17 (1984): 123–139.

Fiske, E. B. *Smart Schools, Smart Kids: Why Do Some Schools Work?* New York: Simon and Schuster, 1991.

Fitzpatrick, J. L., and R. E. Hero. "Political Culture and Political Characteristics of the American States: A Consideration of Some Old and New Questions." *Western Political Quarterly* (1987): 145–153.

Florida Department of Education et al. "Final Report on Guiding Principles Developed by the Juvenile Justice Forum." Tallahassee: Florida Department of Education, 1994.

Forcey, L. R. "Peace Studies." In *Protest, Power, and Change: An Encyclopedia of Nonviolent Action from ACT-UP to Women's Suffrage*, ed. R. S. Powers and W. B. Vogele, 407–408. Hamden, CT: Garland Press, 1997.

Forcey, L. R., and I. M. Harris, eds. *Peacebuilding for Adolescents: Strategies for Educators and Community Leaders*. New York: Peter Lang, 1999.

Fraga, L. R. and B. E. Anhalt. "The Politics of Educational Reform in San Francisco." A paper presented at the Annual Meeting of the Western Political Science Association in San Francisco, CA, 1996.

Frank, T. "State Coffers Brim with Possibilities." *Denver Post*, Jan. 5, 1997, 1A, 13–14A.

Frohock, F. M. *Public Policy: Scope and Logic*. Englewood Cliffs, NJ: Prentice-Hall, 1979.

Furlong, M. J. and G. M. Morrison. "Introduction to Miniseries: School Violence and Safety in Perspective." *School Psychology Review* 23, no. 2 (1994): 139–150.

Galinsky, E. "Do Working Parents Make the Grade?" *Newsweek*, Aug. 30, 1999, 52–56.

Garbarino, J. *Lost Boys: Why Our Sons Turn Violent and How We Can Save Them*. New York: Free Press, 1999.

Geertz, C. "Thick Description: Toward an Interpretive Theory of Culture." In *The Interpretation of Cultures*. New York: Basic Books, 1973.

George, A. L. "Case Studies and Theory Development: The Method of Structured, Focused Comparison." In *Diplomacy: New Approaches in History, Theory, and Policy*, ed. P. G. Lauren, 43–68. New York: Free Press, 1979.

George, M. "Armed Kids in Special Ed Aided by Law: Expulsion Prohibited if Disability at Fault." *Denver Post*, Dec. 12, 1996. 1A, 22A.

Gilbert, S. "Child Deaths: Violence Rises as Accidents Fall." *New York Times*, June 12, 1996, C10.

Goodenow, R. K. and D. Ravitch, eds. *Schools in Cities: Consensus and Conflict in American Educational History*. New York: Holmes and Meier, 1983.

Goodlad, J. I. *A Place Called School: Prospects for the Future*. New York: McGraw-Hill Book Co., 1984.

Goodsell, C. T. *The Case for Bureaucracy: A Public Administration Polemic*. 3rd ed. Chatham, NJ: Chatham House, 1994.

Gottlieb, A. "Dance Ends in Beating by Cops: Black Kids, School Outraged by Action." *Denver Post*, May 17, 1996, 1A, 20A.

——. "DPS Seeks More Guards: Call Spurred by Rise in Violence Reports." *Denver Post*, Nov. 14, 1996, 1A, 18A.

——. "Schools to Get Ultimatum: Produce or Face Shakeup, DPS Saying." *Denver Post*, Feb. 13, 1997, 1A, 13A.

——. "DPS' Get-Tough Policy Product of Frustration." *Denver Post*, Feb. 16, 1997, 1B, 5B.

Greenberg, D. F. "The Cost-Benefit Analysis of Imprisonment." *Social Justice* 17, no. 4 (1992): 49–65.

Greene, M. W. "Viewpoints on School Violence in the Boulder Valley School District: Identifying Conflict and Consensus." Master's thesis, University of Colorado at Boulder, 1993.

——. *School Violence: Changing the Debate*. Denver: Education Commission of the States, 1995.

——. "Viewpoints on School Violence in the Boulder Valley School District: Identifying Conflict and Consensus." A paper presented at the Annual Meeting of the Western Political Science Association in Portland, OR, 1995.

——. "Redefining School Violence in Boulder Valley Colorado." In *Peacebuilding for Adolescents: Strategies for Educators and Community Leaders*, ed. L. R. Forcey and I. M. Harris, 57–88. New York: Peter Lang, 1999.

Guggenheim Foundation. *1993 Report of the Harry Frank Guggenheim Foundation: Research for Understanding and Reducing Violence, Aggression and Dominance*. New York: Guggenheim Foundation, 1993.

Gusfield, J. *The Culture of Public Problems*. Chicago: University of Chicago Press, 1981.

Haas, E. B. *When Knowledge Is Power: Three Models of Change in International Organizations*. Berkeley: University of California Press, 1990.

Haas, P. M. "Introduction: Epistemic Communities and International Policy Coordination." *International Organization* 46, no. 1 (Winter 1992).

Haas, R. N. *The Power to Persuade: How to Be Effective in Any Unruly Organization*. Boston: Houghton Mifflin Co., 1994.

Hajer, M. A. *City Politics: Hegemonic Projects and Discourse*. Aldershot, UK: Avebury, 1989.

Hall, P. "Policy Paradigms, Social Learning, and the State: The Case of Economic Policymaking in Britain." *Comparative Politics* 25 (April 1993): 275–296.

Hallett, A. C., ed. *Reinventing Central Office: A Primer for Successful Schools*. Cross City Campaign for Urban School Reform, 1995.

Handelsman, W. *New York Times*, Aug. 29, 1999, 4.

Harris, I. M. "Teachers' Response to Conflict in Selected Milwaukee Schools." Manuscript, 1995.

———. "From World Peace to Peace in the 'Hood: Peace Education in a Postmodern World." *Journal for a Just and Caring Education* 2, no. 4 (October 1996): 378–395.

Harris, L. *Metropolitan Life Survey of the American Teacher, 1993: Violence in America's Public Schools*. New York: Louis Harris and Associates, 1993.

———. *Metropolitan Life Survey of The American Teacher 1994, Violence in America's Public Schools: The Family Perspective*. New York: Louis Harris and Associates, 1994.

Hawkins, D., and R. Catalano, Jr. *Communities That Care*. San Francisco: Jossey-Bass, 1992.

Hawkins, D., J. M. Jenson, R. F. Catalano, and E. A. Wells. "Effects of a Skills Training Intervention with Juvenile Delinquents." *Research on Social Work Practice* 1, no. 2 (April 1991): 107–121.

Hawkins, D., D. Lishner, and R. F. Catalano. "Childhood Predictors and the Prevention of Adolescent Substance Abuse." In *Etiology of Drug Abuse: Implication for Prevention*, ed. C. L. Jones and R. J. Battjes, 75–125. Rockville, MD: National Institute on Drug Abuse, 1985.

Heclo, H. "Issue Networks and the Executive Establishment." In *The New American Political System*. Washington, DC: AEI, 1978.

———. "Ideas, Interests, and Institutions." In *The Dynamics of American Politics: Approaches and Interpretations*, ed. L. C. Dodd and C. Jillson. Boulder: Westview Press, 1994.

Heintz, H. T., Jr., and H. C. Jenkins-Smith. "Advocacy Coalitions and the Practice of Policy Analysis." *Policy Sciences* 21, nos. 2–3 (1988): 263–277.

Henig, J., L. R. Fraga, A. DiGaetano, and B. E. Anhalt. "Restructuring School Governance: Reform Ideas and Their Implementation." A paper presented at the Annual Meeting of the American Political Science Association in New York, NY, 1994.

Hero, R. *Latinos and the U.S. Political System: Two-Tiered Pluralism.* Philadelphia: Temple University Press, 1992.

Hero, R., and C. J. Tolbert. "A Racial/Ethnic Diversity Interpretation of Politics and Policy in the States of the U.S." *American Journal of Political Science* 40, no. 3 (1996): 851

Hess, D. "Massive 20-Year Crime Crackdown Had Little Effect." *Denver Post,* Jan. 25, 1994, 9A.

Hilgartner, S., and C. L. Bosk. "The Rise and Fall of Social Problems: A Public Arenas Model." *American Journal of Sociology* 94 (1988): 53–78.

Hirschman, A. O. "Two Hundred Years of Reactionary Rhetoric: The Case of the Perverse Effect." *The Tanner Lectures on Human Values* 10 (1989): 3–31.

Innes, J. I. *Knowledge and Public Policy: The Search for Meaningful Indicators.* New Brunswick, NJ: Transaction Publishers, 1990.

Jamison, K. R. *Night Falls Fast: Understanding Suicide.* New York: Alfred A. Knopf, 1999.

Janofsky, M. "A Fresh Coat of Paint and a Fresh Start," *New York Times,* Aug. 15, 1999, A20.

———. "Columbine Killers, on Tape, Thanked 2 for Gun," *New York Times,* Nov. 13, 1999, A1.

Jenkins-Smith, H. C. "Analytical Debates and Policy Learning: Analysis and Change in the Federal Bureaucracy." *Policy Sciences* 21, nos. 2–3 (1988): 169–211.

———. *Democratic Politics and Policy Analysis.* Monterey, CA: Brooks/Cole, 1990.

Jenkins-Smith, H. C., and P.A. Sabatier. "The Study of Public Policy Processes." In *Policy Change and Learning: An Advocacy Coalition Approach,* ed. P. A. Sabatier and H. C. Jenkins-Smith, 1–9. Boulder: Westview Press, 1993.

Johnson, D. W., and R. T. Johnson. *Reducing School Violence through Conflict Resolution.* Alexandria, VA: Association for Supervision and Curriculum Development, 1995.

Johnston, M. D. "Youth Jail Proposed for Lowry: State Considers Range for 500-Bed Facility." *Denver Post,* Nov. 20, 1996, 1A, 10A.

———. "School Tests Pass: Panel Won't Limit Psychological Tools." *Denver Post,* Jan. 30, 1997, 1A, 22–23A.

Jones, C. O. *An Introduction to the Study of Public Policy.* 3rd Ed. Monterey, CA: Brooks/Cole, 1984.

Jones, T. "Comprehensive Peer Mediation Evaluation Project: Overview for Participating Schools." Memorandum. Philadelphia, Temple University, 1995.

Kadel, S., and J. Follman. "Reducing School Violence." SouthEastern Regional Vision for Education, 1993.

Karr-Morse, R., and M. S. Wiley. *Ghosts from the Nursery: Tracing the Roots of Violence.* New York: Atlantic Monthly Press, 1997.

Kathlene, L. "Incredible Words! Gender, Power, and the Social Construction of Legitimacy in the Policy-Making Process." A paper presented at the Western Political Science Association Annual Meeting in Portland, OR, 1995.

Katz, A. "Rally against Violence: Wounded Adams Student Spreads Message." *Denver Post*, 1993, 1A, 10A.

King, R. A., and M. Gomez. *Student Discipline and Expulsions: Schools' Responses to a Revised State Statute.* Greeley, CO: Division of Educational Leadership and Policy Studies, University of Northern Colorado, 1994.

Kingdon, J. *Agendas, Alternatives, and Public Policies.* 2nd ed. New York: HarperCollins, 1995.

Kingsbery, L., and L. Hunt. "Changes to Student Discipline Laws Focus on Expulsion Prevention, Intervention." *Policy Parameters: A School Board Policy Newsletter (Colorado Association of School Boards)* 7, no. 2 (1996): 1–5.

Kirst, M. W. *State, School, and Politics: Research Directions.* Lexington, MA: Lexington Books, 1972.

———. *Who Controls Our Schools? American Values in Conflict.* New York: W. H. Freeman and Co., 1984.

Knight, A. "Violence Spawns Theories: Information Is Still Scarce." *Denver Post,* Nov., 7, 1993, 1D, 5D.

Kozol, J. *Savage Inequalities: Children in America's Schools.* New York: Crown Publishers, 1991.

Kraetzer, A. V. *Fall 1995 Budget Priorities Survey Comparison with Fall 1994 Results.* Colorado Springs: Colorado Springs Public Schools, Department of Planning, Evaluation, and Measurement, 1996.

Kruschke, E. R., and B. M. Jackson. *The Public Policy Dictionary.* Santa Barbara, CA: ABC-CLIO, 1987.

Kuhn, T. S. *The Structure of Scientific Revolutions*. 2nd ed. Vol. 2, *International Encyclopedia of Unified Science*, ed. O. Neurath. Chicago: University of Chicago Press, 1970.

Lam, J. "Evaluating the Program." Manuscript, 1992.

Lasswell, H. D. *A Pre-View of Policy Sciences*. New York: Elsevier, 1971.

———. *The Decision Process; Seven Categories of Functional Analysis*. College Park: University of Maryland Press, 1956.

———. *Psychopathology and Politics*. Chicago: University of Chicago Press, 1977.

Lasswell, H. D., and A. Kaplan. *Power and Society: A Framework for Political Inquiry*. New Haven: Yale University Press, 1950.

Lasswell, H. D., D. Lerner, and I. deS. Pool. *The Comparative Study of Symbols: An Introduction*. Stanford: Stanford University Press, 1970.

Leeuw, F. L., R. C. Rist, and R. C. Sonnichsen, eds. *Can Governments Learn? Comparative Perspectives on Evaluation and Organizational Learning*. New Brunswick, NJ: Transaction Publishers, 1994.

"Legislature '97: Agenda." *Denver Post*, Jan. 9, 1997, 11A.

Levitt, B., and J. G. March. "Organizational Learning." *Annual Review of Sociology* 14 (1988): 319–340.

Levy, J. S. "Learning and Foreign Policy: Sweeping a Conceptual Minefield." *International Organization* 48, no. 2 (Spring 1994): 279–312.

Lijphart, A. "The Comparable-Cases Strategy in Comparative Research." *Comparative Political Studies* 8 (July 1975): 158–177.

Lindblom, C. E. *The Intelligence of Democracy: Decision-making through Mutual Adjustment*. New York: Free Press, 1965.

Lippman, W. "The World Outside and the Pictures in Our Heads." In *Public Opinion*, 3–20. New York: Free Press, 1965.

Lipsher, S. "Juvenile Agencies Baffled: New System Stirs Confusion on Roles." *Denver Post*, Nov. 17, 1993, 1B, 3B.

———. "Violence Fires Legislative Debate." *Denver Post*, Feb. 2, 1994, 1B, 4B.

Lorr, M. *Cluster Analysis for Social Scientists*. San Francisco: Jossey-Bass, 1987.

MacKinnon, C. A. "Pornography as Defamation and Discrimination." *Boston University Law Review* 71 (1991): 793–815.

Majone, G. *Evidence, Argument, and Persuasion in the Policy Process.* New Haven: Yale University Press, 1989.

"Making Education Work for Chicano/Latino Students: An Action Plan for Our Students." Submitted to Denver Public Schools, Board of Education, 1994.

Mann, D. E. "Environmental Learning in a Decentralized Political World." *Journal of International Affairs* 44, no. 2 (Winter 1991): 301–337.

March, J., and J. Olsen. *Rediscovering Institutions.* New York: Free Press, 1989.

March, J. G. "Theories of Choice and Making Decisions." *Society* (Nov./Dec. 1982): 29–39.

Marshall, C., D. Mitchell, and F. Wirt. *Culture and Education Policy in the American States.* New York: Falmer Press, 1989.

May, P. J. "Policy Learning and Failure." *Journal of Public Policy* 12, no. 4 (1992): 331–354.

Mayhew, D. R. *Congress: The Electoral Connection.* New Haven: Yale University Press, 1974.

Mayne, J. "Utilizing Evaluation in Organizations: The Balancing Act." In *Can Governments Learn? Comparative Perspectives on Evaluation and Organizational Learning,* ed. F. L. Leeuw, R. C. Rist, and R. C. Sonnichsen, 17–44. New Brunswick, NJ: Transaction Publishers, 1994.

Mayor's Office. "Mayor Wellington E. Webb's Report to the Citizen's of Denver, July 1994 to June 1996: 1996 State of the City Address." Denver: Mayor's Office, 1996.

Mazzoni, T. L. "State Policy-Making and School Reform: Influences and Influentials." In *Politics of Education Association Yearbook 1994,* 53–73. Taylor and Francis Ltd., 1994.

McCart, L., ed. *Kids and Violence.* Washington, DC: National Governors' Association, 1994.

McCloskey, D. N. *The Rhetoric of Economics.* Madison: University of Wisconsin Press, 1985.

McCoy, J. L. "Political Learning and Redemocratization in Latin America." A paper presented at the 19th International Congress of the Latin American Studies Association in Washington, DC, 1995.

Medler, A. "Reconciling the Two Directions of Reform." *Education Commission of the States: State Education Leader* 13, no. 3 (1995): 9–11.

Meier, K., J. Stewart, and R. England. "Black Representation and Educational Policy." In *Race, Class, and Education: The Politics of Second-Generation Discrimination*, 28–29. Madison: University of Wisconsin Press, 1989.

Meier, K., J. Stewart, and D. R. McFarlane. "The Politics of Funding Abortion: State Responses to the Political Environment." *American Politics Quarterly* 21, no. 1 (1993): 81–101.

Meier, K., and J. Stewart. "Hispanic Representation and Equal Education." In *The Politics of Hispanic Education*. Albany: State University of New York Press, 1991.

Methvin, E. H. "The Dirty Little Secret about Our Crime Problem: Locking Criminals Up Solves It." *Washington Post National Weekly Edition*, Jan. 13–19, 1992, 24–25.

Metis Associates, Inc. "The Resolving Conflict Creatively Program: 1988–1989, Summary of Significant Findings." New York, Metis Associates, Inc., May 1990.

Michaud, D. L., and T. P. Haney. "Letter to Ronald D. Stephens, Executive Director, National School Safety Center." Department of Safety, City and County of Denver, 1996.

Mickish, J., and P. Hinish. "Family Violence: An Overview." In *Violence in Colorado: Trends and Resources*, 71–77. Denver: Colorado Department of Public Health and Environment, 1994.

Milburn, M. *Persuasion and Politics: The Social Psychology of Public Opinion*. Monterey, CA: Brooks/Cole, 1991.

Miller, E., ed. *Ready to Learn: How Schools Can Help Kids Be Healthier and Safer*. HEL Reprint Series No. 2. Cambridge, MA: Harvard Education Letter, 1995.

Mintrom, M. "The Politics of Ideas versus the Power of Self-Interest: The Case of School Choice." A paper presented at the New York State Political Science Association Annual Meeting in New York, NY, 1993.

———. "Policy Entrepreneurs and Institutional Change: The Case of School Choice." Manuscript, 1995.

———. "Policy Entrepreneurs and Policy Innovation: The Case of School Choice." A paper presented at the Workshop in Political Theory and Policy Analysis at Indiana University, Bloomington, IN, 1995.

———. "Policy Innovation Diffusion: Exploring the State-Local Nexus." A paper presented at the 53rd Annual Meeting of the Midwest Political Science Association in Chicago, IL, 1995.

Mintrom, M., and J. T. Kaji. "Selling Ideas: A Strategic Analysis of Policy Entrepreneurship." Draft, 1995.

Moe, R. C. "The 'Reinventing Government' Exercise: Misinterpreting the Problem, Misjudging the Consequences." *Public Administration Review* 54, no. 2 (1994): 111–122.

Morrison, G. M., M. J. Furlong, and R. L. Morrison. "School Violence to School Safety: Reframing the Issue for School Psychologists." *School Psychology Review* 23, no. 2 (1994): 236–256.

Moskowitz, I. "Open Letter from Superintendent Irv Moskowitz to the Faculty and Staff of Denver Public Schools." *Board News* 2, no. 13 (Feb. 1997).

Myrdal, G. *An American Dilemma: The Negro Problem and Modern Democracy.* Vol. 2. New York: Harper and Bros., 1944.

National Association for Mediation in Education. *The Fourth R.* 15 (June/July 1988): 1.

National Center for Injury Prevention and Control, Centers for Disease Control and Prevention. *The Prevention of Youth Violence: A Framework for Community Action.* Atlanta: Centers for Disease Control and Prevention, 1993.

National Education Association, ed. *Discipline and Learning: An Inquiry into Student-Teacher Relationships.* Rev. ed. Washington, DC: National Education Association, 1977.

National Education Goals Panel. *The National Education Goals Report: Building a Nation of Learners.* Washington, DC: National Education Goals Panel, 1996.

National Institute of Education. *School Crime and Disruption: Prevention Models.* Washington, DC: National Institute of Education, 1978.

———. *Violent Schools—Safe Schools: The Safe School Study Report to the Congress.* Washington, DC: National Institute of Education, 1978.

National School Boards Association (NSBA). *Violence in the Schools: How America's School Boards Are Safeguarding Our Children.* Alexandria, VA: NSBA, 1993.

National School Safety Center. *School Crime and Violence Statistical Review.* Westlake Village, CA: National School Safety Center, 1994.

———. *School Safety Assessment of Denver Public Schools, Denver, Colorado.* Westlake Village, CA: National School Safety Center, 1996.

"New York's Schools: Class Action." *Economist*, Nov. 30, 1996, 26.

Nicholson, K. "City Will Drop Charges against 2 in TJ Incident." *Denver Post*, Feb. 22, 1997, 1B.

Nye, J. S., Jr. "Nuclear Learning and U.S.-Soviet Security Regimes," *International Organization* 41, no. 3 (Summer 1987): 371–402.

O'Kane, R. H. T. "The Ladder of Abstraction: The Purpose of Comparison and the Practice of Comparing African Coups d'Etat." *Journal of Theoretical Politics* 5 (April 1993): 169–193.

O'Neill, A. "An Overview of Promising Violence Reduction Strategies." Working Paper, Denver, CO, Hunt Alternatives Fund, 1994.

Oberman, M. "Sex, Drugs, Pregnancy, and the Law: Rethinking the Problems of Pregnant Women Who Use Drugs." *Hastings Law Journal* 43 (March 1992): 505–547.

Office of Program Evaluation. "The Alternative Middle School: Program Evaluation." Denver, CO, Denver Public Schools, 1996.

Office of School/Community Relations. "Colorado Springs Public Schools, 1996–97, District 11 Calendar and Annual Report." Colorado Springs, CO, Colorado Springs Public Schools, 1996.

Office of Student Discipline Services. "Suspension Referral and Discipline Reports." Colorado Springs, CO, Colorado Springs Public Schools, 1988–1996.

Osborne, D., and T. Gabler. *Reinventing Government: How the Entrepreneurial Spirit Is Transforming the Public Sector.* Reading, MA: Addison-Wesley, 1992.

Painter, M. "Policy Diversity and Policy-learning in a Federation: The Case of Australian State Betting Laws." *Publius: The Journal of Federalism* 21 (Winter 1991): 143–157.

Pappas, G., M. Guajardo, and E. Ablin. *Voices from the Heart: The Community Speaks Out about Student Expulsions and Suspensions in Colorado.* Denver: Latin American Research and Service Agency, 1995.

Peters, B. G. *American Public Policy: Promise and Performance.* 3rd ed. Chatham, NJ: Chatham House, 1993.

Pickel, A. "Authoritarianism or Democracy? Marketization as a Political Problem." *Policy Sciences* 26 (1993): 139–163.

Posner, M. "Research Raises Troubling Questions about Violence Prevention Programs." *The Harvard Education Letter* 10, no. 3 (1994): 3.

Project PAVE, Inc. "1995 Project PAVE Fact Sheet." Denver, CO, Project PAVE, 1995.

Prothrow-Stith, D. *Deadly Consequences: How Violence Is Destroying Our Teenage Population and a Plan to Begin Solving the Problem.* New York: HarperCollins Publishers, 1991.

Prothrow-Stith, D., H. Spivak, and A. J. Hausman. "The Violence Prevention Project: A Public Health Approach." *Science, Technology, and Human Values* 12, nos. 3–4 (1987): 67–69.

Purdum, T. S. "Clinton Plans to Get around Ruling: Court Overturned U.S. Ban on Having Guns Near Schools." *Denver Post*, April 30, 1995, 2A.

Quarles, C. L. "School Violence: A Survival Guide for School Staff with Emphasis on Robbery, Rape, and Hostage Taking." Monograph. West Haven, CT: National Education Association, 1989.

Quinney, R. *The Problem of Crime.* New York: Dodd, Mead and Co., 1970.

Rabinow, P., and W. M. Sullivan, eds. *Interpretive Social Science: A Second Look.* Berkeley: University of California Press, 1987.

Rapp, R. L. "A State Policy Maker's Guide to Education Decentralization." Working paper, Denver, CO, Education Commission of the States, 1996.

Ravitch, D., and M. A. Vinovskis, eds. *Learning from the Past: What History Teaches Us about School Reform.* Baltimore: The Johns Hopkins University Press, 1995.

Reese, W. J. "*Reefer Madness* and *A Clockwork Orange.*" In *Learning from the Past: What History Teaches Us about School Reform,* ed. D. Ravitch and M. A. Vinovskis, 355–381. Baltimore: The Johns Hopkins University Press, 1995.

Reiman, J. H. *The Rich Get Richer and the Poor Get Prison: Ideology, Class, and Criminal Justice.* New York: John Wiley and Sons, 1984.

Reiss, A. J., and J. A. Roth, eds. *Understanding and Preventing Violence.* Washington, DC: National Academy Press, 1993.

Rhodes, R. "What Causes Brutality? The People Nurturing It," *New York Times*, Oct. 16, 1999, B7.

Richards, T. J., and L. Richards. "The NUD*IST Qualitative Data Analysis System." *Qualitative Sociology* 14, no. 4 (1991): 307–324.

Richards, T., and L. Richards. "Using Computers in Qualitative Analysis." In *Handbook of Qualitative Analysis*, ed. N. Denzin and Y. Lincoln. Berkeley: Sage, 1993.

Rist, R. C. "The Preconditions for Learning: Lessons from the Public Sector." In *Can Governments Learn? Comparative Perspectives on Evaluation and Organizational Learning*, ed. F. L. Leeuw, R. C. Rist, and R. C. Sonnichsen. New Brunswick, NJ: Transaction Publishers, 1994.

Robey, R. "After-School Tutoring, Access to Computers Top Survey Wish List." *Denver Post*, Feb. 22, 1997, 1B, 6B.

Robinson, M., and J. Kirksey. "Reported Crime Dives 10.9 Percent." *Denver Post*, 1993, 1A, 12A.

Rochefort, D. A., and R. W. Cobb, eds. *The Politics of Problem Definition: Shaping the Policy Agenda*. Lawrence: University Press of Kansas, 1994.

Roderick, T. "Johnny Can Learn to Negotiate." *Educational Leadership* 4, no. 45 (1987–88): 86–90.

Roe, E. *Narrative Policy Analysis: Theory and Practice*. Durham, NC: Duke University Press, 1994.

Rogers, E. M. *Diffusion of Innovations*. 4th ed. New York: Free Press, 1995.

Rohter, L. "Brazil, High in Shootings, Is Proposing to Ban Guns." *New York Times*, June 13, 1999, A19.

Rose, R. *Lesson Drawing in Public Policy: A Guide to Learning across Time and Space*. Chatham, NJ: Chatham House, 1993.

Rothstein, S. W., ed. *Handbook of Schooling in Urban America*. Westport, CT: Greenwood Press, 1993.

Rubin, H. J., and I. S. Rubin. *Qualitative Interviewing: The Art of Hearing Data*. Thousand Oaks, CA: Sage Publications, 1995.

Sabatier, P. A. "An Advocacy Coalition Framework of Policy Change and the Role of Policy-Oriented Learning Therein." *Policy Sciences* 21, nos. 2–3 (1988): 129–168.

———. "Toward Better Theories of the Policy Process." *PS: Political Science and Politics* (June 1991): 147–155.

Sabatier, P. A., and H. C. Jenkins-Smith. "Symposium Editors' Introduction." *Policy Sciences* 21, nos. 2–3 (1988): 123–127.

———. *Policy Change and Learning: An Advocacy Coalition Approach.* Boulder, CO: Westview Press, 1993.

Safe and Drug-Free Schools and Communities. "Resiliency Flyer." Denver, CO, Denver Public Schools, 1996.

Safe City Office. "Building a Safe City: Denver's Response." Mayor's Office, City and County of Denver, CO, 1996.

Sarason, S. B. *School Change: The Personal Development of a Point of View.* New York: Teachers College Press, Columbia University, 1995.

———. *Barometers of Change: Individual, Educational, and Social Transformation.* San Francisco: Jossey-Bass Publishers, 1996.

———. *Revisiting "The Culture of the School and the Problem of Change."* New York: Teachers College Press, Columbia University, 1996.

Saussois, J. M., and H. Laroche. "The Politics of Labeling Organizational Problems: An Analysis of the Challenger Case." *Knowledge and Policy: The International Journal of Knowledge Transfer* 4 (spring–summer 1991): 89–106.

"Saving Youth from Violence." *Carnegie Quarterly* 39, no. 1 (Winter 1994): 3.

Scanlon, B. "Juvenile Crime Filings Hit Record 17,500 in 1996: Youth Offenses Mushrooming Faster than Prison Capacity." *Rocky Mountain News*, Dec. 27, 1996, 4A, 6A.

Schneider, A., and H. Ingram. "Behavioral Assumptions of Policy Tools." *Journal of Politics* 52, no. 2 (1990).

Schön, D. A. "Generative Metaphor: A Perspective on Problem-Setting in Social Policy." In *Metaphors and Thought*, ed. A. Ortony, 254–283. Cambridge: Cambridge University Press, 1979.

———. *The Reflective Practitioner: How Professionals Think in Action.* New York: Basic Books, 1983.

"Schools and Violence." *National Network of Violence Prevention Practitioners Sample Fact Sheet* 1, no. 3 (May 1996).

Schram, S. F. "Post-Positivistic Policy Analysis and the Family Support Act of 1988: Symbols at the Expense of Substance." *Polity* 24, no. 4 (summer 1992): 633–655.

———. "Postmodern Policy Analysis: Discourse and Identity in Welfare Policy." *Policy Sciences* 26 (1993): 249–270.

Schwartz, J. D. "Participation and Multisubjective Understanding: An Interpretivist Approach to the Study of Political Participation." *Journal of Politics* (1984): 1117–1141.

Sebastian, M. "Boulder High Principal Says She Will Retire: Bonelli's 'Involuntary' Transfer Stirs Parent, Pupil, Teacher Protest." *Denver Post*, Dec. 13, 1996, 1B, 5B.

Sedlak, M., C. Wheeler, D. C. Pullin, and P. A. Cusick. *Selling Students Short: Classroom Bargains and Academic Reform in the American High School.* New York: Teachers College Press, 1986.

Shakur, S. *Monster: The Autobiography of an L.A. Gang Member.* New York: Atlantic Monthly Press, 1993.

Shilling, H. "Boot-Camp Jails Not Quick Fixes: Study: Offenders Return to Prison." *Denver Post*, April 14, 1994.

Simon, H. A. *Models of Man.* New York: John Wiley and Sons, 1957.

———. *Reason in Human Affairs.* Stanford: Stanford University Press, 1983.

Skocpol, T., and M. Somers. "The Uses of Comparative History in Macrosocial Inquiry." *Comparative Studies in Society and History* 22 (April 1980): 174–197.

Smith, D. "Memorandum to Potential Grant Recipients Regarding Application for Pilot School Funding; and Pilot School for Expelled Students Request for Proposals, 1996–97." Memorandum. Denver, CO, Colorado Department of Education, 1996.

———. "Memorandum to Superintendents and BOCES Directors—Health Education Contacts—Social Studies/Civics Contacts Regarding Grant Program for In-School or In-Home Suspension." Memorandum. Denver, CO, Colorado Department of Education, 1996.

Smothers, R. "Rumors of Violence Close School and Put Police and Educators on Alert." *New York Times*, Oct. 30, 1999, B5.

Stake, R. E. *The Art of Case Study Research.* Thousand Oaks, CA: Sage Publications, 1995.

State of Colorado, Office of the Governor. "Governor's Expelled Student Task Force Report." Denver, CO, Office of the Governor, 1995.

Stein, J. G. "Political Learning by Doing: Gorbachev as Uncommitted Thinker and Motivated Learner." *International Organization* 48, no. 2 (Spring 1994): 155–183.

Steinberg, J. "Barricading the School Door: Disaster Drills and Intercoms." *New York Times*, Aug. 22, 1999, A5.

Stephens, C. "Memorandum to Supervisors for Mayor's Youth Workers Regarding Evaluations Forms." Safe City Office, Mayor's office, City and County of Denver, CO, 1996.

Stephens, R. D. *Congressional Testimony: Weapons in School*. Westlake Village, CA: National School Safety Center, 1992.

Stone, C. "Efficiency versus Social Learning: A Reconsideration of the Implementation Process." *Policy Studies Review* 4, no. 3 (February 1985): 484–496.

―――. "School Reform and the Ecology-of-Games Metaphor." *Journal of Urban Affairs* 17, no. 3 (1995): 303–307.

―――. "Some Notes on the Civic Capacity and Urban Education Project." Research notes. University of Maryland, 1995.

Stone, D. A. "Causal Stories and the Formation of Policy Agendas." *Political Science Quarterly* 104, no. 2 (1989): 281–300.

Student Discipline Services. "House Bill 96-1203." Colorado Springs, CO, Colorado Springs Public Schools, 1996.

―――. "Senate Bill 96-63." Colorado Springs, CO, Colorado Springs Public Schools, 1996.

Stutman, R. K., and S. Newell. "Beliefs versus Values: Salient Beliefs in Designing a Persuasive Message." *The Western Journal of Speech Communication* 48 (Fall 1984): 362–372.

Terrill, J. L. "An Executive Summary of the Action Plans Submitted to the Colorado Department of Education Safe and Drug-Free Schools and Communities Act Program, 1995." Colorado Department of Education, Denver, CO, 1996.

Teske, P. "Interests and Institutions in State Regulation." *American Journal of Political Science* 35, no. 1 (1991): 139–154.

Thomas, P. "Our 'Subculture of Violence.'" *Washington Post National Weekly Edition*, Mar. 26–30, 1995, 37.

Throgmorton, J. A. "The Rhetorics of Policy Analysis." *Policy Sciences* 24 (1991): 153–179.

Tilly, C. *Big Structures, Large Processes, Huge Comparisons*. New York: Russell Sage, 1984.

Toby, J. *Violence in School.* Washington, DC: National Institute of Justice, 1983.

――. "The Schools." In *Crime,* ed. J. Q. Wilson and J. Petersilia, 141–170. San Francisco: ICS Press, 1995.

Tolan, P., and N. Guerra. "What Works in Reducing Adolescent Violence: An Empirical Review of the Field." No. F-888. Boulder, CO, Center for the Study and Prevention of Violence, 1994.

Torgerson, D. "Book Review Essay: Reuniting Theory and Practice." Review of *Technocracy and the Politics of Expertise,* by Frank Fischer. *Policy Sciences* 25 (1992): 211–224.

Trujillo, L., and N. Aaronson. "A Better Way to Handle 'Disruptive Students.'" *Denver Post,* Mar. 9, 1996, 7B.

Tyack, D., and L. Cuban. *Tinkering toward Utopia: A Century of Public School Reform.* Cambridge, MA: Harvard University Press, 1995.

Tyack, D., R. Lowe, and E. Hansot. *Public Schools in Hard Times: The Great Depression and Recent Years.* Cambridge, MA: Harvard University Press, 1984.

Tyler, T. R., K. A. Rasinski, and E. Griffin. "Alternative Images of the Citizen: Implications for Public Policy." *American Psychologist* 41, no. 9 (1986): 970–978.

U.S. Bureau of the Census. *Current Population Reports: Population Projections of the United States by Age, Sex, Race, and Hispanic Origin: 1995 to 2050.* #P25-1130. Prepared by the Department of Commerce, Economics and Statistics Administration. Washington, DC, 1996.

U.S. Departments of Agriculture, Education, Health and Human Services, Housing and Urban Development, Justice, and Labor. *Partnerships Against Violence: Promising Programs, Resource Guide.* Vol. 1. Washington, DC, 1994.

――. *Partnerships Against Violence: Information Sources, Funding, and Technical Assistance, Resource Guide.* Vol. 2. Washington, DC, 1994.

U.S. Department of Education. *America 2000 Communities: Getting Started.* Washington, DC, January 1992.

U.S. Department of Education, Office of Elementary and Secondary Education. *Safe and Drug-Free Schools and Communities Act, State Grants for Drug and Violence Prevention Program: Guidance for State and Local Educational Agency Programs.* Washington, DC, 1995.

Ventriss, C., and J. Luke. "Organizational Learning and Public Policy: Towards a Substantive Perspective." *American Review of Public Administration* 18, no. 4 (Dec. 1988): 337–357.

Vickers, G. *The Art of Judgment: A Study of Policy-making.* New York: Basic Books, 1965.

Violence Prevention Advisory Committee et al. "Violence in Colorado: Trends and Resources." Denver, CO, Colorado Department of Public Health and Environment, November 1994.

Walker, J. L., Jr. "The Diffusion of Innovations Among the American States." *American Political Science Review* 63 (1969): 880–899.

Wallis, A., and D. Ford. *Crime Prevention through Environmental Design: The School Demonstration in Broward County, Florida.* Washington, DC: Department of Justice, 1980.

Weaver, R. K. "The Politics of Blame Avoidance." *Journal of Public Policy* 6, no. 4 (1986): 371–395.

Weber, M. *The Theory of Social and Economic Organization.* Trans. A. M. Henderson. Ed. T. Parsons. New York: Free Press, 1947.

Weiss, J. A. "The Powers of Problem Definition: The Case of Government Paperwork." *Policy Sciences* 22 (1989): 97–121.

Weyant, J. P. "Is There Policy-Oriented Learning in the Analysis of Natural Gas Policy Issues?" *Policy Sciences* 21, nos. 2–3 (1988): 239–261.

"What a lot of sterEUtypes." *Economist*, Oct. 23, 1999, 60.

Wheeler, S. R. "Six Clubs to Focus on Career Choices: Webb Offers Teens After-School Plan." *Denver Post*, Sept. 4, 1996, 2B.

White House. *Comprehensive Strategies for Children and Families: The Role of Schools and Community-Based Organizations, Report of the July 15, 1994 White House Meeting.* Washington, DC, 1994.

White House, Office of the Press Secretary. "Gun-Free School Zones Amendments Act of 1995." Fact sheet. White House, 1995.

Wildavsky, A. "Choosing Preferences by Constructing Institutions: A Cultural Theory of Preference Formation." *American Political Science Review* 81, no. 1 (March 1987): 3–21.

Wilson, J. Q. "A Gap in the Curriculum." *New York Times*, April 26, 1999.

Wilson, W. J. "*The Truly Disadvantaged* Revisited: A Response to Hochschild and Boxill." *Ethics* 101 (April 1991): 593–609.

Wirt, F. M. *Power in the City: Decision-making in San Francisco.* Berkeley, CA: University of California Press, 1974.

———. *The Polity of the School: New Research in Educational Politics.* Lexington, MA: Lexington Books, 1975.

Wirt, F. M., and M. W. Kirst. *Political and Social Foundations of Education.* Berkeley, CA: McCutchan Publishing, 1972.

———. *The Politics of Education: Schools in Conflict.* Berkeley, CA: McCutchan Publishing, 1982.

Witcher, T. R. "Forward to the Past: What Will Happen When Denver's Model of Integration, Manual High, Returns to the Old Days of Segregation?" *Westword*, Jan. 23–29, 1997, 17–25.

Woodson, R. L. *Youth Crime and Urban Policy: A View from the Inner City.* Washington and London: American Enterprise Institute, 1981.

———. *A Summons to Life: Mediating Structures and the Prevention of Youth Crime.* Washington, DC: American Enterprise Institute, 1989.

Yoder, E. "Obsession with Crime Plagues the U.S." *Denver Post*, Jan. 5, 1997, 1F.

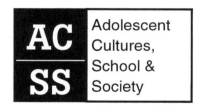

Adolescent Cultures, School & Society

General Editors: Joseph & Linda DeVitis

As schools struggle to redefine and restructure themselves, they need to be cognizant of the new realities of adolescents. Thus, this series of monographs and textbooks is committed to depicting the variety of adolescent cultures that exist in today's post-industrial societies. It is intended to be a primarily qualitative research, practice, and policy series devoted to contextual interpretation and analysis that encompasses a broad range of interdisciplinary critique. In addition, this series will seek to provide a pragmatic, pro-active response to the current backlash of conservatism that continues to dominate political discourse, practice, and policy. This series seeks to address issues of curriculum theory and practice; multicultural education; aggression and violence; the media and arts; school dropouts; homeless and runaway youth; alienated youth; at-risk adolescent populations; family structures and parental involvement; and race, ethnicity, class, and gender studies.

Send proposals and manuscripts to the General Editors at:

Joseph & Linda DeVitis
Binghamton University
Dept. of Education & Human Development
Binghamton, NY 13902

To order other books in this series, please contact our Customer Service Department at:

(800) 770-LANG (within the U.S.)
(212) 647-7706 (outside the U.S.)
(212) 647-7707 FAX

or browse online by series at:

WWW.PETERLANG.COM